Modern Britain since 1906

TAURIS HISTORY READERS

British Imperial History, 1773-1960
edited by *Douglas M. Peers*
Hardback 1 86064 159 8
Paperback 1 86064 160 1

British Women's History to 1914
edited by *Alison Twells*
Hardback 1 86064 161 X
Paperback 1 86064 162 8

Modern Britain since 1906
edited by *Keith Laybourn*
Hardback 1 86064 298 5
Paperback 1 86064 237 3

Modern Britain since 1979
edited by *Keith Laybourn*
Hardback 1 86064 596 8
Paperback 1 86064 597 6

Race and Nation
edited by *Clive Christie*
Hardback 1 86064 195 4
Paperback 1 86064 194 6

Twentieth Century International History
edited by *Stephen Chan & Jarrod Weiner*
Hardback 1 86064 301 9
Paperback 1 86064 302 7

Modern Britain since 1906
A Reader

Edited by

Keith Laybourn

I.B. Tauris *Publishers*

LONDON • NEW YORK

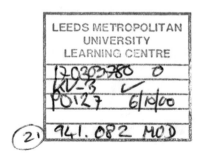
Published in 1999 by I.B.Tauris & Co Ltd
Victoria House, Bloomsbury Square, London WC1B 4DZ
175 Fifth Avenue, New York NY 10010
Website: http://www.ibtauris.com

In the United States and Canada distributed by St. Martin's Press
175 Fifth Avenue, New York NY 10010

ISBN   Hardback   1 86064 298 5
ISBN   Paperback   1 86064 237 3

A full CIP record for this book is available from the British Library
A full CIP record for this book is available from the Library of Congress

Library of Congress catalog card: available

Typeset in Caslon by Dexter Haven, London
Printed and bound in the UK by WBC Book Manufacturers, Bridgend

Contents

Preface and Acknowledgments

Many people have helped me in the production of this book. Most obviously Dr Lester Crook, of I.B. Tauris, has been an excellent and patient editor. Although there are more than 45,000 words of introductory material to the nine main chapters of about 108,000 words, the rest of the book is made up of both secondary and primary documents. I would particularly like to thank all those who have given permission for these documents to be published. They include Brian Brivati (for extracts on his book on Hugh Gaitskell), Andrew Glyn and John Harrison (for an extract from *The British Economic Disaster*), J.A. Jowitt (for an extract from a joint article with Keith Laybourn on 'War and Socialism'), Keith Laybourn (for various items), Bill Lancaster (for an extract for his book *Radicalism, Cooperation and Socialism*), Professor Ann Oakley (for the use of extracts from the writings of her father Richard Titmuss), Cyril Pearce (for an extract from an article on the pacifist movement in Huddersfield during the First World War), Dr John Stevenson (for extracts from *The Slump: Society and Politics During the Depression*); Dr Jay Winter (for an extract from his book *Socialism and the Challenge of War 1912–1918*; and Jilly Wright (for an extract from David G. Wright's pamphlet on *The Great War: A Useless Slaughter?*), and Charles Webster (for an extract from his *History Workshop Journal* article of 1982, 'Healthy or Hungry Thirties'). The extract from José Harris, 'Political Thought and the Welfare State 1870–1940: An Intellectual Framework for British Social Policy', *Past and Present* 135 (May 1992), pp 118–123, is reprinted with the kind permission of World Copyright: The Past and Present Society, 175 Banbury Road, Oxford, England. Professor José Harris, of St Catherine's College, Oxford, also gave her permission for me to use this extract. The Metropolitan Police copyright material in the Public Record Office is reproduced by permission of the Commissioner of Police of the Metropolis. Crown copyright material in the Public Record Office is reproduced by permission of the Controller of Her Majesty's Stationary Office. I would like to thank Stephen Bird, archivist at the National Museum of Labour History for permission to quote from Labour Party documents and the records of the National Union of Railwaymen. A.P. Watt Ltd, Literary Agents, have given permission on behalf of Sir Martin Gilbert CBE, and David Higham Associates have given permission on behalf of David Marquand.

Numerous other institutions and publishers have also given their permission for the use of extracts. They include those listed hereafter: Addison Wesley Longman; Arnold Division, Hodder Headline; Archives Division, Batsford; Berg Publishers; Blackwell Publishers (including Polity Press); Bradford Trades and Labour Council; British Library of Political and Economic Science (for Beveridge Collection); *Bulletin of the Institute of Historical Research*; Cambridge University Press; Cassell plc (including Leicester University Press), Victor Gollancz imprint; Hambledon Press; HarperCollins Publishers; David Higham Associates (on behalf of David Marquand); Heinemann Educational Publishers Ltd, a division of Reed Educational and Professional Publishers Ltd; *History Workshop Journal*; I.B. Tauris Publishers; Institute of Historical Research; Lawrence and Wishart; Macmillan Publishers; Manchester University Press; Merlin Press; John Murray Publishers Ltd; Open University; Oxford University Press (Journals); *Past and Present*; Penguin UK; Pluto Press; Prentice Hall; Random House; Routledge; *Social History*; Tribune; The Edwin Mellen Press Ltd; Times Newspapers Ltd, 1917; and the Trades Union Congress.

Every effort has been made to track down the copyright owners of the quoted documents. In three cases, despite repeated efforts – letters and phone calls (of which a record has been kept), I have had no replies. In these cases the full sources are quoted in the text. Nevertheless, the author and publishers would like to apologise for any inadvertent infringement of copyright and have sought to keep within the Publishers' Fair Dealing Convention in the use of some recently published secondary sources. In every case, the documents have been fully attributed.

Keith Laybourn

List of Abbreviations

ASE	Amalgamated Society of Engineers
BUF	British Union of Fascists
ILP	Independent Labour Party
CPGB	Communist Party of Great Britain
LRC	Labour Representation Committee
MFGB	Miners' Federation of Great Britain
NEC	National Executive Committee (of the Labour Party)
NUWM	National Unemployed Workers' (Committee) Movement
PLP	Parliamentary Labour Party
UDC	Union of Democratic Control
NUR	National Union of Railwaymen
TGWU	Transport and General Workers' Union
TUC	Trades Union Congress
WEC	War Emergency Committee

Introduction

Twentieth-century Britain has experienced a remarkable political, social and economic transformation. The British Empire has gone, social class is more mutable than it once was and, in association with the rest of the world, there has been a communications revolution. Social values and aspirations have changed almost beyond recognition in the course of the twentieth century. From the multitude of changing experiences in Britain three major developments have produced debate amongst contemporaries and between historians. These focus upon the changing nature of politics, the development of a welfare state and the economic decline of Britain. These problems also affect many social problems that are more confined or specific in their impact.

The first, and by far the major, issue that will dominate this text, is one of political realignment. It has produced many questions. Why, for instance, did the Labour Party rise and the Liberal Party decline? Why was it that the Conservative Party was the dominant political party of British twentieth-century politics? Why did the Labour Party's fortunes dip between 1951 and 1979, when compared with the Conservative Party's success? Why have minority parties, such as the British Union of Fascists and the Communist Party of Great Britain, failed to break the British two-party political mould? The ever-changing nature of British politics has been the subject of constant and detailed discussion – not least in the present climate when political divisions over Britain's relations with Europe are once again to the fore.

What is increasingly obvious is that the twentieth century has seen significant political change. It is clear that the first-past-the-post system of British politics has ensured that two major political parties have dominated. On the Right this has meant the Conservative Party, on the Left a sharing of influence by the Liberal and Labour Parties. What is also clear is that under the present electoral system there is no possibility for two different progressive political parties to wield major political influence. The Liberals were declining in political presence from the beginning of the century, although historians have not yet agreed upon the date from which it was no longer politically viable: 1910, 1916, 1924 and 1931 have been offered. As for Labour, its growth appeared almost inexorable from the beginning of the twentieth century, checked only by the post-war election of 1918 and the political debacle of 1931, when Ramsay MacDonald left the Labour Government to form the National Government. Since then, the Attlee years have been regarded as the apogee of Labour's development. However, even here there is a significant difference of opinion between writers such as Kenneth Morgan on the one hand, and writers such as Steven Fielding, Peter Thompson and Nick Tiratsoo on the other, over the nature of the achievements of the Attlee governments.[1] The latter group tend to see Labour as performing badly in controlling the economy but offering a socialist agenda ahead of the electorate's demand, the former see it as performing well in difficult circumstances.

Since the Labour Party left office in October 1951, there has been an increasing tendency for it to modify its socialism. Despite the attempt by Bevanites, in the early 1950s, to get the Labour Party to accept the need for a set of reinvigorated socialist policies the trend, ever since, has been for Labour to withdraw from further public ownership. Hugh Gaitskell, who replaced Attlee as leader in 1955, moved towards the abandonment of Clause Four (the public ownership clause) of the Labour Party Constitution. Indeed, at the 1959 Blackpool Conference, he made a determined attempt to drop it, although his efforts were thwarted by the trade unions. Anthony Crosland's *The Future of Socialism* (1956) had earlier margued for a substantial modification of Labour's objectives, since the secret of production had been mastered by new technology and capitalism tamed by Attlee's policies. Therefore, Labour had to change and develop to recognise that nationalisation was irrelevant to the creation of equality. Since the 1950s and 1960s, there has indeed been the gradual move away from Clause Four: Roy Hattersley and Neil Kinnock paved the way for change and Tony Blair changing it beyond all recognition in the mid 1990s.

Whilst Labour has suffered much anguish about its future, there have been few such concerns in the Conservative Party. It was the dominant political party of the inter-war years (1918–1939), only failing to be the largest British political party between May 1929 and October 1931, the period of the second Labour Government and the early months of Ramsay MacDonald's National Government. It continued to dominate government throughout the Second

World War and, although it shared power equally with Labour between 1945 and 1979, it then dominated British politics from May 1979 until April 1997. This has been the basis of much discussion, although most authors, as will be seen, suggest that this success had much to do with the flexibility and pragmatism of Conservative policies, supported by the view of the party as defenders of tradition. Only Margaret Thatcher, with her commitment to a set of principles, seems to some historians to have veered away from this political style. Indeed, in the post-war years the two major political parties, Labour and the Conservative, seem to have operated almost a consensus in politics – until Thatcher challenged it by attempting to diminish the role of the state in British politics and society.

As for the other political parties, they have suffered defeat and decline. The British Union of Fascists did not survive the 1930s, The Communist Party of Great Britain rarely had more than 3000 or 4000 members before the mid 1930s and, though it had 56,000 members in 1956, membership gradually declined until it ceased to exist in 1991. The Liberals, as already indicated, continued to decline, although they experienced some political revivals in the 1960s and 1970s, before improving their position throughout the 1980s and 1990s.

The second issue revolved around the welfare state, and raises a number of questions. How and why did the British welfare state expand in the twentieth century? To what extent did the social and economic problems of the inter-war years drive the need for an extension of welfare provision? Why did a universalistic welfare state provision, albeit of a limited social security nature, replace a more selective form of welfare in the late 1940s? What impact did the Second World War exert? What was the impact of the Beveridge Report? Why was the National Health Service formed? To what extent was the development of the welfare state a break with the pluralism of the past? How did the concept of welfare provision change with the monetarist policies of Denis Healey in 1975 and 1976, and the views and statements of James Callaghan, as Prime Minister between 1976 and 1979? More recently, concepts of welfare have changed fundamentally as the Thatcher and Major Conservative Governments privatised the National Health Service and then went some way in privatising the personal social services sector of the economy. The welfare state has changed dramatically in recent years, although one must reflect that it was James Callaghan who admitted that the expenditure levels required for full employment were not possible, and gibbed at the cost of the State Earnings-Related Pension Scheme (SERPS). His views were given in a Ruskin lecture, but were also presented at the Labour Party Conference in 1976. On this occasion he stated:

> We used to think that you could just spend your way out of a recession and increase employment by cutting taxes and boosting government spending. I tell

you in all honesty that [that] option no longer exists and that, insofar as it ever did exist, it worked by injecting inflation into the economy. And each time that happened, the average level of unemployment has risen. High inflation followed by higher unemployment. That is the history of the last twenty years.[2]

Callaghan's comments came relatively late in the debate, and called into question the type of commitment that the Labour Party was prepared to make to the future welfare state. This was a step in the direction of the 'New Right' of the Conservative Party, which felt that the economic burden of the welfare state was so great that it had hindered Britain's economic growth and had to be dismembered. There is a resonance of debate on this topic well beyond the confines of this book, which deals only with the short twentieth century, from 1906 to 1979.

Thirdly, there is the issue of Britain's industrial decline: why has Britain declined industrially throughout the twentieth century? Was decline inevitable, a product of other industrial nations catching up, from the late nineteenth century onwards? Or was it due to the fact that, as Corelli Barnett would have us believe, that Britain declined because of the financial burden which the Beveridge Report of 1942 imposed on Britain?[3] Has Britain failed to educate its population properly or neglected industrial training? Did poor industrial relations and industrial conflict, such as the General Strike of 1926 and the serious strikes of the post-Second-World-War period, undermine Britain's economic performance?

These three major themes, along with numerous sub-debates, weave through this book. Nevertheless, there are omissions. Although there is some discussion about women, in connection with wartime work and inter-war health, there is no specific discussion about whether or not they experienced fundamental or cosmetic changes in their economic, social and political position in twentieth-century Britain. There is also little discussion of the events and consequences of Commonwealth immigration, which occurred on a vast scale in Britain between 1948 and the early 1960s. Equally, specific policies such as housing and foreign policy – except in the case of the latter in relation to the appeasement in the 1930s and Ernest Bevin's commitment to forming NATO in the late 1940s – are not examined. To do justice to these areas would require a much larger history than the one undertaken, although they may appear in a subsequent work.

Essentially, then, this book seeks to examine the major trends and developments that shaped British domestic policy between 1906 and 1979. It examines the various debates in detailed introductions and, although many debates are still open, suggests three main points. First, that British politics became increasingly based upon the Labour and Conservative Parties between 1906 and 1979, almost to the exclusion of other parties. Secondly, that a minimalist social security welfare state developed, on which there was remarkable political consensus until 1979. Thirdly, that the relative industrial decline of Britain was inevitable, and had little to do with the burden of the welfare state or the restrictions imposed by trade unions. Indeed it may have had more to do with Britain's failure to develop industrial training.

Notes on Introduction

1   Steven Fielding, Peter Thompson and Nick Tiratsoo, 'England Arise!' in *The Labour Party and Popular Politics in 1940s Britain* (Manchester, Manchester University Press, 1995); Kenneth O. Morgan, *Labour in Power: 1945–51* (Oxford, Clarendon Press, 1984).
2   Labour Party, *Report of the 75th Annual Conference* (London, Labour Party, 1976), p 188.
3   Correlli Barnett, *The Audit of War: The Illusion and Reality of Britain as a Great Nation* (London, Macmillan, 1986).

Chapter 1

The Liberal Reforms 1905–14: Voluntary Help and the State

Introduction

The emergence of state intervention, through the medium of the Liberal social reforms of 1905–14, was the most important development in the decade before the First World War, largely because it challenged both the local control and the philanthropic efforts (particularly by the Charity Organisation Society) that had been the basis of British social policy until the early twentieth century. Indeed, Derek Fraser reflects that 'Whatever historical perspective is used, one cannot escape the conclusion that Liberal social policy before the First World War was at once at variance with the past and an anticipation of radical changes in the future'.[1] Nevertheless, one should be cautious of suggesting that there was any clean break between the past and the present: relations between the two styles of social policy overlapped for a number of years, and the state tended to strengthen the responsibilities, if not the independence, of local administration.

The Edwardian years were clearly ones of transition which saw the state assume new and wider responsibilities. But why did state intervention widen? In recent years, historians have been divided, though perhaps not bitterly so, in explaining the emergence of the Liberal welfare state. Some, such as José Harris, have seen the explanation of state growth in the influence of ideas and idealists[2] (Document 1). Others, such as Keith Laybourn, have focused on the failures of philanthropic and traditional forces in society which necessitated state involvement despite the reluctance of state administrators and government to intervene (Document 2). Yet others, like Joseph Melling and J.R. Hay, have suggested that welfare capitalism might have exerted an impact, although a declining one, on the evolution of the British welfare state[3] (Documents 3–4). A fourth group, including Henry Pelling, Pat Thane and J.R. Hay, have been at pains to challenge any notion that the Liberal welfare state emerged as a result of the pressure of a newly-enfranchised working class demanding increased state intervention. Rightly, however, they point out that the working class was initially suspicious of the new state intervention because of a variety of experiences and association, one of which was the linkage of state intervention with the operation of the feared Poor Law. Evidently, only once the new Liberal reforms were at work did attitudes change[4] (Documents 5–6). To some writers, it was more the concerns of the middle classes, rather than the working classes, that led to efforts to patch up poverty rather than to tackle it. Thane focuses upon the concerns of David Lloyd George and the New Liberals to support the existing political and economic system[5] (Document 6). David Vincent has also commented perceptively upon this middle-class, rather than working-class, concern, and noted that it imposed its own limits in sustaining the existing social and political structure of society (Document 7).

In this whirl of ideas and debates it is becoming obvious that many forces helped to shape the evolution of the welfare state, although the Liberal governments appear to have convinced themselves of the need to both tackle the obvious social failings of society and to stem Labour and socialist threats, whose vision of social change was far wider than anything they would contemplate. However, the evolution of state intervention through the Liberal reforms did not follow one trajectory. The pressure of the working class, the reactions of employers and the need for efficiency were all important factors in its development. Philanthropy also made a contribution, albeit a declining one, in the decade prior to 1914 in a desperate attempt to convert the state to its ideas about how society should tackle poverty.

The Voluntary and Charitable Sector: The Past and the Future

The early twentieth century saw a debate within both the philanthropic community and government as to the best way to deal with the problem of poverty. As the old philanthropy, of the Charity Organisation Society, gave way to the new there was serious debate and overlapping concerns on such issues as unemployment, old-age pensions, national insurance, the future of the Poor Law and other related issues, all of which became the focus of attention of David Lloyd George, Winston Churchill and the Liberal Governments. Although philanthropic influence was limited, due largely to both its inability to form an effective pressure group and to the immense social problems it encountered, it did contribute to the debate that shaped the role of the state before 1914, and indeed the policies that were developed. Philanthropy was considered an essential part of the process by 'which individuals and political groups found themselves pulled in several contrary directions at once'.[6] The older philosophy of the Charity Organisation Society of the nineteenth century, hostile to the state, was not immediately swept away by the newer one of the twentieth century, and the Guild of Help, at least until 1914, attempted, with some limited impact, to balance the two forces of philanthropy and the state (Documents 2 and 9). This was the 'new philanthropy' which also adopted the idea of organising the forces of philanthropy through a clearing house system and attempting to find work for the poor, though not the destitute, and helping to tackle the health problems of the poor.

The Guild of Help was the chief proponent of the new philanthropy, and sought to establish a working relationship with the state in dealing with health, unemployment, pensions and the Poor Law, although its efforts were febrile. Nevertheless, the Guild was far more concerned with recognising some of the failings of British society than the Charity Organisation Society had been. It showed far more respect for the impoverished individual, and accepted that it was often economic circumstances, rather than personal failings, that caused poverty.[7] Indeed, a central feature of the Guild was its commitment to working with public bodies in a partnership to tackle poverty – and its emphasis was always placed upon action by the local community. In Bradford, this connection was reflected in the fact that F.H. Bentham, the chairman of the Bradford Board of Guardians and a member of the Royal Commission on the Poor Laws, was also a founder member of the Guild, a member of its executive committee and a vice-president during the First World War. The Bradford Guild also noted that, in 1908, 28 percent of its cases had been reported by official bodies such as the Guardians and the local education authority.[8] Thereafter, relevant information was passed between the two bodies.

The whole purpose of the guilds was to build up an effective community structure with which to tackle poverty and unemployment (Documents 5, 9 and 10). Apart from an extensive pattern of social casework designed to alleviate the sufferings of the poor by giving advice, arranging necessary health, clothing and holiday provision, it sought to act as a form of labour exchange. The idea was to rescue the poor and to prevent destitution.[9] This desire led guilds into a wider range of activities. Indeed the Halifax Guild encouraged the local authority to appoint health visitors, and in Bolton, Bradford and Halifax, as well as other areas, the guilds contributed to the provision and the distribution of school meals. In Bolton, there was relief for consumptives, provision of spectacles for children, a scheme to deal with juvenile offenders who would otherwise be imprisoned, and one which provided maternity kits for mothers-to-be.[10] Habits of thrift were encouraged amongst the poor, including the membership of friendly societies and trade unions, and health weeks and anti-beggar campaigns were also organised.

In order to undertake these activities, the guilds created an administrative structure based on divisions and districts, the latter normally equating to municipal wards in each town or community. In Bradford, there were four divisions, broadly in line with the parliamentary divisions, and ten districts within each division. There was an Executive Committee which presided over the entire scheme, and a Central Board consisting of all the district heads appears to have met from time to time. Ideally, there were to be ten helpers within each division apart from the district head and secretary. Theoretically, and indeed in practice, this meant that the Bradford Guild would have at least 450 helpers. These people would deal with the 500–1000 applicants per year who applied for help through the helpers and the central office of the Guild, through individuals such as ministers of religion, or through the Guardians, Education Department, or similar official bodies.

The new philanthropy differed little from the old in the range of activities it offered. Both undertook casework and had many other activities in common. Yet the Guild of Help looked more favourably on the state, was more a collection of autonomous bodies than the highly centralised Charity Organisation Society, and was far more respectful of the individual in society. Together, these three factors constituted what it called its 'scientific approach' to poverty (Documents 2, 9 and 10).

Yet in the end, the Guild failed to provide the answer to Edwardian poverty, since its approach was chiefly designed to endorse existing class distinctions, the moral responsibility of the middle classes to the poor, and the moral discipline of the recipient. In other words, the guilds were far more concerned with palliatives than solutions, and unwilling to tackle the high levels of poverty, resulting from unemployment, that occurred in many northern towns during the Edwardian years. They simply lacked the resources for the task. Indeed, the Halifax Guild had to admit that after dealing with 1398 cases in 1908–9 it had consciously kept the number down to fewer than 600 in 1909–10 due to the 'feeling that in the previous year much of our resources and strength were expended in attempting too much'.[11] Local civic consciousness was also riddled with dissent, poor relations existed between the guilds of the Charity Organisation Society, and there were many problems with religious charities. In addition, there were few members of the working class involved in the Guilds. Only Farnworth Guild of Help, a small guild located near Bolton, appears to have had about 50 percent working-class membership,[12] and the main Guilds – such as Bolton, Bradford and Reading – of whom at least 205 of its 300–400 members were professional

people,[13] all drew largely from the middle classes. Indeed a very large proportion of guild members appear to have been the daughters of the middle
classes.[14] In addition, the Guild of Help was never able to establish a full and
harmonious relationship with the state. It lacked an effective national organisation with which to influence the central state, and was limited in its impact
upon the local agencies of state activity.

Neither the old nor the new philanthropies were able to deal with the
rising pressures of unemployment and poverty that afflicted Edwardian society.
The old had failed to obtain sufficient support and resources to deal with the
massive social problems which Victorian and Edwardian societies faced,
while the new was unable to elicit enough local support or resources in its
endeavour to work with the state in dealing with the social problems of
British society at the beginning of the twentieth century.

The Edwardian years were thus ones of transition. They reflected a new
consensus that was emerging to deal with the social problems of the day, the
development of women's suffrage, the issue of labour and the consequent
development of a New Liberal ideology. The Guild of Help was at the centre
of these activities. It wished to act as a half-way house, using voluntary
help to control and influence the direction of state intervention, keeping
Edwardian society within a restricted and recognisable mould. In some
respects the Liberal reforms were similar, although they involved some redistribution of wealth.

The State and the Liberal Reforms of 1905–14

Causes of Reform

The reason for the Liberal reforms has been the subject of intense debate,
contentions ranging from the impact of the emergent Labour Party (Documents 5 and 6 challenge this) to New Liberalism, the need to deal effectively
with the failings of the Poor Law, and the rising concern about the poor,
whose needs were not being met through voluntary help. All these factors
undoubtedly contributed to the final blend of reforms.

The issue of New Liberalism has, of course, assumed immense importance in the debate that has focused upon the rise of Labour and the decline
of Liberalism (see Chapter 2 for further discussion). It has been argued that
L.T. Hobhouse, J.A. Hobson and David Lloyd George attempted to retain
working-class support for the Liberal Party by offering a variety of social
reforms and compromises to the working classes that became known as New
Liberalism.[15] It is further maintained that their prime concern was to reconcile the demands of labour with the need for Liberal Party unity, an equation

that was never going to be easily arranged, given Liberal reliance on industrial and capitalist wealth. The party offered industrial conciliation for industrial conflict, public ownership when efficiency would be served and communal responsibility over sectional interests.[16] The distinctive feature of these, and other, New Liberal policies was that they offered a framework whereby harmony rather than class or sectional conflict would be promoted. Indeed, Lloyd George stressed to the National Reform Union in 1914 that 'it is better that you should have a party which combined every section and every shade of opinion, taken from all classes of the community, rather than one which represents one shade of opinion alone or one class of community alone'.[17] Community, compromise and agreement were thus seen as the alternative to a socialist-type Labour Party committed to changing society in favour of the working class. New Liberalism was to be the referee in British society, not the harbinger of class interest.

As will become obvious in Chapter 2, P.F. Clarke has been the clearest exponent of the view that New Liberalism was responsible for the Liberal revival before the First World War. His regional study of Lancashire suggests that the improving fortunes of the Liberal Party in the country were very largely a product of the New Liberal ideas offered to the electorate. But one must remember that the Liberals did not fight the December 1905 general election on the issue of social reform and that there is little evidence to suggest that New Liberalism had any meaningful presence in the provinces or outside Westminster.[18] Yet, as Thane has suggested, one should not assume that social reform of the type developed by the Liberals was at the top of Labour's political agenda[19] (Document 6). Indeed, issues such as fair wages and the right to work carried far more weight in the first four years of the Liberal administration when a considerable amount of work was done in connection with social reform. New Liberalism and the social reform it implied might thus have been untypical of Liberal Party attitudes at this time and out of tune with the concerns of the working classes and their institutions.

Even if New Liberalism did not necessarily confer political advantage, it could be seen as a working out of the tensions between the old Gladstonian Liberalism of free trade and individualism and the New Liberal tendency towards collective and state responsibility for social reform. The latter was particularly concerned with the question of national efficiency, and its cause was clearly advanced by evidence of the poor quality of the British volunteers for the Boer War and Rowntree's work on poverty in York.

The importance of New Liberal ideas is clearly under scrutiny, even though these ideas must have contributed to the general thrust for social reform. The emergence of a Labour Party with 30 MPs made state action by the Liberal Government even more imperative, both because of the need for Labour's political support and in order to defuse the potential claim of the

Labour Party to the working-class vote. The Liberal Government was not dependent upon Labour's political support in 1906, but became increasingly so from 1910 onwards. Indeed, given the Liberals' thumping parliamentary majority of 356 it would be surprising if the they had thrown anything more than a nod in the direction of Labour, at least until 1910. Thane develops an argument which Henry Pelling first presented in the 1960s (Document 6), that the working classes were hostile to state intervention because they saw in it the experience of the Poor Law and the middle-class control which it presented, and that until the legislation was introduced the only real pressure for reform came from Liberal politicians such as Asquith and Lloyd George, who saw it as desirable. She suggests that the evidence of friendly societies and socialist organisations, such as the Social Democratic Federation, tends to endorse this viewpoint.

Whilst Lloyd George and his immediate supporters obviously felt, rightly or wrongly, the need to respond to what they saw as a serious Labour chal- lenge, there were also more pressing factors such as the greater awareness of social problems and the obvious failures of the Poor Law and philanthropy driving the New Liberals to advocate social reform. Yet it was the Poor Law in combination with philanthropy that presented the major problem. The 1834 New Poor Law offered a solution to destitution, not to poverty, and there was now increasing evidence, from Rowntree and others, that between 25 and 30 percent of the population of England and Wales were living in a state of poverty (Document 8). This revelation came at a time when the Poor Law was in serious crisis, and when it was soon to become the subject of a Royal Commission investigation. Thus, concerned by the failures of philan- thropy, threatened by the burgeoning Labour Party and faced with an obvious concern about the health and well-being of the nation, David Lloyd George, Winston Churchill and others took expedient action not to solve poverty but to reduce its virulence. As Fraser suggests,

> electoral advantage, New Liberal ideology and national efficiency – combined
> with humanitarian concern, bureaucratic initiative, social investigation and popu-
> lar demand to produce a comprehensive programme which, some Liberals today
> assert, represented the 'creation of the welfare state'.[20]

Nevertheless, the possibility that fundamental social reform and income redistribution would actually create genuine freedoms within an expanding state was never seriously considered, except by socialists such as Fred Jowett, the Independent Labour Party/Labour Party MP for Bradford West in 1906, who reflected in *The Socialist and the City* upon the need for slow gradual change in line with the wishes of the people (Document 11).

The Liberal reforms were also hardly part of a preconceived plan, although they were conditioned by the need to improve the lot of the working classes, to tackle poverty and to do something about the parlous state of the

Poor Law, and to obtain political advantage in the face of the perceived threat from the Labour Party. The first welfare reforms of the December 1905 Liberal Government – the provision of school meals in 1906 and the medical inspection of school children in 1907 – arose from campaigns that had been going on before the return of the Liberals, and made only a marginal difference to poverty.

The Poor Law

The pivotal problem was the condition of the Poor Law. The 1834 Poor Law Amendment Act, and the New Poor Law it bequeathed, was no longer relevant to the Edwardian age and the twentieth century. The task of deterring the poor by the imposition of a workhouse test was no longer feasible in a climate where the extension of democratic rights was on the political agenda and when the Guild of Help recognised the inadequacies of its attempt to get the community to rescue the poor, if not the destitute. The 1834 Poor Law seemed even less appropriate after 1894, when any ratepayer could vote to stand for election and when the socialists began to challenge for seats on the boards of guardians in Poplar, Bradford and other areas. The New Liberal reformers were thus forced to accept that they had to intervene to organise a coherent attack upon poverty and inequality. The opportunity to do so arose as a result of the deliberations and findings of the Royal Commission on the Poor Laws (1905–9).

The Royal Commission had been set up by a Conservative Government, which had seen high unemployment force more than two million people per year under the Poor Law in the early twentieth century. The poor economic conditions of the winters of 1902–3 and 1903–4 led to the creation throughout the country of Lord Mayors' funds and the use of public money to bring about relief. In this situation, the labour test seemed inappropriate, but Government was reluctant to acknowledge that unemployment, and consequent poverty, was of an involuntary nature. However, faced with unemployment demonstrations, Walter Long, President of the Local Government Board, persuaded the Government to introduce the Unemployed Workmen's Act of 1905. Under this, distress committees could be established in all metropolitan boroughs and in all urban districts with a population of more than 50,000. In other areas they could be set up at the discretion of the Local Government Board when distress was acute. Yet this did not mollify the Trades Union Congress, and the demonstrations of the unemployed continued, especially given that the Act was only applied for three years and demonstrated the unwillingness of Government to take permanent responsibility for the unemployed. It was in this context that in early August 1905, A.J. Balfour announced the formation of a Royal Commission on the Poor Laws and the Relief of Distress which would report on 'Everything which appertains to the problem of the poor, whether poor by their own fault or by temporary lack of employment'. Apart from the obvious problem of unemployment, the Commission was provoked into existence by the fact that Poor Law expenditure had risen from £8.1 million in 1881 to £8.6 million in 1906 and was increasing rapidly. The Commission finally reported to the Liberal Government in February 1909.

The Majority Report of the Royal Commission on the Poor Laws accepted that the Poor Law could remain an all-embracing social institution and sought to reverse the trend towards removing categories of social need from it. Yet acknowledging that the Poor Law was held in bad odour, it decided that all social services would be united under Public Assistance Committees (PACs) composed of elected councillors and with co-opted members drawn from philanthropic agencies. The PACs were to make effective use of voluntary charities and social casework agencies. It was clearly critical of the existing arrangements for dealing with poverty and destitution, noting the immense local variation that had occurred. In common with the Minority Report it was concerned about the overlapping duties of local authorities and boards of guardians.

Both the Majority and Minority Reports were critical of the existing system, and advocated the introduction of labour exchanges and the raising of the school-leaving age in order to reduce the size and to increase the quality of the labour market. On other matters, they varied greatly. The Minority Report wanted the break-up of the Poor Law into specialist bodies (dealing with sickness, old age and the like) administered by a committee of the elected local authority, but recommended that unemployment, a vast problem beyond the means of local administration, should be dealt with by central government. It maintained that it was possible to tackle the evils of unemployment and poverty only if the people, and particularly the middle classes, were aware that the solutions it offered were realistic (Document 17).

In the end, it proved impossible to change the Poor Law before the First World War. There was resistance to change from the civil servants of the Local Government Board and there were problems of ensuring that local finance was changed in order to bring about rate equalisation between different areas. In the end, the Poor Law was dismantled by the removal of needy groups through a series of measures such as old-age pensions, the creation of Labour Exchanges, the introduction of the National Insurance Act of 1911, and child legislation.

Old–Age Pensions and Children

After three decades of debate over the provision or non-provision of old-age pensions, and contributory and non-contributory pensions, Lloyd George, Chancellor of the Exchequer, finally introduced a non-contributory scheme in 1908, to become effective on 1 January 1909. It offered five shillings (25p) per week at the age of 70 and introduced a sliding scale arrangement for those with incomes between 8s and 12s (40–60p) per week, or between £21 and £31/10s per annum, provided that they had not been imprisoned for any offence, including drunkenness, during the ten years preceding their claim. These pensions were to be paid through the Post Office rather than through the Poor Law. In other words, pensions were given as a right of citizenship, and were not tainted with the moral stigma of the Poor Law.

As Thane suggests, 'It was a pension for the very poor, the very respectable and the very old'.[21] In fact, this meant that a small number of people qualified for the pension, whose level was too low to provide more than the absolute minimum for survival. At best, the sliding-scale pension was a supplement to those who had some means of subsistence, and at worst it kept a small number of the aged from the Poor Law.

Liberal legislation also attempted to tackle the problems of child poverty. The concern for national efficiency, provoked by the poor physical condition of recruits in the Boer War, was one of the major events that forced the state to show concern that future generations of schoolchildren be properly fed and maintained in a healthy condition. Public concern at the so-called 'national deterioration' was further aroused in 1903 when a Royal Commission on Physical Training in Scotland recommended that both education authorities and voluntary bodies combine to provide school meals. In the following year, the Report of the Interdepartmental Committee on Physical Deterioration recommended that medical inspection and feeding should be undertaken by the state educational system. In fact, all that the Tory administration did was to advise the Guardians to take up the duty of school feeding. It was not until the Liberals came to power that this matter was first considered seriously. Towards the end of 1906, local authorities were empowered to provide free school meals for needy children up to the cost of half a penny after efforts had been made to raise money from the community and the Education (Administrative Provisions) Act of 1907 promoted medical inspection by local education authorities.

Yet the most significant development was the introduction of the Children's Act of 1908. This complex act consolidated and codified 21 acts and portions of 17 others. It established separate juvenile courts, remand homes with Treasury grants, and prevented children under sixteen being placed in an adult prison. It also set out the Poor Law responsibility for visiting and supervision, in its own and other institutions, children who had been subject to cruelty proceedings. It imposed penalties for the neglect of, as well as cruelty to, children, who were to be guarded from immorality. It also dealt with Infant Life Protection and demanded that any person taking reward for the nursing and maintenance of a child under seven years of age had to inform the Local Authority within 48 hours.[22]

Indeed, childcare became the great focus of the act and in 1909 the Local Government Board carried out its responsibilities by obliging each Poor Law Union to set up a boarding-out committee. Two years later it was decided that a third of the members should consist of women, who were assumed to be more sensitive to the needs of children. The boarding-out committees were to appoint salaried female visitors to visit those children who were boarded out and to visit women with children who were on outdoor relief. They also undertook the life-protection visiting required by the act. The Local Government Broad also appointed a superintendent woman inspector to supervise all these activities.

The Children's Act of 1908 unleashed a whole range of improvements in the position of children, designed to encourage parental responsibility and to focus the efforts of the state. This was the intention of the Liberal administration but was also a wider progressive view which obtained the Labour Party's widest support.

The National Insurance Act, 1911 – Health

The old-age pensions removed a small number of people from the Poor Law, and the Children's Act removed one of the largest groups directly associated with it. Yet Lloyd George went further, and attempted to reduce the large number of respectable people thrown onto it because of ill-health.

On 4 May 1911, Lloyd George, as Chancellor of the Exchequer, offered his scheme to the House of Commons, stating, 'In this country... 30 percent of pauperism is attributable to sickness,' noting that a considerable number would have to be added for unemployment[23] (Document 16). Stressing that death was an event for which the working classes attempted to make financial contingency, he pointed out that 'Sickness comes in the next order of urgency in the working-class mind. Between six and seven million people in this country have made some provision against sickness, not at all adequate and a good deal of it defective.' However, he observed that in sickness insurance there was a very high number of policies that lapsed, and he emphasised that to obtain death, sickness and unemployment insurance a working-class man would have, at least, to provide between 1s/6d and 2s per week, clearly beyond his means. Lloyd George concluded, referring to both parts of the scheme – Part I Health Insurance and Part II Unemployment Insurance – that a system of national insurance, with the aid of the state and employers, was the best solution to the problem of unemployment and ill-health.

Lloyd George's health scheme did, however, work within strict constraints. The vested interests of friendly societies, trade unions and the 'House of Industrial Insurance interest' operated the scheme. However, the existing insurance system did provide a cheap and established system of insurance, and could be supplemented by the purchase of stamps through a Post Office for those workers who were not in a friendly society or a trade union. Yet, the general supervision of the scheme fell under the control of Robert Morant, a government official who had previously been responsible for the implementation of the 1902 Education Act, and the 'approved' societies were guaranteed that the state would not intervene with their traditional business.

For those workers who were insured, there was guaranteed full medical treatment by a doctor who they would select from a local list or 'panel'. They were eligible for free treatment in TB sanatoria, but were not entitled to free hospital treatment. The doctors would be paid on a per-patient basis.

The contributors had to pay 4p per week (3p for females), the employer 3p, and the state 2p into an accumulating fund to finance benefits. Contributors were to be between the ages of sixteen and sixty-five, and had to earn less than £150 per year. When it came into operation on 15 January 1913, the scheme provided sickness benefits of 10s (50p) per week for men or 7s 6d for women for the first 13 weeks of sickness, although nothing was paid for the first three days. After the first 13 weeks, 5s per week was paid to men and women. There was a disability pension of 5s per week, and a maternity benefit of 30s was paid to the wives of insured men.

According to Thane, the cumulative effect of the measures for the aged and sick was to reduce the number of paupers from 916,377 in 1910 to 748,019 in 1914.[24] The Poor Law was finding its burden dramatically reduced even at a time of relatively good economic conditions.

National Insurance Act 1911 – Unemployment

The Conservative Government's Unemployed Workmen Act of 1905 had done little to relieve unemployment, and Ramsay MacDonald, Ernest Bevin and the emergent Labour Party were campaigning in favour of the 'right to work' in 1908. It was at this point that the young William Beveridge emerged to provide a clear policy for tackling the problem of the unemployed. He was a university student who had spent the years 1903–7 as a sub-warden of the Toynbee Hall East End settlement, where university graduates worked amongst the poor in their spare time. He felt that the settlement scheme was a failure, but it put him into contact with the Webbs (Beatrice and Sidney) and George Lansbury. In fact, Beatrice Webb drew upon his expertise to counter the Charity Organisation Society's negative attitude towards dealing with the able-bodied unemployed on the Royal Commission on the Poor Law[25] (Document 12).

Drawn into the study of poverty and unemployment at many levels, Beveridge quickly became the expert on unemployment, and directed and influenced affairs. His ideas greatly influenced both the Majority and Minority Reports of the Royal Commission on the Poor Laws, both of which accepted that there were differences between the temporary unemployment of skilled workers in periods of depression and the permanent underemployment of the unskilled or semi-skilled in an overstocked labour market. Both reports proposed the establishment of national labour exchanges at which all unemployed workmen would be registered, and where all vacancies would be notified, the Minority Report suggesting programmes of public works, the Majority Report accepting such measures as necessary only in times of depression.

Obviously Beveridge influenced the Poor Law Commission, but Winston Churchill, who was to become President of the Board of Trade in 1908, was already contemplating a package of changes, including labour exchanges, the decasualisation of the docks, training for juvenile labour and other related activities. Beveridge's influence was plainly visible here, for Churchill recruited him to the Board of Trade in July 1908 with responsibility for putting these proposals into effect. The Commons approved the formation of labour exchanges, and by June 1909 they had become a reality. There were 423 such exchanges by February 1914, with appointed management boards containing worker representatives.

It is debatable how successful they were. By 1914, they were registering over two million workers per year and finding 3000 jobs per day. Nevertheless, three-quarters of those registered never got a jobs through the exchanges, and there was always a lurking suspicion among trade unions that the labour exchanges could be used for strike-breaking. It is certainly questionable whether or not they achieved the 'organised fluidity of labour' aimed for by Beveridge in his *Unemployment: A Problem of Industry* (1909).

In 1909, Churchill introduced the Trades Boards Act, establishing boards of employers and employees to fix minimum wages in the unionised 'sweated trades'. Again, the effectiveness of this legislation is debatable. Less so was the introduction of unemployment insurance, which became part II of the 1911 National Insurance Act. Once again, the idea came from Beveridge, who felt that unemployment insurance could be provided for most workers, if not for the chronically unemployed. Beveridge developed the idea that certain trades should be covered by a compulsory system of contributory insurance. Churchill presented their ideas to the Commons on 19 May 1909 (Document 14).

The Act faithfully followed through Churchill's outline. Each insured workmen contributed 2.5d (1p) per week, as did each employer, and the state provided 1.67d. The scheme was compulsory for certain industries (such as building, mechanical engineering and ironfounding), and benefits were to be 7s (35p) per week for up to 15 weeks, with the possibility of subsidies to trade unions which ran their own schemes. About 2.25 million men were to be protected against unemployment and the scheme came onto the statute book without much parliamentary rancour. The first contributions were paid on 1 July 1912, and the first benefits from 1 January 1913.

Nevertheless, there was considerable opposition in the country, some trade unionists still feeling that it was part of an attempt to regiment labour and to break strikes. In the end, like George Lansbury, many workmen felt that the scheme was not a solution to unemployment but just a shifting around of the problem. Thane rightly points out that it increased the burden on the poor rather than the rich. She estimates that a poor family on 18s per week would be paying 10.2 percent of its income through a combination of indirect taxes (7.1 percent), National Health (2 percent) and Unemployment Contributions (1.1 per cent), whereas a family on a wage of 35s per week was paying only 5.27 percent in taxes and contributions (3.65 percent in indirect taxes). Part of the cost of the new state legislation came from the pockets of the poor, but nevertheless the state had committed some considerable sums of money to its new social reform ventures.

The 'People's Budget', 1909

Although some measures, such as the National Insurance Acts, involved a contributory arrangement to pay for the reform measures, the state contribution to insurance, old age pensions and other measures – as well as rising naval spending – did involve a considerable increase in state expenditure. As the new Chancellor of the Exchequer, Lloyd George faced a £16 million deficit which he sought to recover through his controversial budget of 1909, which raised issues of constitutional rights (Document 17). This was resisted by the House of Lords, and not passed until April 1910, amidst a constitutional crisis. Once passed, this budget raised the basic rate of income tax on earned income to 1s/6d in the pound and imposed a supertax on incomes above £3000 per year. Death duties were also increased on estates of over £5000, and taxes were levied on land. It was these land taxes that provoked the wrath of the Lords, for they were charged at a rate of 20 percent on any increase in the value of land when sold. In order to help families on lower incomes, Lloyd George also introduced a £10 tax allowance for each child under sixteen for taxpayers earning £500 per annum or less. This established firmly the principle of progressive taxation. He also provided a development fund, to be devoted to increasing job opportunities by financing such measures as afforestation and the provision of smallholdings in the countryside. This was part of Lloyd George's commitment to diminish rural poverty and to offer some wider ownership of land in the countryside, building up on his Smallholdings and Allotments Act of 1908.

The 'People's Budget' was clearly designed to make some small redistribution of the wealth of the country through taxation, and was indicative of the Liberal commitment to reducing the poverty of the mass of the people by a relatively modest taxing of the rich. Indeed, at the end of the budget speech, Lloyd George stated,

> This is a War Budget. It is for raising money to wage implacable warfare against poverty and squalidness. I cannot help hoping and believing that before this generation has passed away we shall have advanced a great step towards the good time when poverty and wretchedness and human degradation which always follow in its camp will be as remote to the people of this country as the wolves which once infested its forests.[26]

It provoked the opposition of the House of Lords, and led to two general elections in 1910 (one connected with the budget and the other in connection with the power of the House of Lords). But eventually, in 1911, the Lords, faced with the Liberal Government's threat to create new peers, agreed that their absolute veto on legislation would be reduced to a two-year blocking power, and that money bills would pass automatically.

Conclusion

The years between 1900 and 1914 saw not only the immense extension of the role of the state in social reform but also a process whereby old and new values were sifted to produce a new balance between the state and philanthropic bodies in the determination of social policy of Britain. It was accepted that voluntary and philanthropic efforts were insufficient to deal with the immense social problem of poverty, despite the best efforts of the Guild of Help to create a community response to replace the almost uncaring approach of the Charity Organisation Society. Yet faced with high levels of poverty and unemployment, and a Poor Law that was obviously wilting under the strain of the economic depression of the Edwardian years, the pre-war Liberal Governments decided to introduce a set of reforms which would reduce the burden upon the Poor Law rather than to reform it along the lines proposed by the Majority and Minority Reports of the Poor Law Commission. Driven by a commitment to New Liberal ideas, the concern for national efficiency and the hope of political advantage, the Liberal Governments produced something which – in a hackneyed phrase – became recognised as the 'foundations of the welfare state'.

Documents
SECONDARY SOURCES AND INTERPRETATIONS

1 – José Harris, 'Political Thought and the Welfare State 1870-1914: An Intellectual Framework for British Social Policy', *Past and Present* 135, May 1992

Over the past forty years a very fertile literature has explored the relationship between changing social policies and such theoretical stances as utilitarianism, idealism, progressivism, Social Darwinism, Marxism, Keynesianism and the theories of business management. Many illuminating and often unexpected perspectives have emerged from these studies, reshaping conventional wisdom. Benthamism, for instance, characterised by Dicey as a predominantly individual philosophy, has been revealed as the seed-bed of the Victorian 'welfare state'. Mid-Victorian social scientists functioning in the supposed heyday of administrative laissez-faire have emerged as overwhelmingly in favour of certain kinds of ameliorative state intervention (albeit on somewhat limited and class-specific terms). Eugenics theory, once viewed as the characteristic stronghold of the hard-line radical right, has been convincingly reinterpreted as a much more widely pervasive philosophy shared with socialism and progressive liberalism. The 1909 Poor Law Commission, classically portrayed by Beatrice Webb as a battleground between socialist and individual ideals, has been recast as a conflict of a very different kind: a conflict in which the rationalising, modernising and professionalising interests of the Webbs appear to have differed very little from those of their arch-enemies, the adherents of 'voluntarism' and family care work in the Charity Organisation Society...

The first thing that strikes the reader of this new wave of social reform literature is that, in marked contrast to comparable writing in the mid-Victorian period, much early twentieth-century social sciences was predominantly 'idealist' in character... The permeation of Edwardian public administration by the political thought of T.H. Green is of course a familiar theme in the history of social policy; but the idealist infiltration of the young élite was merely the tip of a much larger iceberg than has usually been acknowledged.

2 – K. Laybourn, *The Guild of Help and the Changing Face of Edwardian Philanthropy: The Guild of Help, Voluntary Work and the State 1904–1919* (Lewiston, NY, The Edwin Mellen Press, 1994), pp 2–4

The Guild of Help was inaugurated in Bradford on 21 September 1904, but first emerged as an idea on 14 October 1903, when the Mayor of Bradford, Alderman David Wade, held a meeting 'for the purpose of discussing the question of Co-ordination of work and workers amongst the poor with a view to the adoption of some such form of system in vogue in Elberfeld as may be successfully carried out in this country'. A Central Board of the town's charities was formed and met monthly to devise a scheme for co-ordinating their charitable provision. A provisional committee of ten people met regularly during the ensuing ten months and publicly launched the Bradford City Guild of Help on 20 September 1904, at a meeting addressed by Dr Boyd Carpenter, the Bishop of Ripon and Seebohm Rowntree. One newspaper reflected that 'The experiment of applying to Bradford the system of poor relief and help which has been so markedly successful in Elberfeld was initiated yesterday'. The idea was to form an alternative to the COS, which had never been a widespread organisation in the North of England, and to gather into a well-organised body 'all the community who have a desire and more or less capacity for social services'. 'Not alms but a friend' was to be the motto of the Guild, reflecting the emphasis which it laid upon the personal service to individuals or families in need. In essence, then, the Guild had three main objectives. First, it wished to organise 'Helpers' who would exercise 'personal responsibility for the poor' by visiting and keeping a social casebook on each poor family, thus reaching the 'darkest corners' of society through social work. These Helpers would assess the family needs of the poor and contact their district, or head, office to consult the register of charitable and public organisations and call up necessary help. The second aim was that the Guild would act as a clearing house for cases of need thus reducing the overlapping charitable effort and rooting out scroungers and beggars. Thirdly, the Guild aimed to form a partnership between the private and public bodies through which its social work would flow. This was to be the basis of the New Philanthropy. These three objectives together were considered to constitute a scientific approach to the assessment and treatment of want, replacing the indiscriminate charity, considered to be the failing of Victorian charity, with a more scientific and discriminate approach. The organisers of the Bradford Guild certainly felt that with these approaches they could effectively tackle, if not solve, the problem of poverty. Similar views were expressed elsewhere. Mr Philip Bagenal of the Harrogate Citizen's Guild of Help, a former Poor Law Inspector in the Knaresborough Union and then a Local Government Board Inspector for the Poor Law, informed the Halifax Guild that the Town Hall ought to be the home of every Guild, and described the Guild as a core movement which was going to lay the foundation of a national movement for cultivating a more scientific interest in what they might call the problem of relief. It is impossible to meet the demand for public assistance merely by State aid... Therefore to organise the voluntary and systematic charity of England was one of the great tasks which had been laid on the shoulders of the present generation.

The Guild of Help emerged at a time when the whole question of poverty, and how to deal with it, was testing the minds of Victorian and Edwardian Britons. Concern about the quality of army recruits for the Boer War, Rowntree's 1899 survey of York, that led to *Poverty: A Study of Town Life*, the high level of infant mortality, and the impending changes in the poor law that were threatened by the formation of the Royal Commission on the Poor Laws and Relief of Distress (1905–9) all made poverty crucial to the municipal and national politics of the age. Poverty was also a factor in the emergence of the New Liberalism, especially with its concern for social harmony. And in Bradford, some of the leading activists in the Guild considered themselves to be advanced, if not especially New, Liberals. They found the New Liberal emphasis upon social harmony and a professional approach in tune with their objectives, which were partly designed to neutralise the class challenge that the emergent socialist and Labour groups presented to their ideals.

3 – J. Melling, 'Welfare Capitalism and the origins of the Welfare State, British Industry, Workplace and Social Reform c1870–1914', *Social History* 17/3 (1992)

The preceding section suggests that the voluntary provision of benefits remained an area of continuing struggle between employers and workers in the late nineteenth century. Workplace welfare can be best understood in terms of the labour contract between capital and labour, when employers sought to secure the compliance of workers to management's conception of the effort bargain. The structure of production in large sectors of British industry gave workers considerable autonomy and bargaining capacity...

Recent scholarship on the formation of welfare states has explained the distinctive character of national policies in terms of the primacy of state structures and political processes in each country. Earlier models of welfare growth which focus on the modernisation of capitalism and the outcome of class conflicts are rejected as inadequate and inconsistent. The strategies and discursive practices of political actors are presented instead as the expressions of the management structure of the state in responses to the electoral politics of risks and needs. Many points in the new orthodoxy can be supported by historical evidence, with British employers complaining to the Board of Trade that they 'have not as many votes as the workmen... and we suffer for it'. Not only were government institutions and electoral shifts clearly important in the peculiar evolution of British welfare, but simplistic views of social insurance, as the businessman's solution to the passing of the Poor Law, are untenable.

The constraints within this analysis arise from the reluctance of such historians to explore the different social resources and political capacities of actors in civil society, and the complex relationship between the growth in the state's infrastructural power and the social relations of the labour market. The maintenance of contractual relations in capitalist society depends on a political infrastructural power and the social relations of the labour market. The maintenance of contractual relations in capitalist society depends on a political infrastructure which acknowledges both the formal and substantive authority of the employer...

By the New Liberal era it was evident that business welfarism was provoking serious resistance and voluntaryism itself was under strain as working-class institutions were struggling to meet the financial and political demands placed on them...

In the event, the remodelling of an infrastructure for the labour market and welfare took the form of integrating existing voluntaryist institutions within the state provisions. If business welfare failed as the fundamental basis for accidents, sickness and unemployment provisions, the scheme succeeded in recruiting employed workers to the cause of responsible behaviour. The exchange between industrialists and government contributed to a common discourse on the rights and responsibilities of the organised working class, with politicians and civil servants as determined as the employers that policy should be based on the principle of contributions and expose the folly of 'unsound Socialist legislation'. Social citizenship was to be earned by instalments rather than delivered by class struggle.

4 – R. Hay, 'Employers and Social Policy in Britain: the Evolution of Welfare Legislation, 1905–14', *Social History* 2 (1977)

The evolution of social policy in capitalist societies is exceedingly complex. Though it has often been treated in isolation, it is better appreciated as part of the whole political process. Social policy may alter the distribution of income in a society in favour of certain defined groups, but it may also act as a means of social control or contribute to the efficiency with which resources are used in society. Indeed for certain influential political groups the value of social policy may lie in its contribution in the latter two respects, not in the former... In Britain, despite the attention given to pressure groups by historians, the attitude of the business community to social welfare legislation has not been seriously examined. The gap is an important one because business interests not only helped shape the climate of opinion in which legislators operated, but also on occasion pressed for the implementation of specific measures of social reform...

British historians have not seriously considered the economic implications of social welfare legislation or the interests of employers in such measures from the late nineteenth century onwards. G.R. Searle's study of the campaign for national efficiency in the years after the Boer War is based largely on statesmen's papers, the press and the periodical literature and does not discuss the attitudes of employers' organisations. Even Gilbert's otherwise useful comments on national efficiency are limited to the pronouncements and influence of the ideologues of the movement, including E.E. Williams and A. Shadwell, rather than the business community. J.F. Harris, in her study of unemployment as a political issue, mentions briefly the interests of a group of radical businessmen associated with Sir John Brunner, Mond Chemicals, the precursor of ICI, in programmes and economic development to absorb surplus labour. She also discusses the attempts by some deputations from employers organisations to alter the details of Liberal legislation. H.V. Emy has some brief passages on employers and emphasises the opposition of the business wing of the Liberal Party to expensive programmes of social reform.

The only exception to the generalisation about limited study of employer attitudes to welfare is that the activities of certain Quaker businessmen and philanthropists like Charles Booth are well known. There has, however, been no systematic study of the attitude of employers to welfare legislation, or their influence upon the evolution of social policy...

The traditional picture of British business in this period is of a hard-headed, unsympathetic group of short-term profit maximising employers, together with a few progressive individuals, who provided welfare benefits for their workers and themselves played leading parts in the movement for social reform. The names which immediately spring to mind are those of Cadbury, Rowntree, Lipton, Lever and Booth...

In fact, some of the attitudes and activities, thought of as characteristic of only a few eccentrics and 'philanthropic' employers, affected in varying degrees a wide range of British businessmen, many of whom faced market and labour situations very different from those of the 'new' and service industries...

The reasons why employers supported state welfare schemes are not always simple and clear cut. Any analysis in terms of an ideological commitment to or against state intervention is quite insufficient. Some employers were influenced by arguments about the declining relative efficiency of the British economy. Even though it may be true, as American revisionist historians have suggested, that the Victorian economy was not 'failing', this is beside the point. At the same time, there were many people who could see that, in relative terms at least, Britain was declining and, under the powerful influence of historical and social Darwinist arguments, they believed that unless something fairly drastic were done then this relative decline might become absolute. This was the message of writers like Shadwell and Williams, of politicians like Joseph Chamberlain, and even economists like Marshall. It can also be found in different forms in the speeches and writings of leading businessmen. The remedies ranged from Fair Trade or Tariff Reform to the encouragement of technical and scientific education and social reform.

Moreover, British employers and the ruling élite faced an internal challenge from the working class through its political and industrial organisations. Working-class groups were pressing for legislation on unemployment – the eight-hour day and the right to work – industrial accidents, old age pensions and more generally for a reduction of the risks and uncertainties of industrial life. The schemes put forward by socialists and trade unionists inevitably appeared costly and dangerous to some employers who became convinced of the need to deflect the attention of the mass of the workers from them.

The efficiency and social control arguments for social reform are analytically separate themes, but the striking thing about much of the debate over welfare measures among employers is the way in which they were regularly used in conjunction. Support for intervention was often based on internal measures developed by firms themselves which employers found to be both productive and effective as a means of social control. There was little idealistic philanthropy in this, more a practical appreciation that in the context of internal and external pressures on British society, social welfare accompanied perhaps by more direct forms of social control, might serve the interests of society as employers saw them.

Many employers, however, worried about the cost of social welfare. They were concerned to minimise the burdens falling directly on them and consequently tended to favour schemes financed by workers' contributions...

The General Purposes Committee of the Birmingham Chamber [of Commerce] was asked to produce a report on the establishment of a system of labour registries, and this was transmitted to the Royal Commission on the Poor Laws in August 1906, together with a request to give oral evidence. On 18 November 1907, the Secretary, George Henry Wright, appeared to put the Birmingham case. Wright stressed the need for permanent national machinery under the auspices of Chambers of Commerce or, in their absence, associations having similar objects and functions. Committees set up to administer the registries should include labour representatives and the whole scheme should be administered by the Board of Trade. Under questioning Wright maintained that the Chamber had no objections to municipal control and labour registries provided they were kept entirely separate from the Poor Law or Distress Committees...

The conclusion of this argument is not that all or even a majority of British employers wished to see state welfare measures introduced in the first decade of the twentieth century, nor yet that welfare reform was a significant reflection of business interest and pressure. Rather it is that a significant and influential proportion of the business community did wish to see changes in the relationship between the employer, the employee and the state, which included measures of social reform as well as attempts to control the political and industrial activities of Trade Unions...

Welfare policy in Britain was initially designed to strengthen the basis of the existing structure of society in face of internal and external crises and it would be difficult to find a period when such motives ceased to be influential.

5 – J.R. Hay, *The Origins of Liberal Welfare Reforms 1906–1914* (London, Macmillan, 1978), pp 25-9

There is a wide measure of agreement among historians and social scientists that political pressure from the working class was one of the main reasons for the origins of social reform. Politicians introduced social reform either to attract electoral popularity or to prevent workers turning to extreme socialist or syndicalist solutions...

But there are some problems with simpler versions of this link between political democracy and social reform. Why, if social reform was so popular, was it never a major election issue? [Bentley B.] Gilbert's answer is that the two major parties were aware that they could get involved in an auction of social reform and made a tacit bargain not to compete...

Gilbert and others stress the effects of the franchise changes in the 1880s, but these made little difference to either the strength or the effectiveness of working-class pressure...

One simple way out of the difficulty is to deny that social reform was popular and insistently demanded by the working class. Pelling has suggested that 'the extension of the power of the state at the beginning of this century, which is generally regarded as having laid the foundation of the Welfare State, was by no means welcomed by members of the working class, was being undertaken over the critical hostility of many of them, perhaps most of them'. He attributes this hostility to the dislike of the existing state institutions, especially the Poor Law...

These arguments have not been generally accepted... Hobsbawm feels that Pelling's hypothesis might apply to the 'ordinary, unskilled uneducated and unorganised masses' but that it is misleading if applied to the organised labour movement. Other historians... emphasise the importance of deference and the acceptance of some middle-class norms by important sections within the working class, especially those who have been granted the franchise. The working-class voter was not interested in a massive redistribution of income, but expressed preference for only limited social changes which were quite within the compass of traditional parties. Social reform was only one element which determined voting patterns and demand for reform was neither insistent nor profound. Moreover support for reform was diffused among competing groups and their influence was reduced. Though politics were conducted on a class basis in the late nineteenth and early twentieth centuries, the major parties were not forced into social reform by massive popular demand or fear of revolution, but were to introduce specific policies to gain tactical advantage over other parties. Given the character of the electorate, there would be a gradual trend towards social reform, no more. This approach which is tending to become the new orthodoxy, is closely bound up with the view that the Liberal Party had established a viable base in the new class politics before the First World War... [Hay believes that many of Hobsbawm's observations are correct and that evidence points to a number of working-class attitudes.]

Some opposed welfare reforms on theoretical grounds, arguing that the economic and political system had to be changed first. Others made a distinction between social and economic reforms. 'To the poor, economic reform means a measure of justice between the "haves" and "have nots", but social reform means "police", whether they are really required or not.' Some had no objection to reform in principle and supported or opposed specific Liberal measures. Finally, there were some who benefited personally from social legislation...

There remains the effectiveness of working-class pressure for reform. Some historians see the Labour Party as an appendage of the radical wing of the Liberals which exerted relatively little pressure for social reform... Others, like K.D. Brown... have argued that it played an important part in Liberal legislation, particularly that relating to unemployment. [Hay believes that social reform is only partly the result of working-class pressure, and that the pressure of individual reforms needs to be examined in detail.]

6 – P. Thane, 'The working class and state "welfare" in Britain 1889–1914', *Historical Journal* 27/4 (1984)

Some years ago Henry Pelling offered one of his stimulating and provocative challenges to a conventional wisdom of labour history. He pointed out that it is often assumed that the significant extension of the welfare activities of the state by the post-1906 Liberal governments were in some way associated with the growth of the organised labour movement; that they were, if not simply responses to pressure from Labour (which has rarely been seriously argued), at least supported and welcomed by a significant proportion of the working class, and therefore could be expected by Liberal politicians to increase their credit with working-class voters, perhaps insufficiently to persuade them to resist the lure of Labour.

Pelling argued that this assumption was incorrect, that the mass of working people were hostile or indifferent to state welfare at least until after measures such as old age pensions and national insurance were introduced; that labour and socialist politicians who proposed welfare reforms, such as the Webbs, or Hyndman, were themselves middle class. Working-class dislike of state welfare, he suggested, derived partly from a deeply rooted preference for independence and self-help, partly from suspicion of the state as a complex of institutions run by or on behalf of the rich (as apparently exemplified by the constraints imposed by the courts upon trade union activity, culminating with Taff Vale), and partly from experience of state social intervention which was seen rather rarely to have brought unmixed benefits to workers. He instances popular hatred of the Poor Law, of compulsory education, which deprived poor families of the vital earnings of their children, and of local authority housing and clearance policies which appeared to dis-house as many as were housed. He added that there is no evidence that social policy issues influenced working-class voters in national elections. He concluded that Liberal reforms came about largely due to middle-class pressures and because Liberal politicians, notably Asquith, Lloyd George and Churchill, 'thought them desirable' and were able to finance them. He did not explore why they thought them desirable, though rather dismissed the possibility that they consciously sought to prevent the loss of working-class votes to Labour.

If Pelling was correct, he offered an important pointer to working-class political attitudes and expectations before 1914 and he opened up new questions: how, and why, did official Labour and working-class attitudes so change in the succeeding generations that by 1945 Labour was popularly identified as the party of social reform and became the party which created the modern 'welfare state'?

There is considerable evidence to support Pelling's contentions, stronger sometimes than he was himself able to offer, since he actually offers rather little...

Radical opposition to proposed reforms was also evident among trades councils. Throughout the 1890s and 1900s, trades councils were in large and small towns throughout the country devoting a large proportion of their time to discussion, investigation and agitation about the need for more and better working-class housing, old age pensions, working-class education at all levels, health care, school meals, poor law reforms, against sweated labour, for railway nationalisation and cheap fares...

But the councils were not generally uncritical in welcoming these measures as symptoms of social progress, though some of their members were inclined to be so; rather they believed in their extreme inadequacy. Like many groups they went through a process of debate about the terms on which they should accept state 'welfare'. [There follows a discussion of class collaboration in welfare measures.]

Many trades council members experienced a similar conflict over collaboration with state welfare measures which they believed might not be in the best long-term interests of their class, but which alleviated short-term need. The way out of this dilemma for many of them lay in increasing belief in the possibility of effecting working-class representation in local and national politics...

So what does this partial, selective and hurried survey tell us about working-class attitudes to welfare before 1914? That there was, as Pelling suggested, widespread suspicion of the policies and action of Liberal and other politicians. The grounds for this suspicion were that they were too limited, too 'intrusive', and a threat to working-class independence both collective and individual. But these views were not universal and probably diminished over time. Many poorer people, throughout, were grateful for any amelioration of hard lives. It is reasonable to conclude that very many people would have preferred, as an ideal, regular work, wages sufficient for a decent life, however defined, allowing them sufficient surplus to save for hard times and perhaps even to choose to pay for their children's education, their own health, or health care, leaving the state the minimal role of providing services which the individual could not... Only a highly politicised minority of liberals and socialists thought with any precision about the desirable extent and nature of state action. Few however could have thought either the individualist or collectivist versions of the desirable state foreseeably attainable before 1914.

7 – David Vincent, *Poor Citizen, The State and the Poor in Twentieth Century Britain* (London, Longman, 1992), p 44

Henceforth it was evident that for the most part reform would not extend far into the realm of wages, nor far beyond the capacity of insurance to deal with the failure of charity and the Poor Law. Increasing national prosperity would be the means rather than the end of legislation. The task was to find a more efficient way of dealing with poverty, not a way of dealing with poverty which was to promote a more efficient economy.

PRIMARY EVIDENCE AND INFORMATION

8 – B.S. Rowntree, *Poverty: A Study of Town Life* (London, Longman, 1901) and second edition (1906), p 295–8, 300

(a) Families whose total earnings were insufficient to obtain the minimum necessaries for the maintenance of merely physical efficiency. Poverty falling under this head was described as 'primary' poverty.

(b) Families whose total earnings would have been sufficient for the maintenance of merely physical efficiency were it that some portion of it was absorbed by other expenditure, either useful or wasteful. Poverty falling under this head was described as 'secondary' poverty...

[Rowntree drew up an absolute poverty line of 21s/8p for food, rent, clothing, lighting and fuel for a family of five, and then calculated the number experiencing primary and secondary poverty in York. Those failing to meet this standard were in primary poverty but investigators, in their house-to-house visits, noted other families who were obviously living in poverty and squalor.]

In this way 20,302 persons, or 27.84 percent of the total population, were returned as living in poverty. Subtracting those whose poverty is 'primary', we arrive at the number living in 'secondary' poverty, viz. 13,072 or 17.93 percent of the total population.

We have been accustomed to look upon the poverty in London as exceptional, but when the results of careful investigation show that the proportion of poverty in London is practically equalled in what may be regarded as a typical provincial town, we are faced with the startling probability that from 25 to 30 percent of the town populations of the United Kingdom are living in poverty.

9 – *Report on the Guilds of Help in England* by G.R. Snowden, An Assistant General Inspector of the Local Government Board (Cd 56664, HMSO, 1911)

Origin and Development of the Movement

1. The first Guild of Help was inaugurated chiefly by the efforts of Mr Bentham and Mrs Moser, in Bradford, in 1904. In 1905 Guilds were founded at Bolton, Eccles, Halifax, Heckmondwike, Salford and Swinton (near Manchester)... Among the number of Guilds of Help are not reckoned the Charity Organisation Societies, or such bodies as the Central Relief Committee at Liverpool, or such bodies as the Central Relief Committee at Liverpool or the Council of Social Services at Hampstead, which pursue the same objects by not dissimilar methods.

2. The idea of the Guild of Help movement no doubt came partly from the Elberfeld poor law system...

General Objects

4. The general objects of the Guilds of Help may be summarised as follows from their published statements:

(1) To deepen the sense of civic responsibility for the care of the poor, and to promote, through personal services, a neighbourly feeling among all classes of the community.

(2) To provide a friend for all those in need of help and advice, and to encourage them in efforts towards self-help.

(3) To discourage indiscriminate almsgiving by private persons, and to organise methods whereby the generosity of such persons may be wisely directed and enabled to secure results of permanent benefit.

(4) To co-operate with all existing charitable agencies in order to prevent overlapping.

(5) To arrest the inroads of poverty in its initial stages in order to prevent the poor from sinking into destitution and to ensure, so far as possible, that no home shall be broken up which can be saved by friendly advice and assistance.

(6) To consider the causes of poverty in the town and to bring influence to bear through public bodies or by private efforts to lessen or remove them.

5. Attention should be directed to two general characteristics common to all Guilds. First, the work is carried on by voluntary assistance and unpaid personal service; and, as in Elberfeld, the person who visits and investigates a case has a voice in deciding what assistance is to be given. Second, a prominent position is given to the idea of a man's civic responsibilities, his special duties to the place in which he lives and to his fellow-citizens as such. It is sought to foster local patriotism and to create an interest in all matters of local importance. The field of the Guild's work coincides usually, with the borough and other areas of municipal government; the Mayor, or the Chairman of the District Council, is its President... In order to emphasise this point of view, some such words as 'The City' or 'Citizens', or 'Civic' are frequently prefixed to the title Guild of Help. It should be added that all Guilds profess absolute independence of all parties in politics and religion.

Organisation and Methods

10. The town is divided into a number of units named 'districts'... The helpers in each district form the 'district committee'.

11. The helpers are drawn from all classes of society; in a few Guilds half or more than half are men and women of the working classes...

Promotion of Co-operation among Charities

25. The promotion of co-operation among charities one of the foremost aims of the Guild of Help movement; and perhaps the most practical step in this direction, as a means to the prevention of overlapping in the distribution of relief, is the establishment of a general register of all persons receiving aid from charitable sources...

Co-operation with Public Authorities

34. The civic ideal of a Guild of Help... comprehends essentially the closest possible co-operation with the public authorities. This ideal, unfortunately, seems at present to be far from attainment, but some advances have been made towards it.

10 – *Help*, the journal of the Bradford City Guild of Help, Vol. IV, 12 November 1908.

The Guild of Help is the practical expression of the civic consciousness and the embodiment of the new philanthropy. The old, was clearly associated with charity in a narrow sense, and between those who gave and those who received was a great gulf fixed; the 'lady bountiful' attitude has received its death blow, the Guild worker does not go in as visitant from another world but as a fellow creature to be helpful.

11 – Fred Jowett, *The Socialist and the City* (London, ILP, 1907), pp 2–3

The future must grow out of the present; it cannot be created to fit with a plan.

The Socialist, in the city life of today, is painfully trying, amidst many difficulties and much misunderstanding, unfortunately accompanied also by a considerable amount of misrepresentation, to change the municipal institutions at present in existence and add to their number, so as to bring them into harmony with the social gospel which he preaches in accordance to his convictions.

He cherishes his ideals because they help him to decide which way true progress lies, but the necessity for carrying public opinion with him at every step confines his power within very narrow limits. Sometimes the Socialist municipal reformer is inclined to chafe at the limitations which the indifference of public opinion imposes upon his activity, since being himself, at his best, moved by strong convictions, he is naturally impatient of delay. But, being by conviction a democrat, his inclination to chafe soon gives way to the feeling that on the whole it is better so, because progress in advance of the public opinion of the day rests on very unsafe foundation...[27]

12 – Letter from Beatrice Webb to W.H. Beveridge, 4 May 1907, asking for assistance in connection with the Poor Law Enquiry, taken from the Beveridge Collection, Letters, IIb, no. 6, in the Archives Division of the British Library of Political and Economic Science

I want your help in respect to the Poor Law Enquiry into the working of the Unemployed Act. We begin this Enquiry next Autumn. But from past experience of the work of the Commission I see that we shall get little else but 'opinion' and those mostly in a negative direction. Messrs Pringle and Jackson's investigation did little else but discredit Relief work and suggested no alternative ways of dealing with the Unemployed. Moreover their investigation was limited by their Reference to the working of the Unemployment Acts and they were not asked to Enquire or Report into the working of the Poor Law alternative to the Workhouse test, the Labour Yard. These alternatives have also been ruled out of our Enquiry next Autumn, as it is assumed that we have dealt with it in our general Enquiry into Poor Law Administration which is now practically concluded. That is not the case, and these alternatives therefore hold the field if we arrive at our unfavourable verdict on Relief Work. What I wanted (but was over-ruled) was an Enquiry into all ways of dealing with the Able-bodied or persons assumed to be able-bodied, including the Casual Ward, and therefore vagrancy. Only in that way shall we get a statesmanlike grasp on the question. The Charity Organisation Society, on the other hand, is to break the subject up into little bits and get a negative conclusion on each division so as to fall back in the 'non Possumous'.

Now what I should like would be some help both in suggestions as to possible reform and actual investigations into fact. Would it be possible to form a little Committee to take each way of dealing with the Able-bodied into consideration, getting all the evidence together on each part, and looking at each by the light of the other? If then we could get a secretary (for a small salary to do the clerk's work and possibly some additional investigation) we might draw up a report of our own which the Progressive members of the Commission might circulate as Memorandum...

13 – Evidence given by Sir William Beveridge on Employment Exchanges (1906) drawing upon the Criticism of the Existing Methods of Relief to Able-Bodied (1906), Beveridge Collection, III, 32 in Beveridge IIb 6, Archives Division, British Library of Political and Economic Science

We have now shown that municipal relief-works have not assisted but rather prejudiced the better classes of workmen they were intended to help. On the other hand they have encouraged the casual labourers, by giving them a further supply of that casual work which is so dear to their hearts and so demanding to their character. They have encouraged and not helped the incapables. Moreover, the provision of artificial work for the unskilled labourers in particular localities can only tend to fix in such localities agglomerations of unskilled labour, to digress, which is one of the solutions of local employment. We regard, therefore, that we must preserve the system of relief-works suggested by the Local Government Board Circular of 1886 a failure, and we support our condemnation of this by the following extract for the Report of our Special Investigators:

The Municipal Relief Works, encouraged by Mr. Chamberlain's circular in 1886 have been in operation for twenty years, and must, we think, be pronounced a complete failure – a failure accentuated by the attempt to organise them by the Unemployed Workmen's Act of 1905. The evidence we have collected seems conclusive that relief works are economically useless. Either ordinary work is taken, in which case it is merely forestalled, and later, throws out of employment the men who are in the more or less regular employ of the council, or else it is sham work which we believe to be even more deteriorating than direct relief. If the 'right to work' is to be construed as the right to easy work, we are directly encouraging the lazy and incompetent and discouraging the trade unionists and the thrifty. The evidence seems very strong that most men on relief work do not do their best, and to pay them less than ordinary wages only encourages the belief that they are not expected to do so. Competence to do the work required should be the basis for selection, not destitution and a large family. These are very good reasons for giving relief but not for giving work.

14 – Winston Churchill, speaking to the House of Commons, 19 May 1909, from *Hansard*, 19 May 1909, on the issue of Unemployment Insurance

So I come to unemployment insurance. It is not practicable at the present time to establish a universal system of unemployment insurance… We have therefore to choose at the very outset of this subject between insuring some workmen in all trades and insuring all workmen in some trades. That is the first parting of the ways upon unemployment insurance. In the first case we can have a voluntary system and in the second a compulsory system. If you adopt a voluntary system of unemployment insurance, you are always exposed to this difficulty. The risk of unemployment varies so much between man and man, according to their qualities… and the risk varies so much between man and man that a voluntary system of unemployment insurance which the State subsidises always attracts those workers who are most likely to be unemployed. That is why all voluntary systems have broken down when they have been tried, because they accumulate a preponderance of bad risks against the insurance office, which is fatal to financial stability. On the other hand, a compulsory system of insurance, which does not add a contribution from outside, has always broken down, because of the refusal of the higher class of worker to assume unsupported a share of the burden of the weaker members of the community. We have decided to avoid these main difficulties. Our insurance scheme will present four main features. It will involve contributions from the workpeople and from the employers; those contributions will be aided by a substantial subvention from the State: it will be insurance by trade, following the suggestion of the Royal Commission; and it will be compulsory within those trades upon all unionists and non-unionists, skilled and unskilled, workmen and employers alike.

15 – Extract from the *Minority Report* of the Royal Commission on the Poor Laws and Relief of Distress (1905–9), p 684

Utopian

[Our] elaborate scheme for national organisation for dealing with the grave social evils of Unemployment, with its resultant Able-bodied Destitution, and the deterioration of hundreds of thousands of working-class families, will seem to many persons Utopian. Experience proves, however, that this may mean no more than that it will take a little time to accustom people to the proposals, and to get them carried into operation. The first step is to make the whole community realise that the evil exists. At present, it is not too much to say that the average citizen of the middle or upper class takes for granted the constantly recurring destitution among wage-earning families due to Unemployment as part of the natural order of things...

We have to report that, in our judgement, it is now administratively possible, if it is sincerely wished to do so, to remedy most of the evils of Unemployment...

16 – Speech by David Lloyd George, Chancellor of the Exchequer, in the House of Commons debate, *Hansard*, 4 May 1911, referring to the health and unemployment aspects of the National Insurance Act of 1911

In this country... 30 percent of pauperism is attributable to sickness. A considerable percentage would probably have to be added to that for unemployment. The administration of the Old Age Pensions Act has revealed the fact that there is mass poverty and destitution in this country which is too proud to wear the badge of pauperism, and which declines to pin that badge to its children. They would rather deprivation than do so...

The efforts made by the working classes to insure against the troubles of life indicate they are fully alive to the need of some provision being made. There are three contingencies against which they insure – death, sickness and unemployment. There are 42,000,000 industrial policies against death in this country... There is hardly a household in this country where there is not a policy of insurance against death. It is no part of our scheme at all, partly because the general ground has been covered...

Sickness comes next in order of urgency in the working-class mind, Between 6,000,000 and 7,000,000 people in this country have made provision against sickness, not all adequate and a good deal of it defective. Then come the third class, the insurance against unemployment. Here not a tenth of the working classes have made any provision against unemployment...

What is the explanation that only a portion of the working-classes have made provision against sickness and unemployment? Is it that they consider it not necessary. Quite the reverse, as I shall prove by figures. In fact, those who stand in need of it make up the bulk of the uninsured. Why? Because very few can afford to pay the premiums, and pay them continually, which enable a man to provide against those three contingencies. As a matter of fact, you could not provide against all those three contingencies anything which would be worth a workman's while, without paying at any rate 1s 6d and 2s per week at the very lowest. There are a multitude of working classes who cannot spare that, and ought not to be asked to spare it, because it involves the deprivation of children of the necessaries of life. Therefore, they are compelled to select, and the vast majority choose to insure against death alone. Those who can afford to take up all three insure against death, sickness and unemployment in that order. What are the explanations why they do not insure against all three? The first is that their wages are too low. The second difficulty, and it is the greatest of all, is that during the period of sickness and unemployment, when they are earning nothing, they cannot keep up premiums... I do not think there is any better method, or one more practicable at the present moment, than a system of national insurance which would invoke the aid of the State and the aid of the employer to enable the workmen to get over all these difficulties and make provision for himself for sickness and, as far as most precarious trades are concerned, against unemployment...

I now come to the machinery of the Bill we have got to work. Collection is the first thing. We shall collect our funds by means of stamps. That is purely the German system... Then comes the question, who is to dispense the benefits? In this country we have fortunately a number of very well-organised, well-managed, well-conducted benefit societies who have a great tradition behind them, and an accumulation of experience which is very valuable when you come to deal with questions like malingering.

I will now briefly outline the unemployment insurance... The scheme only applies to one-sixth of the industrial population. We propose to apply it only to the precarious trades, which are liable to very comfortable fluctuations. The benefit will be of a very simple character; it is purely a weekly allowance... The machinery will be the Labour Exchanges and the existing unions which deal with unemployment...

We have started, first of all, by taking two groups of trades, and we propose to organise them individually – the engineering group and the building group. They include building, construction of works, shipbuilding, mechanical engineering and the construction of vehicles. These are trades in which you have the most serious fluctuations... I ought to say here that you have not the same basis of actuarial calculation that you can in sicknesses that a certain fund will produce such and such benefits. In the case of sickness you have nearly 100 years' experience behind you, and you have the facts with regard to unemployment...

I have explained as best I could the details of our scheme – the system of contributions and benefits and the machinery whereby something like 15,000,000 people will be insured at any rate against the acute distress which now darkens the homes of the workmen, wherever there is sickness and unemployment.

17 – David Lloyd George and the People's Budget, quoted in *Hansard*, 10 October 1909.

The question will be asked 'Should 500 men, ordinary men chosen accidentally from the unemployed, override the judgement – the deliberate judgement – of millions of people who are engaged in the industry which makes the wealth of the country?' That is one question. Another will be, who ordained that a few should have the land of Britain as a perquisite; who made 10,000 people owners of the soil, and the rest of us as trespassers in the land of our birth; who is it – who is responsible for the scheme of things whereby one man is engaged through life in grinding labour... and another man who does not toil receives every hour of the day, every hour of the night, whilst he slumbers, more than his neighbour receives in a whole year of toil?

Notes on Chapter 1

1   D. Fraser, *The Evolution of the British Welfare State* (London, Macmillan, first edition 1973), p 163.
2   J. Harris, 'Political Thought and the Welfare State 1870–1914: An Intellectual Framework for British Social Policy', *Past and Present* 135, May 1992.
3   J. Melling, 'Welfare capitalism and the origins of Welfare States: British Industry, Workplace, Welfare and Social reform, c. 1870–1914', *Social History* 17/3 (1992), pp 453–78.
4   H. Pelling, 'The Working Class and the Welfare State' in H. Pelling, *Popular Politics and Society in Late Victorian Britain* (1968); P. Thane, 'The Working Class and State "Welfare" in Britain, 1880–1914', *Historical Journal* 27/4 (1984), pp 877–900.

5 Thane, 'The Working Class and State "Welfare" in Britain, 1880-1914'.

6 J. Harris, 'Society and State in Twentieth-century Britain' in *The Cambridge Social History of Britain 1750–1950* Volume 3: *Social Agencies and Institutions* (Cambridge, Cambridge University Press, 1990), p 70.

7 M.B. Simey, *Charitable Effort in Liverpool* (Liverpool, Liverpool University Press, 1951), pp 124–36.

8 Reported in the Borough of Poole League of Help, minutes, 13 April 1908.

9 Poole League of Help, minutes, 18 November 1907.

10 County Borough of Bolton Guild of Help, Third Annual Report, November 1907, pp 5–10.

11 Halifax Citizen's Guild of Help, *Fifth Annual Report* 1909–10 (Halifax, Halifax Guild of Help, 1910), p 4.

12 *Croydon Guild of Help Magazine*, no. 20, July 1912, p 98.

13 *The Citizen* (organ of the Reading Guild of Help), Vol. 1, no. 2, July 1912.

14 K. Laybourn, *The Guild of Help and the Changing Face of Edwardian Philanthropy* (Lampeter, Edwin Mellen Press, 1994), ch. three.

15 K. Laybourn and J. Reynolds, *Liberalism and the Rise of Labour* (London, Croom Helm, 1984), ch. one; P.F. Clarke, *Lancashire and the New Liberalism* (Cambridge, Cambridge University Press, 1971); D. Powell, 'The New Liberalism and the Rise of Labour, 1886–1906', *Historical Journal* 19/2 (1986).

16 Powell, 'The New Liberalism and the Rise of Labour, 1886–1906', pp 376, 379, 382.

17 *Manchester Guardian*, 7 November 1914.

18 K. Morgan, 'The New Liberalism and the Challenge of Labour: The Welsh Experience' in K.D. Brown (ed.), *Essays in Anti-Labour History* (London, Macmillan, 1974); A.W. Purdue, 'The Liberal and Labour Parties in North-East Politics, 1900–1914: The Struggle for Supremacy', *International Review of Social History* Vol. xxvi, pt. 1 (1981), pp 1–24; P. Thompson, *Socialists Liberals and Labour: The Struggle for London 1885–1914* (London, 1967), p 170.

19 Thane, 'The Working Class and State "Welfare" in Britain, 1880-1914'.

20 Fraser, *The Evolution of the British Welfare State*, p 174.

21 P. Thane, *The Foundations of the Welfare State* (London, Longman, 1982), p 83.

22 *The Helper*, Vol. 1/2. February 1909, pp 6–8.

23 *Ibid.*, 4 May 1911.

24 Thane, *The Foundations of the Welfare State*, p 91.

25 *Ibid.*, letter from Beatrice Webb to Beveridge, 4 May 1907.

26 *Ibid.*, 29 April 1909, and also quoted in Fraser, *The Evolution of the British Welfare State*, pp 145–6.

27 F.W. Jowett, *The Socialist and the City* (London, ILP, 1907), pp 2–3.

Chapter 2

Class Politics or Accident of War? Liberalism and the Rise of Labour 1906–18

Introduction

The years between 1906 and the end of the First World War saw a fundamental change in the balance of political power, particularly within the progressive politics of Britain. The general election of 1905–6 brought the Liberal Party back to office with 400 MPs, after a period of 11 years in opposition. Although the Conservative Party was still the second largest parliamentary party, it had been defeated and the real political danger to the Liberals lay in the fact that the Labour Representation Committee, soon to be the Labour Party, had returned 29, soon to be 30, MPs at the election, thus enormously increasing its pre-election strength amongst the progressive electorate. This development, more than the subsequent revival of the Conservative Party, was to be the dominating political theme of these years and the cause of much contemporary and current debate. This was especially the case because the Liberals experienced a period of decline which saw the number of its MPs fall to 40 in the general election of 1924, ten months after the Labour Party had formed its first government. Not surprisingly, G.R. Searle regards this political change as 'the most important single development in early twentieth-century political life',[1] a sentiment echoed by many other writers.[2]

The major events of Labour growth and Liberal decline are well known. The Labour Representation Committee was formed in 1900, redefined its aims to capture wider working-class and trade-union support at its Newcastle Conference in 1903, was tied into a secret Lib-Lab pact to avoid competition between it and the Liberal Party in over 30 seats in 1903, and improved its parliamentary representation substantially at the December 1905–January 1906 general election. Thereafter, it operated a policy of supporting the Liberal Party and became increasingly important in that role after the 1910 general election when the Liberal Party began to lose parliamentary seats. During the First World War, in May 1915, it was drawn into the wartime Coalition Government, and looked well positioned to assume the mantle of the progressive party in British politics at the end of the war when the Liberal Party was divided and Lloyd George was only sustained by the Conservatives.

The Liberal Party seemed to be omnipotent in 1906. It had achieved a landslide victory in the general election and was intending to build up its political support amongst the working classes by offering social reforms which were more intrusive than any they had offered before, and which sought to tackle some of the major social problems of unemployment, ill-health, old age and poverty. Social harmony was its objective, but this was both its perceived strength and weakness. Whilst social reform did help to attract working-class support in some areas, and kept the Labour Party on its side, this philosophy also meant that it sought not to choose sides in an industrial dispute. The lack of New Liberal support for trade unions in disputes thus led to a reaffirmation of trade-union commitment to the emergent Labour Party. The First World War further weakened the Liberal Party by raising issues of policy and leadership which divided, rather than united, it. The Liberal shibboleths of peace, retrenchment and free trade were all challenged and undermined by the war, there were Liberal doubts about the formation of the Coalition Government and some disquiet on the conduct of the War, which saw Lloyd George replace Asquith as Prime Minister in December 1916. In the end, it was a divided Liberal Party which fought the general election of December 1918. As a result, the Liberal Party under Asquith declined to a rump of MPs while the Liberal Party under Lloyd George helped to form a Coalition Government with the dominating and overwhelming Conservative support.

Debates

Historians have sought to explain the rise of Labour and the decline of Liberalism, and to establish the precise timing of the change. They have asked a number of related questions. Was it class politics or the First World War that caused the decline of Liberalism? More precisely, was it the trade-union and working-class support for the Labour Party that pushed the Labour Party forward, or was it simply the split within the Liberal Party, most obviously seen in the way in which David Lloyd George replaced

Asquith as Prime Minister? In other words, was the shift in political support before 1914 decisive, or was it later internal party politics which brought a change in progressive politics in Britain?

The primary cause of Liberal decline and Labour growth is obvious: the voters had abandoned the Liberal Party in favour of its Labour and Conservative rivals. But why had this occurred? Some historians – such as George Dangerfield, Henry Pelling, Ross McKibbin and Keith Laybourn – argue that Labour's growth was rapid before 1914 largely because it had captured trade-union, and thus working-class, support from the Liberal Party. A variation of this argument is put forward by both Bill Lancaster and Keith Laybourn, who maintain that the growth and development of the Labour movement must recognise the local variations that occurred, Lancaster noting 'the organic growth of the party rooted in local political and economic conflict and the corresponding decline in working-class Liberal support'.[3] Lancaster also maintains that there was a close connection between radicalism and socialism, and emphasises, in the case of Leicester, the persistence of the social base of cultural radicalism. At the other extremes there are historians such as Trevor Wilson, Michael Bentley and Duncan Tanner who reject such views and maintain that the First World War helped to destroy the Liberal Party and created a political vacuum within progressive politics which was filled by the Labour Party. Even here, there are divisions, though, for whilst most of this group see the First World War as decisive, some, particularly Bentley, feel that the Liberal Party could have retrieved the situation if it had been willing to be flexible in the policies it pursued: the fixity of the 'Liberal mind' prevented the revival of the Liberals.

The contentious debate about the rise of Labour and the decline of Liberalism began almost 60 years ago, at a moment when the Liberal Party had all but expired. George Dangerfield's *Strange Death of Liberal England* announced that the 'death knell of Liberalism' was ringing well before 1914, and that after the 1906 general election the Liberal Party was 'no longer the party of the left'.[4] Although Dangerfield's book is mainly a literary confection of assertions, 'an entrancing historical novel' gathered around the view that the Liberal Party was incapable of dealing with the challenge of Labour, female suffrage, Ireland and constitutional change, it provides the context of the debate which still rages today.[5] Period piece or not, what Dangerfield did was develop the ideas of Fabian writers who had tended to accept the almost Whiggish belief in the continuous and inevitable rise of Labour. Dangerfield merely perpetuated the belief that the Liberal Party had fallen victim to the development of class politics as the working class attached itself to the political ambitions of the Labour Party.

It was almost 20 years before Henry Pelling took the argument further when he provided evidence of the way in which the Independent Labour

Party (ILP) and the Labour Party began to cultivate trade-union support at the expense of the Liberals, who had neglected to attend to the needs of their trade-union supporters and were unwilling to consider their candidates for parliamentary and municipal support[6] (Document 1). His later work gave the impression that pre-war contemporaries accepted the inevitability of Labour replacing the Liberal Party as the progressive force in British politics.[7] Since the 1970s, Ross McKibbin has been the leading spirit of this class-politics explanation (Document 2). Examining the history of the Labour Party for the period 1910–24, he has maintained that Labour's increasing association with the trade-union movement captured for it the support of the working class: 'Yet the Labour Party was not based upon broadly articulated principles, but rather upon a highly developed class-consciousness and intense class loyalties…'[8] This process of rising working-class attachment to the Labour Party was, apparently, well entrenched before the First World War, and spelled the decline of the Liberal Party, although in recent years McKibbin has softened his attitude to the irrelevance of the First World War in Labour's growth.[9] The more recent works of Laybourn, Reynolds and Bernstein endorse such a view.[10]

Nevertheless, since the mid-1960s this class-based explanation has been challenged by the Liberal 'revisionists'. In 1966, Trevor Wilson produced a remarkable book, *The Downfall of the Liberal Party* (Document 3), which has influenced books and articles by Roy Douglas, P.F. Clarke (Document 4), K.D. Brown, Chris Cook, Michael Bentley, Duncan Tanner and others, all of which have all attempted to explain the demise of the Liberal Party in reference to the cultural and social change wrought by the First World War.[11] The 'rampant omnibus' of war – which exposed that the Liberal Party was ideologically ill-equipped to deal with 'total war' – apparently ran over it and created the internal tensions that led to the replacement of Asquith by Lloyd George as Prime Minister in 1916.[12] Bentley made much the same point when he wrote that 'the First World War not only buried the Liberal future but rendered hopeless the past by which Liberals had chartered the course which took them there'.[13] Nonetheless, Bentley's approach is far more positive than Wilson's, and accepts that war sifted out the type of Liberalism most suited to the occasion, although it thereby led to a parting of the ways between the Asquithian Liberalism of the centre and David Lloyd George's left-of-centre variety. To Bentley, 1916 saw the almost permanent parting of the ways, and was proof positive that the internal conflict between Liberal leaders could destroy a party just as much as any external threat from Labour.[14]

These historians have needed to prove that the Liberal Party was politically healthy in 1914, that the Labour Party was performing badly, and that New Liberal ideas were permeating the Liberal ranks in the pre-war years. These needs have led Clarke to suggest that New Liberalism, with its greater emphasis upon social reform, was the key to the Liberal revival from 1906 to 1914.[15] He thus stresses the strength of Liberalism, and accepts that class politics had established itself by 1910, and that the Liberal Party had adapted and survived. It did so because it embodied new progressive ideals, with their connotations of 'social justice, state intervention and alliance with Labour', the basis of Liberal policy after 1906.[16] The fact that Clarke's study was based upon Lancashire, a peculiar county where in the 1890s the Conservative Party held more sway than the Liberals, who were thus forced to change their political approach, did not inhibit him from making the claim that Lancashire was the 'cockpit' of British politics.[17] Indeed, he developed his ideas in a second book which examined the lives of ideas of social-democratic intellectuals.[18] Other Liberal revisionists have noted the failures of the Labour Party before the war, particularly in parliamentary by-elections.[19]

Sub-Debates

The debate about the rise of Labour and the decline of Liberalism has spawned several sub-debates. The three most important concern the issues of the franchise, the New Liberal ideology and local developments.

The sub-debate on the impact of the pre-war parliamentary franchise has become extremely complex in recent years, and is now studded with speculative calculations about the proportions and numbers of middle-class and working-class males excluded from the parliamentary vote before 1914. Matthew, McKibbin and Kay argued that if the 4,800,000 or so largely working-class men who were kept from voting by the 1884 franchise had been on the register, as they were under the 1918 Franchise Act, then the Labour Party would have presented a more serious political challenge to Liberalism than was apparent in its pre-war parliamentary representation.[20] Clarke, M. Hart and Tanner disagree, their views being represented by the statement 'The war caused the Liberal party to break up intellectually, in the constituencies (especially after the election), and in Parliament.'[21] Furthermore, they argue that the pre-war franchise imposed random inequality and denied the vote to male members of both the middle and working classes alike. Clarke also denigrates Labour's parliamentary by-election performances between 1910 and 1914, noting that Labour came third in 14 three-cornered contests in industrial constituencies between 1910 and 1914.[22]

How are we to assess these claims and counter-claims regarding the impact of the pre-war franchise? Despite recent criticism, there is much evidence that Labour was much stronger than its parliamentary performances would suggest. Indeed, Labour did not do as badly in parliamentary by-elections as Clarke suggests. Despite the defeat of Labour candidates, the party was making significant headway in some constituencies like Holmfirth (where its proportion of the vote doubled between 1910 and 1912) and Crewe (where there was a similar advance). It is also easy to underestimate the burden imposed upon Labour by the complex property-based pre-1918 parliamentary franchise. It was essential that political parties had full-time agents in order to garner their full political strength. The Labour Party, unlike its major opponents, had few full-time agents before the war – a mere 17 in 1912.[23] It was only when the national party provided a grants-in-aid scheme in May 1912, promising to pay 25 percent of the agents' salaries, that the situation was transformed. By 1918, there were 80 agents, and in 1922 the figure reached 133. Nevertheless, the Labour Party had few agents before the war, while the Society of Certificated and Associated Liberal Agents recorded 299 members in December 1915.[24] Given this situation, it was Labour supporters, rather than those of the Liberal and Conservative Parties, who were likely to fail to obtain the parliamentary franchise from registration courts simply because they were not effectively represented or put forward. Also, the financial limitations imposed upon Labour by the infamous Osborne judgement in 1908 and 1909, which also blighted Labour's parliamentary fortunes by preventing trade unions contributing a political levy to the Labour Party, also made the party's position more difficult: it was unable to give many of its enfranchised supporters the opportunity to vote for it because it could not afford to put up candidates.

In the final analysis, Labour's parliamentary performance was hardly indicative of the true level of its pre-war appeal. The franchise, financial restrictions and the absence of full-time agents conspired against Labour's ability to turn its rising trade-union vote to parliamentary effect. Yet a truer measure of Labour's appeal can be gained from the annual round of local elections. Although there is, as yet, no fully detailed survey of Labour's total political challenge in local and municipal politics, one survey of municipal election contests in England and Wales has suggested that Labour was making deep inroads into Liberal support from about 1909 onwards, and that 'this material casts grave doubt on the notions that both Labour and Liberalism may be subsumed in progressivism', Labour 'fared abysmally' in all contests with the Liberals from December 1910 to the outbreak of war, or that it was 'in decline'.[25] Indeed, its number of municipal victories in England and Wales rose from 82 in 1909 to 171 in 1913, and about 500 of the 8000 municipal seats were held by Labour on the eve of war. In addition, there were other significant signs of growth, for the Labour Party had increased the number of its MPs from two in 1900 to 30 in 1906 and 42 in December 1910.

Less speculative, but certainly more contentious, is the second sub-debate, which focuses on the impact of New Liberalism. It was L.T. Hobhouse, J.A. Hobson and Lloyd George who, attempting to retain working-class support within the Liberal Party, offered the working classes a variety of 'social reforms' and compromises which became known as New Liberalism.[26] Their prime concern was to reconcile the demands of labour with the need for Liberal Party unity, an equation which was never going to be easily arranged, given Liberal reliance upon industrial and capitalist wealth. They offered industrial conciliation for industrial conflict, public ownership where it would lead to efficiency, and communal responsibility over sectional interests.[27] The distinctive feature of these, and other New Liberal, policies was that they offered a framework whereby harmony, rather than class or sectional conflict, would be promoted. Indeed, Lloyd George stated to the National Reform Union in 1914 that 'it is better that you should have a party which combined every section and every shade of opinion, taken from all classes of the community, rather than one which represents one shade of opinion alone or one class of community alone'.[28] On another occasion, he added, 'Liberals are against anything in the nature of class representation and I think it was a mistake for the Labour party to commit to go in for anything like independent class representation. They will realise that sooner or later.'[29] Community, compromise and agreement were thus seen as the alternatives to a socialist-type Labour Party committed to changing society in favour of the working class. New Liberalism was to be the referee in British society.

Clarke has been the clearest exponent of the view that New Liberalism was responsible for the Liberal revival before the First World War (Document 4). His regional study of Lancashire suggests that the changing fortunes of the Liberal Party in the country were very largely a product of the New Liberal ideas that were offered to the electorate by C.P. Scott, editor of the *Manchester Guardian*, Winston Churchill and Lloyd George. Other writers have developed similar views and suggested that New Liberal ideas adapted well to the emergence of class politics.[30] Indeed, there has been some evidence of the development and continuation of plebeian radicalism within the working-class sections of the Liberal Party.[31] The difficulty for Clarke is that he asserts that Lancashire was the 'cockpit' of Edwardian politics, and that developments that were important in Lancashire were important elsewhere.[32] The fact is that there is little supporting evidence for his viewpoint, even from those who maintain that the Liberals were performing well up until 1914. Welsh Liberalism was, apparently, successful because of Old Liberalism, with its traditional commitment to peace, retrenchment, free trade, nonconformity and Welsh nationalism: 'new Liberalism barely existed'.[33] It was, apparently, Old, rather than New, Liberalism that was responsible for the Liberal Party's political successes in the North East, West Yorkshire and London, and there seems little evidence that it was capable of resolving the industrial conflicts which so dominated the years immediately before the First World War.[34] Kenneth Morgan makes a telling point about David

Lloyd George, one of the chief architects of New Liberalism: 'After 1908, he was a New Liberal in England and an Old Liberal in Wales'.[35] Indeed, regional demands appear to have counted for far more than the personal desires of even the most prominent of politicians.

Chris Wrigley has also assembled convincing evidence that the Liberal Party could not cope with the demands of trade unions.[36] He acknowledges that the Labour Party was not the only mouthpiece of the TUC in 1906 – the TUC also supported the trade-union mining MPs who were Lib-Lab at that time – but that it rapidly became so. Many trade unionists were still suspicious of socialists, and both Liberal and Conservative Parties vied for trade-union support despite the fact that many trade unions paid political funds to Labour; but the Osborne judgement put the matter beyond doubt, for it created problems for both the Liberal and Unionist parties. The trade unionists wanted a reversal of the judgement, and the Liberals were torn between resisting an action which could lead to the strengthening of ties between the trade unions and the Labour Party and presenting too hostile a reaction which would alienate trade unionists.

None the less, Lloyd George entered secret negotiations with the Unionists to block a reversal of the Osborne judgement, and the 1913 Trade Union Act did not reverse the judgement but rather permitted unions to hold a secret ballot on the issue. The fact is that neither the Liberal nor the Unionist parties had much motivation to reverse the Osborne judgement. In the end, it rebounded upon them as union after union held secret ballots under the 1913 Trade Union Act and voted for the political fund, which in practice was to endorse Labour representation. By the beginning of 1914, trade unions with a membership of 1,207,841 had voted on the issue of establishing political funds for the Labour Party. Of more than 420,000 members who voted, 298,702 voted in favour, 125,310 against.[37] As Wrigley suggests, 'These votes ensured Labour's post-First World War electoral finances, and in themselves reflect an element of the explanation for the rise of the Labour party and the decline of the Liberal party in the twentieth century.'[38] The trade-union appeal of New Liberalism seems to have been very limited.

New Liberalism could find few takers, but it is clear that Liberalism, Old Liberalism, still carried some influence and allowed the Liberal Party to retain its pre-eminence in progressive politics until the First World War. There was obviously immense regional and local variation in the development of Liberal and Labour support, and this forms the basis of the third, and currently topical sub-debate, about the extent pattern of Liberal and Labour support throughout the country and the type of factors that supported those political traditions. The fact is that most regional and local surveys have demonstrated a variety of experiences. Lancashire Liberalism may have revived on a diet of New Liberalism, but Welsh, North East and Yorkshire

Liberalism survived on Old Liberal values and support. In some towns, such as Bradford, Halifax and Leicester, the ILP and the Labour Party made significant inroads into areas where Liberalism had once been omnipotent partly as a result of the strength of trade-union support, according to Keith Laybourn and Jack Reynolds (Document 7). The Labour Party made headway in Colne Valley, although this was due to the power of ethical socialism, Labour's club organisation and the individualistic appeal of socialism, according to David Clark (Document 5). The patchwork of experience is not open to easy interpretation.

One problem in assessing the local and regional evidence is that most attention is still focused upon parliamentary politics. On that basis, even the strongest of Labour areas would appear to have presented a limited challenge to an entrenched Liberal Party. In West Yorkshire, for instance, the Labour Party held only three or four parliamentary seats at any one time between 1906 and 1914, while the Liberal party normally took the other 19, except for in the 1895 and 1900 general elections, in which it won only 14.[39] Concentration on the results of parliamentary by-elections lead to a similar conclusion, as is evident in Roy Douglas's essay 'Labour in Decline 1910–1914' and Michael Bentley's book *The Climax of Liberal Politics* (Document 9). The trouble is that such pre-occupation with parliamentary results alone hides the substantial evidence of Labour's growth at the local level. Recent research indicates that Labour's success in local contests cannot be lightly dismissed as representing 'no more than the natural result of increased intervention'.[40]

The precise extent and meaning of Labour's local and regional successes has been the subject of two recent major studies. David Howell's book *British Workers and the Independent Labour Party 1888–1906* surveyed the main ILP areas and acknowledged that ILP and Labour Party support was patchy (Document 6). But far more controversial has been Duncan Tanner's book, *Political Change and the Labour Party* (Document 10), which examines the wider framework of the Liberal versus Labour debate, surveys the state of the Labour Party between 1900 and 1918, and concludes that by 1914 there was an uneven pattern of political control between Labour and the Liberals, although Tanner argues that Labour support 'was comparatively strong where Liberal party support was weak and unable to seriously rival it in more Liberal areas. Co-operation was therefore possible.'[41] In the end, he maintains that Labour was not posed to replace the Liberal Party in 1914, and that Labour had no generally successful area of support.

In reflecting upon Tanner's comments, it is first wise to recognise that he is dealing with the wider debate, dismissing the class politics explanations and supporting the view that the war brought the Liberal Party to a state of collapse. There are many critics of this approach who point out that the problem is that the evidence does not support his claims.

In the first place, his conclusion that Labour was powerful in areas where the Liberals were weak will come as a surprise to those who have studied the powerful growth of the Labour Party and ILP in West Yorkshire, for here was an area where the ILP/Labour Party was making significant gains in a Liberal stronghold. Also, a good half of his Yorkshire material deals with South Yorkshire and the East Riding, and this has the effect of playing down the importance of Labour's breakthrough in its West Yorkshire heartland. This tendency to underplay West Yorkshire's significance is coupled with a lack of detailed work on municipal and local politics. We are told that 'In Bradford and Leeds, Labour made most progress before 1906, when the Liberals were extremely conservative'.[42] Yet this hardly squares with the increase in Labour councillors in Bradford from 11 in 1906 to 20 in 1913, or a similar increase in Leeds from nine to 20. Other local results are not examined. Apart from this electoral under-estimation, there is also a lack of discussion on the key institutions of Labour, such as the Clarion movement, the Labour Church, socialist Sunday schools, picnics and all the social activities that served to sustain the early Labour Party, and rendered the political break with Liberalism permanent. Similar charges have been levelled against Tanner's treatment of other areas.[43]

If Clarke's weakness was his concentration upon parliamentary events, Tanner does not seem to have served his cause well in his sweeping survey of both parliamentary and municipal elections. It may be true that Labour's growth was uneven, a patchwork of responses which might have to be interpreted in the organic development of local politics, but it is simply wrong to suggest that the Liberal Party was containing the Labour challenge, as was indicated in an earlier section on municipal politics.[44] Bill Lancaster is also right to stress the importance of examining the organic development in different regions which produced the rich mosaic of local socialisms (Document 8).

Some of Tanner's main claims also seem inconsistent. Although he argues that the Liberal and Labour Parties would have come to some type of electoral arrangement if war had not broken out, because of the ways in which the two parties complemented each other by tapping different types of support, he nevertheless emphasises the division between the parties. Given the differences of programme and class appeal which he emphasises, one questions the view that the Liberal Party had been committed to 'social democracy' in any meaningful way. He further admits that New Liberalism had no institutional base within the Liberal Party. Given these points, was it really likely that the Liberals could have rebuffed the Labour challenge?

Tanner has also attempted to undermine the validity of municipal evidence in an article in which he stresses its importance but suggests that it has not been used properly. Instead of looking at the number of municipal seats Labour were winning, he suggests that the percentage of Labour's municipal vote should be compared at some consistent stage in the parliamentary cycle.[45] The fact is that he is attempting to throw some doubt upon the value of municipal records without actually doing any serious study on these himself. Given the inaccuracy of his information referred to earlier, and the fact that other areas of local representation have not been tapped, one can discount the suggestion that local election results tell us very little. The fact is that Labour was making rapid progress in this sphere, and had speeded that process up before 1914.

A Balanced Approach

From these sub-debates, it becomes clear that the unifying strategies divide these two major groups of historians. Those who maintain that the Labour Party was rising rapidly before the war invoke the class conflict of the pre-war years, the formation of the Labour Party and the attachment to it of trade unionism as evidence of the failure of Liberalism. They argue that the inequalities of the franchise means that Labour under-performed in parliamentary elections and that it was this factor, not New Liberalism nor Old Liberalism, that confined the pre-war Labour Party to limited parliamentary success and fitful, though significant, advance in local elections. In sharp contrast, those who stress that the pre-war Liberal Party was destroyed by the war assume that the random inequalities of the franchise meant that the Liberal Party was just as disadvantaged as the Labour Party, and that it was New Liberalism or Old Liberalism, or a combination of the two, which explains the healthy state of Liberalism on the eve of war. Lacking common ground, the two schools of thought have been trenchant in debate. They rarely perceive the weakness of their own presumptions, or allow for the evidence of their opponents. The marked divisions between the two major approaches to the Liberal-versus-Labour debate, plus Lancaster's more organic approach, are evident in the following extracts (Documents 1–10)

A more balanced approach is necessary, one which accepts that the First World War was responsible for significant political and social change but admits that the Liberal Party was finding great difficulty in containing Labour's pre-war challenge. The Liberal Party's problems were largely a product of its own inability to absorb the organised working class within the caucus system which had developed in the 1860s and 1870s. In the end, the lack of a positive response from the Liberal Party drove working men to look towards the Labour Party, not for socialism so much as simply representation of their own sectional interests.

Indeed, the crunch question for this debate is at what point did the working class transfer their allegiance from the Liberal Party to the Labour

Party? Evidence suggests that this occurred before 1914, and through the trade-union movement. In part, the reason for that would appear to be the unwillingness of local Liberal Parties to permit working-class candidates to stand as Liberals in local, and indeed parliamentary, elections. What the national Liberal Party, and its local organisations, failed to appreciate was the seething discontent which had erupted among trade unionists from the mid-1880s onwards. This neglect, combined with working-class anger and frustration, helped to produce an independent Labour movement.

Few historians doubt the importance of industrial conflict in creating the climate of independent political action by the working classes. E.P. Thompson noted this, and even many of the sceptics of Labour's pre-war political growth concur.[46] The strikes amongst the girls at Bryant and May match factory in 1888, the London dockers of 1889, the gasworkers in 1889 and 1890, and the textile workers of the Manningham Mills of 1890–1 have thus attracted the attention of historians who have seen them as uniting skilled, semi-skilled and unskilled workers into an economic conflict with their employers which had political implications. Indeed, the Manningham Mills strike had immense political importance in Bradford, and the textile area of the West Riding, for 'The struggle took on the character of a general dispute between capital and labour',[47] and 'Labour had so associated itself that even defeat must be victory'.[48] Indeed, the wider Labour movement identified with the several thousand Manningham strikers, and paved the way for the formation of the Bradford Labour Union, the embryonic Bradford Independent Labour Party, in May 1891.

In the wake of such events, local labour unions and independent labour parties were formed, leading to the formation of the national Independent Labour Party in January 1893. Within seven years, following the disastrous general election performance in 1895, the ILP had pushed for the formation of the LRC in 1900, which became the Labour Party in 1906.

The formation of the LRC was seen as an affirmation of the alliance with trade unions, and the capture of the support of the Miners' Federation of Great Britain in May 1908, leading to its affiliation in January 1909, confirmed the success of the Labour Party's attempt to widen its trade-union support. By that time, Labour had increased its membership to over one million, from 353,700 in 1901.[49] Yet how much of this support was genuinely committed to the party? As K.D. Brown suggests, political allegiances are very difficult to break, and a vote for Labour was something of a political aberration.[50] Yet there is much evidence to suggest that once the Labour Party came into existence it offered an alternative focus of activity. Even the emergence of a loosely-based Lib-Lab arrangement in Edwardian politics distanced the Liberal Party from the trade unions, since their influence on trade unions was to be increasingly directed through the LRC/Labour Party.

In addition, the very formulation of the Lib-Lab pact in 1903 – whereby both parties agreed not to contend certain seats, leaving the other to mount an undivided challenge to the Conservative candidate – was anathema to the New Liberal idea of a harmony of interests operating within the Liberal Party. Its very existence was a recognition of the distinctions that were growing and the increasing popularity of the LRC. But above all, it was rapidly becoming clear that the Liberal Party could not embrace trade unionism after 1900, and by 1914 British trade unionism was firmly identified with the Labour Party. This made the Labour Party politically and led to an inevitable falling away of Liberal Party support.

Conclusion

In this introduction the emphasis has been on the dangers of oversimplification. The rise of Labour and the decline of Liberalism are not events which are easily susceptible to monocausal explanations. The rise of class politics, as evidenced through the increasing trade-union support of Labour and local organic developments, was just as much a factor in the transformation of progressive politics in Britain as was the First World War. The problem is one of assessing the point at which the process of change became inexorable. In this respect, it is clear that the process of political change was well established before the First World War. Local research combines with national evidence to suggest that a powerful Labour Party had emerged with MPs, rising trade-union membership and increasing financial support. In addition, Old Liberalism, which was unreceptive to the demands for direct working-class representation, remained the dominant strand in most regions throughout the country. Only in areas where the Liberal Party needed to change in order to increase its political support was there much evidence of a New Liberal presence, and even there its influence may have been impaired by the obvious equivocation of its leaders towards reversing the Osborne judgement, in case that action should further encourage the growth of the Labour Party. The fact is that the Labour Party was a significant political party on the eve of war, though it obviously under-performed in parliamentary elections because of the difficulties of the pre-war franchise. How much difference the 1918 franchise made is still open to speculation, but there is no doubt that Labour was making significant progress in local elections and in parliamentary by-elections between 1910 and 1914.

On the eve of war the Labour Party was well established and threatening the hegemony of the Liberal Party in progressive politics, a process which was undoubtedly speeded up by the Asquith-Lloyd George split of 1916. It is difficult to believe, given the pre-war developments, that the war was solely responsible for the decline of the Liberal Party or, conversely, that it came 'just in time to save the Labour Alliance'.[51] Nevertheless, war did speed up the political change which had been brought by the emergence of class politics before 1914. But the Liberal Party realised too late that it had neglected the working class and the left in British politics. The problem for the Liberal Party is that its neglect of labour interests had been evident for more than three decades before the 1924 general election, and that its perception of this failing had come too late for it to recapture the left.

It is clear that the debate will continue. In this, the proponents of rival interpretations remain as fixed in their views as they have ever been. The secondary extracts (Documents 1–10) below reveal this; the primary evidence (Documents 11–16) acts as both evidence and corrective.

Documents
SECONDARY SOURCES AND INTERPRETATIONS

1 – Henry Pelling, *The Origins of the Labour Party* (London, Macmillan, 1954), pp 235–6, 238, 241

All along, there is little doubt that most of the non-Socialist trade-union leaders would have been happy to stay in the Liberal Party – which most of them had belonged to in the past – if the Liberals had made arrangements for a larger representation of the working class among their Parliamentary candidates. Again and again, it was the fault of the official Liberal Party constituency caucuses that this did not happen; and it was the behaviour of these caucuses that set many of the leaders of the workers thinking in terms of a separate party. Even Keir Hardie's revolt at Mid-Lanark in 1888 had been directed, not against the policy of Gladstone, but against the system by which the local association chose its candidates...

For these reasons [the Liberal rejection of trade union candidates, the Osborne Judgement, and other factors] it is not difficult to see why the Liberal Party had failed to retain the popularity that it had once had among the responsible leaders of trade unionism. There was justice in Ramsay MacDonald's observation to Herbert Samuel: 'We didn't leave the Liberals. They kicked us out and slammed the door in our faces...'

Still by 1903 the new party machine was in existence, and whatever the political views, it soon began to build up among them a vested interest in its maintenance. The officials of the great trade unions had made up their minds in favour of a distinct party of their own, and so long as their industrial strength continued to grow, the strength of the political organisation would also increase. In the years that followed, there were doubts at times about the value of political action, there were personal feuds among the leaders as well as disagreements on policy... Some of the unions, such as the Miners, suffered much in the vicissitudes of the British economy and became more radical; others, such as the new unions of 1889, moved in the opposite direction. But the unity of the party once established remained substantially intact, and in the first half-century of its life, every General Election but two that it fought resulted in an increase in the aggregate Labour poll. The association of Socialist faith and trade-union interest, of hope for an ideal future and fear for an endangered present, seemed to point to disruption at times; yet it survived... for a variety of reasons which lie outside the compass of this book, but also because in the years before the party's birth there had been men and women who believed that the unity of the working-class movement, both in industry and politics, was an object to be striven for, just as now most of their successors regard it as an achievement to be maintained.

2 – R. McKibbin, *The Evolution of the Labour Party 1910–1924* (Oxford, Oxford University Press, 1974), pp 240, 241, 244

It becomes, therefore, difficult to avoid the conclusion that the war itself was not of first importance in the Labour Party's post-war successes. Everything points to Labour's enduring *ante-bellum* character: continuity of leadership and personnel at all levels, effective continuity of policy, and, above all, continuity of organisation. The Labour Party, the 'old' pre-1931 Party, remained as it had been before 1914 – propagandist and evangelical. It saw its function as the political mobilisation of an already existing industrial class-consciousness: in practice, it concentrated more upon the extension of organisation than upon the perfection of policy. But this organisation, particularly in the constituencies, was itself only the political side of an industrial organisation that had grown rapidly in the late nineteenth and early twentieth centuries. Almost everywhere the proliferating trades councils became local agencies of the Labour Party...

[The war widened the vote and strengthened trade unionism] but why was it Labour, and not the Liberal Party which benefited from these changes?

The answer is to be found in the nature of the relationship between the Labour Party and the trade unions on the one hand, and between the trade unions and the industrial working-class on the other. Since the Labour Party was inextricably linked with the unions, it, like them, followed the main lines of British economic development. Because it had no life apart from the unions it gained electorally from their growth...

Within the Labour Party itself the preponderance of the unions meant that class loyalty drove out socialist class doctrine. The war, far from representing a general movement to the left, was responsible for a confident and aggressive attack from the right. This attack was partly successful: clause IV, the 'socialist objective, was inserted in a constitution that conformed the triumph of the unions and the defeat of the socialists'.

3 – Trevor R. Wilson, *The Downfall of the Liberal Party, 1914–1935* (London, Collins, 1966), pp 16–18, 23–4, 96–8

The most menacing problem for the Liberals before August 1914 was relations with Labour. The Liberal party contained a substantial element of wealthy businessmen, many of whom held individualistic views on economic matters and looked askance at the trade union movement... To maintain a working alliance with Labour, the Liberals would probably have been obliged to shed some of the more 'conservative' elements. But such a shedding process had occurred before without causing irrevocable disaster. The real danger to the Liberals was that in seeking to retain their 'whigs' they might lose contact with Labour. Yet in 1914 this was not happening. The social reforming wing of the Liberal government was making the running. Advanced Liberals were still looking to Liberalism to implement their ideas. And Labour had put forwards no major policy items which the Liberal party was unable to implement.

Nor in purely electoral terms was there any sign that Labour was supplanting the Liberals. In the general elections of 1910 and the by-elections from 1911 until the outbreak of war, Labour fared abysmally in contests with the Liberals. Twice in by-elections during these years Liberals contested Labour-held seats, and on both occasions Labour came bottom of the poll. Thus even in constituencies where Labour could not be dismissed as a 'hopeless' party (because it happened to be in occupation), it could not hold its own against the Liberals. By and large, the Labour parliamentary party still existed in 1914 by Liberal indulgence – that is, because the Liberals deemed it advantageous to give Labour a free run against the Conservatives in certain seats...

The whole notion that 'liberal England' died 'strangely' between 1910 and 1914 is based upon the assumption that during these years the nation experienced a cataclysm of internal violence to which the war provided a fitting climax. The elements in this cataclysm were the intransigence of the House of Lords, wide-scale industrial unrest, the excesses of the suffragettes, and the imminence of bloodshed in Ireland... [He argues that none of these are sufficient to create a system of violence and conflict which were to bring about the end of Liberalism.]

To make clear the view taken here about when the Liberal party 'reached the point of no return' it may be permissible to resort to allegory. The Liberal party can be compared to an individual who, after a period of robust health and great exertions, experience symptoms of illness (Ireland, Labour unrest, the suffragettes). Before a thorough diagnosis could be made, he was involved in an encounter with a rampant omnibus (the First World War), which mounted the pavement and ran him over. After lingering painfully, he expired. A controversy has persisted ever since as to what killed him. One medical school argues that even without the bus he would soon have died; the intimations of illness were symptoms of a grave disease which would shortly have ended his life. Another school goes further and says that the encounter with the bus would not have proved fatal had not the victim's health already been seriously impaired. Neither of these views is accepted here. The evidence of them is insufficient, because the ailments had not yet reached a stage where their ultimate effect could be known. How long, apart from the accident, the victim could have survived, what future (if any) he possessed, cannot be said. All this is known is that at one moment he was up and walking and at the next he was flat on his back, never to rise again; and in the interval he had been run over by a bus. If it is guess-work to say that the bus was mainly responsible fore his demise, it is the most warrantable guess that can be made...

The outbreak of the First World War initiated a process of disintegration in the Liberal party which by 1918 had reduced it to ruins. As Liberals were often to recognise, the onset of war jeopardised the existence of a party whose guiding principles were international conciliation, personal liberty, and social reform. On the fateful 4th August 1914 Christopher Addison, a junior member of the Liberal government, foretold his party's demise in words which, with one variation or another, were to be repeated many times in the following years. Addison was talking with Sir John Simon, the Attorney-General, about possible resignation from the government, and Simon said that he was reluctant to see too many ministers resign because that would necessitate a coalition government, 'which would assuredly be the grave of Liberalism'. Addison gloomily replied that in the opinion of most Liberals, and certainly of himself, Liberalism was in the grave already. A few months later a prominent Scottish Liberal wrote privately: 'I meet many good Liberals in Midlothian and elsewhere who are prone to take a view that we pacifists made a mistake and the Jingos were right all along'.

For a Liberal government to lead Britain into war, and to direct a wartime administration, seemed almost a contradiction in terms. Its task of international pacification had automatically disappeared. And it had little hope of preserving intact those principles and practices identified with Liberalism: free trade, protection of minorities, the 'pacification' of Ireland, liberty of individuals and voluntary services in the armed forces. Yet once a Liberal government began to modify its ideals under stress of war, how long would it be before the liberal position was abandoned altogether and that of the Conservatives adopted? In short, war and the conduct of war threatened to eliminate liberalism as a coherent political position.

While some Liberal values were being suspended for the duration, others seemed unlikely (except to devout Liberals) ever to become important again. Issues on which Liberals possessed a distinctive and militant attitude, like temperance, denominational education, and Welsh disestablishment, suddenly seemed irrelevant both now and for the future...

[Asquith, the Prime Minister, found difficulty prosecuting the First World War and came into conflict with Lloyd George.]

On 5 December 1916... Asquith brought the crisis to a head. Lloyd George, Bonar Law, and all the other Conservative ministers resigned, and the coalition automatically collapsed... Asquith resigned from the premiership and the king, after a token gesture to Bonar Law as Conservative leader, commissioned Lloyd George on 6 December to form a government...

For the Liberal party this constituted a shattering defeat – even though some excellent Liberals considered it necessary for the success of the war... In December 1916 the Liberal party as such was conclusively ejected from office, and a section of Liberals established an alliance with their party's traditional enemies to which there appeared no certain point of termination. Towards the new, basically non-Liberal regime, which Lloyd George had formed, it was difficult for Liberals to behave either with sympathy or hostility... Now not even success in battle would make any difference. Indeed, every step the Allies advanced towards victory brought catastrophe closer to the Liberal party.

4 – P. F. Clarke, *Lancashire and the New Liberalism* (Cambridge, Cambridge University Press, 1971), pp vii, 151, 274, 339, 406–7

... the argument is less over Lancashire than over a general theory which can subsume Lancashire as a special case. For Lancashire was the cockpit of Edwardian elections. It was, above all, the way north west England voted that kept a Liberal Government in office. Now it is often argued that in so far as the Liberals did well in Lancashire it was for peculiar reasons; that the cotton bosses were staunch Free Traders and hence Liberals; and so on. I shall argue that what follows cannot be fitted into the conventional interpretation of British politics in this period; that it is not the old story with some modifications but a new story altogether...

The Liberal revival gave evidence of its scale in 1906 and of its durability in 1910. In one sense this represented the triumph of the progressive idea.

The basis of progressive policy, as elaborated after 1906, was formulated in the 1890s, and the career of C.P. Scott is of particular significance here. Scott's efforts in Manchester politics did not bear fruit in the short term; but he and L.T. Hobhouse were educating their party. The Boer War had the effect of reconciling Gladstonians, collectivists and organised labour – three elements in the progressive coalition which ruled Britain from 1905. In the era of Liberal success Scott found, first in Churchill and then in Lloyd George, sympathetic exponents of his kind of views... [Continuing about C.P. Scott, editor of the *Manchester Guardian*, and L.T. Hobhouse he stresses the importance of their new or progressive Liberalism which sought to offer collective solutions to social problems and to meet some of the demands of working men and organised labour. Indeed, Scott had become President of the newly formed Manchester Corporation Workmen's General Union in 1891.]

It is usually asserted that the Liberals did well in Lancashire from 1906 onwards because of Free Trade; with the implication that laissez-faire Liberalism enjoyed a freak revival. On this reading, the Liberal party remained essentially a bourgeois instrument and the millowners rallied to it in defence of the precepts of the Manchester School. Now this chapter will not seek to deny that for many Lancashire men Free Trade was the most fundamental of political truths, not that Lancashire as a whole was unenthusiastic about Tariff Reform. But whatever was the case in 1906, it is grossly misleading to attribute the Liberal victories of 1910 in any significant degree to the business-men's preference for Free Trade...

The electoral importance of the Labour vote can be exaggerated; it was still an aristocracy of labour that was allowed to send its sectional representatives to Parliament with Liberal cooperation – albeit one rapidly being expanded. It was Labour's propensity to 'grow' which had led to the further inference that it would inevitably 'grow up' and 'grow out' of progressivism. But there were severe constraints upon a party based on trade unionism. In the progressive view, the legitimate grievances of labour were a special case of a more general maldistribution of resources in the community. On the other hand, it was more difficult to generalise particular trade-union interests into prescriptions for society as a whole. One way of doing so, of course, was to adopt a thoroughgoing socialist critique; but that was hardly the formulation towards which the workingmen of Lancashire were groping. Labour, then, could form no more than a section of a party representative of the poor against the rich; it was not of itself the true church of the working class. It fulfilled itself after 1900, not through rivalry with Liberalism, such as it had earlier displayed, but through a cooperation that grew increasingly close. 'I should like to say this,' Churchill once said, taunted with the prospect of Labour's inexorable march. 'A great many men can jump four feet, but very few can jump six feet.' Under these conditions, it was, of all the electoral pressure groups, Labour which brought the new strength to the Edwardian Liberal revival. Despite all the obvious shortcomings of the arrangement, the national understanding between Liberalism and Labour was a considerable advantage on both sides; its rupture would have been a considerable disaster on both sides...

Thus the first quarter of the twentieth century saw two sorts of change in British politics. The first sort centred upon the emergence of class politics in a stable form; the second sort upon the effective replacement of the Liberal party by the Labour party. But the first – with which this book is concerned – does not in any simple way explain the second. For one thing, the chronology is wrong. By 1910, the change from class politics was substantially complete. That from Liberalism to Labour had not really begun. Nor were there signs that it must begin. It was a light thing to overturn one party and make another to put in its place. At the beginning of the second decade of the twentieth century it looked as though both Labour and Liberalism would be subsumed in progressivism. It seemed that social democracy in England was bound up with the prospects of the Liberal party; and in the generation after its downfall the social democratic record is not one of achievement. But that is another question. Tomorrow is another day. It is upon how Edwardians voted (as distinct from how Victorians voted) that the case of this book rests. For by the time of the General Election of January 1910, during which Liberals eagerly celebrated the Gladstone centenary, politics had entered a world in which the Grand Old Man would not have been at home.

5 – David Clark, *Colne Valley: Radicalism to Socialism: The Portrait of a Northern Constituency in the Formative Years of the Labour Party 1890–1910* (London, Longman, 1981), pp 181, 182, 195

The emergence of Socialism in Colne Valley came not as a rupture with the past but as a natural progression of radical thought which had been associated with advanced Liberalism...

The situation in Colne Valley appears to have been reflected in other parts of the country and this reinforces the claim that the ILP was not primarily a Marxist party. Indeed it would have been surprising if it had been so. It might be argued that the SDF failed because it attempted to impose an alien political culture on the British voter. By the same argument the ILP's success in the early years was because it adapted its beliefs to part of the prevailing political culture, that of advanced Liberalism. This appears significant, for by its nature, culture entails continuity and embodies such concepts as tradition and history... The ILP's success was based on the gradual adaptation of part of the existing political culture and by the acceptance of some key concepts of that culture. This approach must be contrasted with that of the SDF which sought to replace the indigenous culture with a Marxian one which embodied concepts which were alien to Britain...

It was the Labour clubs which were to be the crucial factors in the successful development of the new political party in Colne Valley and elsewhere. Not only did they provide the permanency upon which the activities of the party could be based but they also symbolised the emancipation of the members from the existing political parties. In turn they were instrumental in persuading the new movement to adopt a Socialist outlook...

The individualistic, ethical branch of Socialism was alien to trade unionism which laid great stress on collective action. In a sense the very *raison d' etre* of such bodies as the Colne Valley Labour League with its objectives in political action was the antithesis of the Lib-Lab-ism of such groups as mining unions... The whole environment in the Colne Valley militated against collective action of the trade-union type...

It can be argued that Colne Valley Labour Party does not provide an ideal type for the comparative purposes although even there, the trade union presence, albeit minimal, still made a contribution. Colne Valley, however, does prove conclusively that trade unionism is not an essential prerequisite for Socialism.

6 – David Howell, *British Workers and the Independent Labour Party 1888–1906* (Manchester, Manchester University Press, 1983), p 389

This lengthy investigation began with some questions about the predictability of the ILP's emergence as the primary expression of British socialism. We have examined the varied implications of attempts to expand the party's influence within particular communities with their own cultural features and balances of political forces, or within unions each with its distinctive industrial tradition, and immediate challenges. We have indicated the complex ways in which local predicaments and solutions interacted with the decisions and squabbles of national leaders. On the one side there stands a tangled web of local opportunities, constraints and responses; on the other stands an increasingly coherent party with an agreed structure, a characteristic mode of operation, and a broad policy which, if it sometimes provoked internal criticisms, nevertheless developed along reasonably coherent lines. Activists might have developed their own local initiative, but they defined themselves increasingly as members of a particular national organisation. Although immediate local concerns remained important, such a definition had a limiting effect on activities. The parameters of the debate were affected significantly by dominant understandings of the ILP tradition. The party's establishment meant inevitably that some priorities and symbols became central to debate on the British left, others became marginal.

The emphasis raises the question of 'suppressed alternatives'... The image of the Social Democratic Federation as a narrow dogmatic sect unsuited to the pragmatic rigours of British politics is a tendentious, partial and misleading one, in which the polemical judgement of some ILP contemporaries have been canonised into firm historical verdicts... Similarly, there was the hope of some ILP leaders that a democratic alliance of Labour, Radicals and Irish Nationalists could become a leading element in a political realignment...

7 – K. Laybourn and J. Reynolds, *Liberalism and the Rise of Labour* (Beckenham, Croom Helm, 1984), pp 10, 149, 204

Like most major debates the one which was focused on the rise of Labour and the decline of Liberalism has led to a good deal of academic pettiness and belligerence which is anathema to compromise. Yet sober opinion would, even at this interim stage, reflect that several main conclusions have emerged. In the first place, no one can be categorical about the timing of the Liberal decline or Liberal growth because of the immense regional variations which have been observed. Secondly, advocacy of New Liberalism as the redeemer of Liberalism is no longer tenable; too much research has indicated the absence of its influence in many regions of the country. Thirdly, although the impact of unequal franchise remains unclear, municipal and parliamentary by-election results suggest that Labour's electoral strength was rising rapidly between 1910 and 1914. But if there is one lesson to learn from this debate, it must be that attempts to apply a general theory to the whole country will not work...

Table 6.1 The Number of Local Representatives on Local Political Bodies in West Yorkshire 1906–14

Year	Municipal	CC, UDC, RDC, PC	Board of Guardians	Total
1906	47	36	6	89
1907	51	39	18	108
1908	44	45	18	107
1909	47	53	21	121
1910	44	60	24	128
1911	61	69	24	154
1912	70	68	24	162
1913	85	70	33	188
1914	85	77	40	202

(Based on the *Halifax Guardian*, *Bradford Observer*, *Labour Leader* and other newspaper sources.)

It was trade unionism which underpinned the burgeoning Labour movement in West Yorkshire. The ILP's capture of many trades councils in the early 1890s paved the way for the extension of its influence amongst trade unions. Even in areas where trade unionism was weak, as in Colne Valley, it is clear that many of the leading local Labour politicians were in fact trade unionists. The only difference between many Labour strongholds and areas of patchy Labour support was the strength of the local trade union movement. In areas where trade unionism was firmly established and closely linked with the ILP, as was the case in Bradford and Halifax, powerful and effective political Labour organisations emerged. In the other areas, where trade unionism was weak and ineffective, or where the ILP's trade union links were now widely established, the ILP and Socialist organisations proved to be less resilient, prone to bouts of frenzied political activity followed by lengthy periods of inactivity in the wake of political adversity...

8 – Bill Lancaster, Radicalism, *Cooperation and Socialism: Leicester Working-class Politics 1860–1906* (Leicester University Press, 1987), p 185

Thus the socialism of the Leicester ILP was an expression of indigenous working-class traditions, contemporary circumstances and socialist ideas. The Labour movement that the new party was attempting to lead and shape both looked back to what increasingly appeared to have been a golden age of workshop production and forward to the collective solution of poverty. The ILP succeeded in winning a substantial section of working-class electoral support because it drew strength from both facets of this apparent ambiguity.

   The themes pursued in this book are manifestly central to the debate currently being waged over the rise of independent Labour politics and the decline of liberalism. One group of historians has argued that the rise of Labour was inevitable, although they differ over the factors which created Labour's inexorable growth. A second group has pointed to the tenacity of liberalism; surviving on its traditional links with nonconformity in Wales, reinvigorated by 'New' Liberalism in Lancashire, or sustained by a combination of 'Old' and 'New' Liberalism in the North-East of England. The evidence presented in this study clearly supports the first group. Continuities can obviously be discerned between Liberalism and Labour in Leicester but grand generalisations on the subject lose sight of particularity, context and the drama of the historical process as it shaped, and was being shaped by, activities of seemingly unimportant people.

9 – Michael Bentley, *The Climax of Liberal Politics: British Liberalism in Theory and Practice 1868–1918* (London, Edward Arnold, 1987), p 138

The doctrines of 'progressivism', or what came to be called 'New Liberalism', played an obvious if ambivalent role in political arguments after 1895... 'Liberalism', as one local newspaper put it in 1905, 'is not a stagnant opinion, but a flowing stream – the expression of Progressive ideas... It will cease to be Liberalism when it ceases to be progressive and becomes fixed.' That progressives comprised an important element in the House of Commons and among journalists or publicists therefore goes without saying. But as well as operating as a contemporary focus for discussion, progressivism has more recently acquired an historical function; and that usage has in turn given rise to sustained argument about the health of Liberal politics before 1914 and the potential of Liberalism for surviving the coming of a mass industrial society.

10 – Duncan Tanner, *Political Change and the Labour Party 1900–1918* (Cambridge University Press, 1990), pp 317, 441–2

Labour had not developed the ideological/political strength to support the expansionist strategy. It had not created a solid 'class' vote, based upon cultural units which were common to working-class voters in all areas. It had not even the uniform support of trade unionists. The assumption that it did is based upon inadequate theory and shaky and partial empirical analysis. In reality, electoral politics followed a pattern in which past political parties and current economic interests combined to create an extremely uneven electoral map. The distribution of support was such that it was comparatively strong where the Liberal party was weak, and unable to seriously rival it in most Liberal areas. Cooperation was therefore possible...

The Labour party was not on the verge of replacing the Liberals in 1914... The Liberal party stood for prosperity, improvement and security. The Labour left had no generally successful region. It had not created a 'class-based' political allegiance which would undermine the Liberal party on a broad front.

PRIMARY EVIDENCE AND INFORMATION

11 – The Labour Vote: Parliamentary Result

Elections	Votes	MPs elected	Candidates	% share of vote
1900	63,304	2	15	1.8
1906	329,748	30	51	5.9
1910 (Jan.)	505,657	40	78	7.6
1910 (Dec.)	371,772	42	56	7.1
1918	2,385,472	63	388	22.2

12 – Labour Representation Committee, *The Aim and Objectives of the Labour Representation Committee, as Amended at the Newcastle Conference February 1903* (London, LRC, 1903)

I

The Labour Representation Committee is a federation of Trade Unions, Trades Councils, the Independent Labour Party, and the Fabian Society, Co-operative Societies are also eligible for membership.

II

To secure, by united action, the election to Parliament of candidates promoted in the first instance, by an Affiliated Society or Societies in the constituency, who undertake to form or join a distinct group in Parliament, with its own whips and its own policy on Labour questions, to abstain strictly from identifying themselves with or promoting the interests of any section of the Liberal or Conservative parties, and not to oppose any other candidate recognised by this Committee. All such candidates shall pledge to themselves to accept this Constitution, to abide by the decisions of the Group in carrying out of the aims of this Constitution, or reign, and to appear before their constituencies under the title of Labour candidate only.

13 – The Liberal-Labour Electoral Pact 1903
[Letter from Jesse Herbert to Herbert Gladstone, 6 March 1903, quoted in Frank Bealey, 'Negotiations between the Liberal Party and the Labour Representation Committee before the general election of 1906, *Bulletin of the Institute of Historical Research* Vol. 29/30, 1956/7. This deals with the Liberal thinking towards the Lib-Lab pact which was concluded in secret between Herbert Gladstone and Ramsay MacDonald in August 1903. The arrangement was to give each other about 30 straight runs each in parliamentary constituencies. In other words Liberal and Labour candidates opposed only Conservatives candidates (from the major parties) in defined constituencies.]

A determination of the course to be followed by the Liberal party is urgently needed for to do nothing is to seem to reject the overtures of the LRC, who may be irretrievably committed to courses during delay which they would avoid if they anticipated future friendly relations.

I am keenly conscious that the matter is not so simple and clear that it may be determined in the off-hand manner in which it is dealt with by many Liberals as well as Labour men. The official recognition of a separate group unpledged to support of the Liberal party, a group which will harass every Government and whose representatives in Parliament will probably decline the Liberal whip, is not lightly to be given. It would be the recognition of a vital change in the organisation of parties. But would it be other than the official recognition of a fact, indisputable, and clear to every politician? There is no difficulty experienced in giving official recognition to the League group which had wealth. Why should there be difficulty in giving official recognition to the Labour group which has numbers? Neither asks for official approval of its objects, but both seek the friendly concession by the party of the liberty to run their candidates by the presence of official candidates…

I am concerned with the electoral prospects of the party, and anxiously ask myself, 'What would be the gain and the loss to the party at the General Election, if a working arrangements were arrived at with the LRC? There are some members of the party in and out of Parliament who would be estranged thereby, but they are few. Those employers of labour who remained with the Liberal party when the Whig seceders went out on the Home Rule excuse, have (with few exceptions) sincere sympathy with many of the objects of the LRC. The severe Individualists of the party who are wholly out of sympathy with the principles of the LRC are very few. The total loss of their financial aid and of their votes would be inconsiderable. The gain to the party through the working arrangement would be great, and can be measured best by a comparison of the results of 'no arrangement' with those of 'an arrangement'

The LRC can directly influence the votes of nearly a million men. They have a fighting fund of £100,000. (This is the most significant fact in the new situation. Labour candidates have had hitherto to beg for financial help and have fought with paltry and wholly insufficient funds.) Their members are mainly men who have hitherto voted against Liberal candidates, and (as they probably would) should they act as advised, the Liberal party would suffer defeat not only in those constituencies where the LRC candidates fought, but also in almost every borough, and in many Divisions of Lancashire and Yorkshire. This would be the inevitable result of unfriendly action toward the LRC candidates. They would be defeated, but so also should we be defeated.

If there be good-fellowship between us and the LRC the aspect of the future for both will be very bright and encouraging.

14 – The Labour Electoral Manifesto 1906

To the Electors –

This election is to decide whether or not Labour is to be fairly represented in Parliament.

The House of Commons is supposed to be the people's House, and yet the people are not there.

Landlords, employers, lawyers, brewers, and financiers are there in force. Why not Labour?

The Trade Unions ask the same liberty as capital enjoys. They are refused.

The aged poor are neglected.

The slums remain; overcrowding continues, whilst the land goes to waste.

Shopkeepers and traders are overburdened with rates and taxation, whilst the increasing land values, which should relieve the ratepayers, go to the people who have not earned them.

Wars are fought to make the rich richer, and underfed school children are still neglected.

Chinese Labour is defended because it enriches the mine owners.

The unemployed ask for work, the Government gave them a worthless Act, and now, when you are beginning to understand the causes of your poverty, the red herring of Protection is drawn across your path.

Protection, as experience shows, is no remedy for poverty and unemployment. It serves to keep you from dealing with the land, housing, old age, and other social problems!

You have it in your power to see that Parliament carries out your wishes. The Labour Representation Executive appeals to you in the name of a million Trade Unionists to forget all the political differences which have kept you apart in the past, and vote for _____ (here is inserted the name of the Labour candidate).

15 – Ben Tillett, *Is the Parliamentary Labour Party a failure?* (London, 1908), pp 11–15

The House of Commons and the country, which respected and feared the Labour Party, are now fast approaching a condition of contempt towards its Parliamentary representatives.

The lion has not teeth or claws, and is losing his growl, too; the temperance section being softly feline in their purring to Ministers and their patronage. Those of the Party who, out of a sense of loyalty to others, refrain from protest, indicate more patience than courage in their attitude...

Labour is robbed of the wealth and means of life created by the genius of toil; the exploiters are on trial for their malefactions; the charge is that capitalist ownership of the land and material wealth is the cause of poverty. When that has been sufficiently explained and taught to people, there will be ample time for side issues, after the real work is done. I do not hesitate to describe the conduct of these blind leaders as nothing short of betrayal especially with the fact in view that they have displayed greater activity for temperance reform than for Labour interests. Of all the farces, these same Labour-Temperance advocates knew the Bill would never pass the House of Lords; if not, they are not merely innocent but they are ignorant of their business, and cannot see an inch before their noses. Every Labour man knew the attitude of the Lords; all the Liberals did, for the game was played with cards on the table. What a mockery it was, and merely to waste time. While Shackleton took the chair for Winston Churchill, thousands of textile workers were suffering starvation through unemployment; his ability and energy could have been well used in Stevenson Square, in Manchester, instead of in mouthing platitudes and piffle in Liberal meetings. The worst of the winter is coming on, time thrown away will never be recovered, and thousands will perish for want of bread. A great many of the victims to destitution will be in their graves before the Liberal Government will have approached the subject of unemployment, which they will sandwich between abolition of the House of Lords and Welsh Disestablishment. The temperance section, in particular, will be seizing on the other 'red-herrings', and the winter will have passed, and these unctuous weaklings will go on prattling their nonsense, while thousands are dying of starvation. Some of these lives might have been saved to the country, the misery consequent to foodless conditions of life averted. Blessed valuable months have been lost; the Labour movement must not tolerate the further betrayal of interests with agitation about the House of Lords, or Welsh Disestablishment.

16 – 'How the Osborne Judgement Dooms Trade Unionism', Labour Party Leaflet, no. 49, 1909.

A few judges have decided that Trade Unions must not defend their members and advance their interests by political means.

Landlords, Railway Directors, can go to the House of Commons. Brewers, Rich men generally. But Labour is forbidden by the Judges to adopt the only means by which working men can get there.

The Rich can draw Cheques for Thousands of Pounds to finance their political friends. That is all right!

Both political parties sell honours to their wealthy followers, and thus maintain secret political funds. That is all right!

People who, under Tariff Reform, will be better able than now to become rich at the Nation's expense, keep the coffers of the Tariff Reform League full. That is all right!

But when combined Labour tries to help the poor by use of its combined funds – the only way the coppers can be made as effective as cheques – the Judges say 'That is illegal!'

Thus there is still one law for the Rich, and another for the Poor.

How can Trade Unions do their work with this power taken from them? Parliament has become the field upon which the great battles between capital and Labour are top be fought. By using its political power, Trade Unionism has won the Workmen's Compensation Act, Factory and Mining Legislation, Unemployed Workmen's Act, Fair Wages in Government Contracts and similar Working-class benefits.

They have secured freedom of combination, and they repelled the last attack made upon their liberties by the unjust Taff Vale Decision.

In the future they are they to be, like shorn Samson, at the mercy of the Philistines.

Notes on Chapter 2

1   G.R. Searle, *The Liberal Party: Triumph and Disintegration 1886–1929* (London, Macmillan, 1992), p 1.

2   Most notably T. Adams, 'Labour and the First World War: Economy, Politics and the Erosion of Local Peculiarity?', *The Journal of Regional and Local Studies* 10 (1990), p 23.

3   Bill Lancaster. 'The rise of Labour', *Labour History Review* 57 (1992), p 98; Bill Lancaster, *Radicalism, Co-operation and Socialism: Leicester Working-Class Politics 1860–1906* (Leicester, Leicester University Press, 1987).

4   George Dangerfield, *The Strange Death of Liberal England* (London, MacGibbon and Kee, 1966 edn), p 22, ch. 2.

5   Michael Bentley, *The Climax of Liberal Politics: British Liberalism in Theory and Practice 1868–1918* (London, Edward Arnold, 1987), p 138.

6   Henry Pelling, *The Origins of the Labour Party* (London, Macmillan, 1954).

7   Henry Pelling, *Social Geography of British Elections 1885–1910* (London, Macmillan, 1967), pp 434-5.

8   Ross McKibbin, *The Evolution of the Labour Party 1910–1924* (Oxford, Oxford University Press, 1974), p 243.

9   Ross McKibbin, *The Ideologies of Class* (Oxford, Oxford University Press, 1990).

10 Keith Laybourn and Jack Reynolds, *Liberalism and the Rise of Labour 1890–1918* (Beckenham, Croom Helm, 1984); George L. Bernstein, *Liberalism and Liberal Politics in Edwardian England* (London, Allen & Unwin, 1986) G.L. Bernstein, 'Liberalism and the Progressive Alliance in the Constituencies, 1900–1914: Three Case Studies', *Historical Journal* 26 (1983), pp 617–40.

11 P.F. Clarke, *Lancashire and the New Liberalism* (Cambridge, Cambridge University Press, 1971); Trevor Wilson, *The Downfall of the Liberal Party 1914–1935* (London, Collins, 1966); Kenneth D. Brown, *The English Labour Movement* (London, 1982); Keith Burgess, *The Challenge of Labour* (London, 1980); R. Douglas, 'Labour in Decline 1910–1914' in K.D. Brown (ed.), *Essays in Anti-Labour History* (London, Macmillan, 1974), pp 116–119; Duncan Tanner, *Political Change and the Labour Party 1900–1918* (Cambridge, Cambridge University Press, 1990).

12 Wilson, *The Downfall of the Liberal Party 1914–1935*, p 18.

13 Bentley, *The Climax of Liberal Politics*, p 152.

14 *Ibid.*, pp 145–51.

15 Clarke, *Lancashire and the New Liberalism*, pp 1–4.

16 *Ibid.*, pp 397–8.

17 *Ibid.*, preface.

18 Peter Clarke, *Liberals and Social Democrats* (Cambridge, Cambridge University Press, 1978).

19 Douglas, 'Labour in Decline 1910–1914', pp 116–19; Brown, *The English Labour Movement*.

20 H.C. Matthew, R.I. McKibbin and J.A. Kay, 'The Franchise Factor in the Rise of the Labour Party', *English Historical Review* xci (1976), p 727.

21 P.F. Clarke, 'The Electoral Position of the Liberal and Labour Parties 1910–1914', *English Historical Review* xc (1975) pp 828–36; M. Hart, 'The Liberals, the War, and the Franchise', *English Historical Review* xcvii (1982), p 381; D. Tanner, 'The Parliamentary Electoral System, the "Fourth" Reform Act and the Rise of Labour in England and Wales', *Bulletin of the Institute of Historical Research Archives* lvi (1983), p 213.

22 P.F. Clarke, 'The Electoral Position of the Liberal and Labour Parties 1910–1914', p 831.

23 McKibbin, *The Evolution of the Labour Party 1910–1924*, p 143.

24 Minutes of the Society of Certified Associated Liberal Agents, 1916–1920, deposited at the Leeds branch (Sheepscar) of the West Yorkshire Archives Service.

25 M.G. Sheppard and John L. Halstead, 'Labour Municipal Election Performance in Provincial England and Wales 1901–13', *Bulletin of the Society for the Study of Labour History* 39 (1979), p 42.

26 D. Powell, 'The New Liberalism and the Rise of Labour, 1886–1906', *Historical Journal* 29 (1986), 369–93.

27 *Ibid.*, pp 376, 379, 382.

28 *Manchester Guardian*, 7 November 1904. Also see Chris Wrigley, *David Lloyd George and the Labour Movement* (Harvester Wheatsheaf, Hemel Hempstead, 1976).

29 *Carnarvon Herald*, 21 October 1904.

30 S. Collini, *Liberalism and Sociology* (Cambridge, Cambridge University Press, 1979); Michael Freeden, *The New Liberals* (Oxford, Oxford Universoty Press, 1978).

31 John Shepherd, 'Labour and Parliament: The Lib-Labs as the First Working-class MPs 1885–1906'; Alastair Reid, 'Old Unionism Reconsidered: the Radicalism of Robert Knight 1870–1900' in Biagini and Reid, *Currents of Radicalism*, pp 187–213, 214–243.

32 Clarke, *Lancashire*, p vii.
33 K.O. Morgan, 'The New Liberalism and the Challenge of Labour: The Welsh Experience, 1885-1929' in Brown, *Essays in Anti-Labour History*, p 164
34 A.W. Purdue, 'The ILP in the North East of England' in D. James, T. Jowitt and K. Laybourn (eds) *The Centennial History of the Independent Labour Party* (Halifax, Ryburn, 1992), pp 17–42; Laybourn and Reynolds, *Liberalism and Labour 1890–1918*; P. Thompson, *Socialists, Liberal and Labour: the Struggle for London 1885–1914* (London, 1963); Powell, 'The New Liberalism and the Rise of Labour, 1886–1906', pp 381. 383, 393.
35 Morgan, 'Welsh Experience', 170.
36 Chris Wrigley, 'Labour and the Trade Unions' in Brown, *The First Labour Party*, pp 129–57.
37 *Ibid.*, p 152.
38 *Ibid.*, p 151.
39 Laybourn and Reynolds, *Liberalism and Labour 1890–1918*, p 127.
40 Douglas, 'Labour in Decline 1910–1914', p 123.
41 Tanner, *Political Change and the Labour Party 1900–1918*, p 317.
42 *Ibid.*, p 259.
43 Bill Lancaster, 'The Rise of Labour', *Labour History Review* 57 (1992), pp 97, 100.
44 Laybourn and Reynolds, *Liberalism and Labour 1890–1918*, pp 109, 149.
45 D. Tanner, 'Election Statistics, and the Rise of the Labour Party, 1906–1931', *Historical Journal* 34, (1991), p 895.
46 E.P. Thompson, 'Homage to Tom Maguire' in *Essays in Labour History*, Asa Briggs and John Saville (eds) (1960), pp 276–316; Burgess, *The Challenge of Labour*, pp 81–95; Brown, *The English Labour Movement*.
47 *Bradford Observer*, 28 April 1891.
48 *Yorkshire Factory Times*, 1 May 1891.
49 Henry Pelling, *The Origins of the Labour Party*, pp 244–5.
50 Brown, *The English Labour Movement*, p 189.
51 James Hinton, *Labour and Socialism: A History of the British Labour Movement 1867–1974* (Brighton, Harvester, 1983), p 81.

Chapter 3

The First World War: the Impact of War upon British Politics and Life 1914–18

Introduction

Recent work on the First World War has emphasised that it was a crucial period of change in British history. It altered the economic relationship between Britain and the rest of the world, changing Britain from a creditor into a debtor nation, it dampened the worst excesses of social differences and fundamentally changed the balance of British politics, ensuring that the Liberal Party would lose support to both the Labour and Conservative Parties. As a result, the First World War has attracted enormous attention from historians and spawned numerous debates. Seven of these are examined, some briefly, in this chapter. One concerns the political events that saw the division of the Liberal Party in 1916, between David Lloyd George and H. H. Asquith, and has already been examined in detail in the previous chapter. A second concerns the process by which Labour placed Clause Four, on the need for the socialisation of industry and services, in its 1918 Constitution. A third focuses upon the peace movement and poses the question can the Independent Labour Party (ILP) be truly considered a peace party, and how pervasive and influential was pacifism during the war? A fourth considers the extent to which there was social levelling within Britain during the war, asking to what extent the lower sections of the working class improved their social and economic circumstances? A fifth concerns the extent to which the rank-and-file industrial protest movement in Glasgow in 1915 and 1916, which gave rise to the phrase and legend of the 'Red Clyde', created a powerful post-war Labour movement in Glasgow and Scotland. Was it this militancy or other factors which accounted for Labour's political tradition in that area? The sixth debate is about the impact of the war experience upon British society. Was the First World War, or Great War, a futile conflict, which led to useless slaughter, or a necessary evil supported by the vast majority of the British people? There is, of course, also a seventh debate about the way in which the First World War changed the social position of women. Did war release women from 'serfdom', or did it merely change their working lives?

The balance of evidence suggests that in most cases the First World War did bring about significant changes in British politics, culture and life. There is no doubt that it necessitated much greater state intervention than had hitherto had been the case. Yet at the same time one must recognise that the Great War often speeded up trends that were already occurring. It exposed the internal weakness of the Liberal Party, forced the Labour Party to sift through the socialist doctrines available to it in order to alight upon one appropriate to Labour in the post-war world, and exposed the well-known weaknesses of a British economy whose industrial and economic supremacy was already under severe examination before 1914. Nevertheless, in its own right it left a deep impression upon British culture for many decades afterwards, the memory of which is evoked annually on Armistice Day, the nearest Sunday to the 11 November, the date on which the war ended in 1918. Naturally, then, it is with the experience of war that we must begin.

The Great War: Useless Slaughter?

The poems of the First World War, particularly those of Wilfred Owen and Siegfried Sassoon, and the other literary contributions on the war, most particularly Robert Graves's classic personal memoir *Goodbye To All That,* have presented the Great War as a farce in which millions of men were needlessly slaughtered. The futility of war is presented in such a way that a generation of British politicians avoided war, as best they could, in the 1930s. More recently, however, some historians have begun to suggest that the war was not futile, that the generals tapped into a widespread desire for victory, and that Field Marshal Douglas Haig was disliked simply because he won.[1]

This debate has seen J.M. Bourne, in his *Britain and the Great War 1914–1918,* reject the tragic and futile view of the Great War. Nevertheless, there are those who disagree with this new approach, most particularly T. Travers who, in *The Killing Ground: The British Army, the Western Front and the Emergence of Modern Warfare* makes a penetrating criticism of Haig and the British High Command. There are probably a hundred or more books and articles which have, in recent years, taken up the debate. They are best summarised and assessed in a short pamphlet by David G. Wright, who is at pains to stress that those involved often did not see the Great War as futile. One extract presented here is thus taken from David Wright's pamphlet *The Great War: A Useless Slaughter?* (Document 1). A similar view has also been expressed by Trevor Wilson in his monumental book *The Myriad Faces of War* (Document 2). The current orthodoxy is, therefore, to suggest that the Great War had a purpose and achieved much, but one should perhaps not totally dismiss the protests of a section of a generation who were horrified by the events and carried, through organisations such as the No More War movement, considerable support for their views, at least until the mid- and late 1930s, when the rise of fascism and the events of the Spanish Civil War saw their influence decline.

War and Politics: the Liberal and Labour Parties and the Progressive Vote, and the Adjustment of the Conservative Party

On the home front the most intense debate has focused upon the impact that the war exerted upon British politics. The major political parties accepted a political truce for the duration of the war, although not all parties and candidates abided by it. Nevertheless, there were major changes in politics, occasioned by the formation of a wartime coalition government, under Asquith in May 1915 and Lloyd George in December 1916. This created its own strains within the Liberal Party, as indicated in Chapter 2, and forced the other political parties to make their own political adjustments. Indeed, Arthur Marwick has written that during the Great War 'The Liberal Party was greatly damaged, the Labour Party was greatly strengthened', and Trevor Wilson, one of the leading proponents of the new orthodoxy which highlights the war as the prime cause of the decline of the Liberal Party has made a similar point.[2] These issues are taken up, and examined in detail, in the previous chapter (see Chapter 2 and Document 3). It has also been elaborated by Michael Bentley (Document 3).

What is most clear, however, is that the Labour Party was faced with having to redefine its position with regard to clearly indicating its distinctiveness from the Liberal Party. It did this through the introduction of Clause Four, the socialisation of industry clause in its 1918 Constitution. Ever since, historians have argued about the precise reasons for its implementation.

Arthur Marwick, Philip Abrams, Ralph Miliband and many others have written on the subject. However, the issue was put into sharp focus in 1974 with the publication of J.M. Winter, *Socialism and the Challenge of War: Ideas and Politics in Britain, 1912–18* (Document 4) and R. McKibbin, *The Evolution of the Labour Party 1910–1924*; these two disagree over whether or not Clause Four should be taken seriously as a statement of Labour's socialism[3] (Documents 5).

It was Winter who developed the orthodox view that the First World War brought about significant changes in British society. He argued that the improved incomes and employment prospects of all workers resulted in the blurring of distinctions within the working class and between classes and maintained that the deep involvement of all sections of society in the war effort led to a decline in the deferential attitudes of the working class and the rising prospect of political and social change. In this environment, Labour leaders were forced to conclude that the restructuring of the Labour Party was essential, and they were forced to sift through a variety of socialist policies in order to select that which would be most appropriate to its post-war growth. In the final analysis, the wartime conditions favoured the collectivist policies of the Webbs and paved the way for the Constitution and Clause Four, Labour's clear commitment to a future socialist state. The more democratic guild socialist policies of G.D.H. Cole and the long-term educational approach of R.H. Tawney did not offer the clarity, immediacy or wartime context that seemed essential to the Labour leaders. The Marxist alternative was never considered.

Such an interpretation is entirely alien to Ross McKibbin, who rejects the view that the wartime economy made much difference to the potential of Labour politics, cannot believe that the men who drew up the new Labour Constitution, most of whom were in their fifties and sixties, were capable of dramatic conversion, or that Clause Four was anything other than an 'uncharacteristic adornment' of the new constitution. To him, the trends in British Labour development were evident before the war, and Clause Four was simply a response to the wider electorate to be created by the Representation of the People's Act of 1918. He believes that it is inconceivable that it could have been otherwise, given that the Labour Party was moving to the right not the left during the war, a fact evidenced by the increased trade-union control of the National Executive Committee of the Labour Party under the 1918 Labour Constitution.[4]

Although both Winter and McKibbin differ in many respects there are only three vital points of divergence. The first is the extent to which the trends evident in the Labour Party were apparent before the First World War. The second is whether or not the wartime economy led to the creation of an homogenous working class, which will be referred to later. The third is the degree to which the Labour Party seriously discussed the socialist alternatives; put more bluntly, was the Labour Party conscious of the need for a distinguishing ideology, concerned with offering a genuine socialist ideology, or simply responding to the political needs of the moment?

The first sub-debate stems from the emphasis which McKibbin placed upon the growth of the Labour Party before the First World War. McKibbin sees that Labour was growing before 1914 with the support of the working class, Winter sees the pre-war Labour Party as being 'rudderless'. The second debate is concerned more with the way in which wartime conditions narrowed the pay differentials and the social divides. However, it is the third sub-debate which is vital to the present discussion.

According to Winter, the lack of direction from the Labour Party forced socialists 'to work out anew political ideas which they hoped would give form and purpose to the growing protests of the labouring population'.[5] This led to a debate about the socialist direction of the pre-war Labour Party which was clarified by the war, which helped to sift the socialist alternatives. Through the agency of the War Emergency: Workers' National Committee, the gradualist and statist policies of the Webbs began to become dominant in the discussion of the 1918 Constitution, and in *Labour and the New Social Order*, Labour's reconstruction programme written by Sidney Webb and published in 1918.

This interpretation contrasts sharply with McKibbin's view that Clause Four has hogged the limelight of debate to the detriment of the corpus of the 1918 Constitution, which 'embodied not an ideology but a system by which power in the Labour Party was distributed'.[6] To McKibbin, it is the practical considerations of the time, with Labour in the wartime coalition governments, events in Russia and the 1918 Representation of the People Act, that dominated Labour's approach to the Constitution. The demands of trade unions were to the fore in the formulation of the new constitution, socialism very much an afterthought.

In contrast, part of the sense of greater working-class unity and possible improvements in living standards which Winter refers to may have come from the activities of the War Emergency: Workers' National Committee. Winter feels that this body did much to promote the state socialist ideas of the Webbs within the Labour Party. His views are not shared by McKibbin, who simply ignores them, nor by Ralph Miliband, S.H. Beer or Royden Harrison, who see the structure of power within the Labour Party as more important than the proclamation of socialist intent in Clause Four.[7]

The War Emergency Committee (WEC) was drawn together on 5 August 1914 after Arthur Henderson, Secretary of the Labour Party, had written to the National Executive Committee (NEC) to call a special meeting 'to consider what action should be taken in the very serious crisis in Europe and any other business that may arise'.[8] It was formed in the context of a Labour Party committed to peace, but within a day it was being called to act for a movement which was committed to the war effort. Its prime function became the defence of the rights and interests of the working class from unreasonable encroachment. It quickly evolved to include not only the NEC of the Labour Party but the Co-operative Union and the Co-operative

Wholesale Society. Its policy of co-option led to invitations to Ramsay MacDonald, and several hundred individuals, to join it, and the absorption of the representatives of many trade unions and socialist societies. In short, it soon became the most representative body in the British Labour movement, incorporating both pro-war and anti-war organisations, although its 'heterogeneous membership ought not to obscure the fact that it was an extension of the Labour Party's national office'.[9]

The primary objective of the War Emergency Committee was to keep the Labour movement from disintegrating under the impact of war. To achieve this end, the WEC concentrated its efforts on assuming a leading role in defending the living standards of the population. It protested at the 70 percent inflation that occurred between 1914 and 1916, participated in the campaign to raise old age pensions from five shillings to seven shillings and sixpence, and worked for rent restriction in 1915 and to ensure that there was an adequate distribution of food supplies.

Towards the end of the war, however, the WEC became far more positive in its policies and aggressive in its approach. The introduction of compulsory military service in 1916 brought about a fundamental change in its strategy. It protested against the Military Service Act in 1916 and developed a campaign for the Conscription of Riches – through income tax, supertax capital tax and sequestration of all unearned income – as a *quid pro quo* for labour's contribution to providing manpower for the trenches.[10]

Both Winter and Harrison agree that the work of the WEC was important. For Winter it meant that the Webbian thought was projected forward, for in the wake of the proposal being formed it was accepted by the Labour Party Executive and various other Labour organisations: 'we may see a complete acceptance of Webbian thought on this measure – the first independent Labour programme during the First World War'.[11] It followed that with Webb's deep involvement in formulating the new Labour Party Constitution, the WEC programme had a direct bearing upon the formulation of Clause Four. Harrison agrees that Webb was the dominant spirit behind the new policy, and that 'In short, the Conscription of Riches demand led on to clause 4'.[12] But from that point onwards there is disagreement. While Winter sees the growing influence of Webbian socialism as the basis of the party's new Constitution, Harrison suggests that Clause Four has to be seen within the context of the political pressures being placed on the Labour Party at the time.

Why did the Labour Party commit itself to the socialist goal? Was it because of the growth of Webbian socialism, thrust forward by war, or was it simply a product of political expediency?

There is no doubting that the socialist ideas of the Webbs were attractive to some sections of the Labour movement, particularly the ILP and the Fabians. It is also possible that the Russian Revolutions of 1917, and particularly the

Bolshevik one which occurred soon after Arthur Henderson's ill-fated trip to Russia, forced Labour leaders to adopt a resolution that would offer a less violent and a more democratic route to socialism. There is also the suggestion that the professional middle classes were being drawn to such a policy in the wake of the government collectivisation policy. In addition, the Lloyd George Coalition Government set up a Ministry of Reconstruction to prepare policies for the post-war years. Of the nine members of the central Advisory Council attached to the Ministry two, Ernest Bevin and J.H. Thomas were trade unionists and active members of the Labour Party. Apart from being in the Coalition, Labour was being drawn into efforts to prepare schemes for housing, health and social welfare policies on a broader front in the post-war years. It must have appeared that old laissez-faire capitalism was dead, and that socialist policies, particularly those of the Webbs, were now more appropriate than ever. To many Labour activists, it appeared that the wartime collectivism would not be dismantled, especially after the formation of the Ministry of Reconstruction: Clause Four was therefore essential.

Clause Four (or Party Object 'd') ran as follows:

> To secure for the producer by hand or by brain the full fruits of their industry by the Common Ownership of the Means of Production and the best obtainable system of popular administration and control of each industry and service.

It was a very imprecise statement of socialist intent, though it was the Labour Party's first official commitment to socialism. McKibbin suggests that it was an 'uncharacteristic adornment' of the new Constitution of the Labour Party not meant to be taken seriously. That may be so, but presumably it meant something to someone. If it is assumed that it was useful in order to distinguish the Labour Party from the Liberal Party, to indicate Labour's political independence, then it is fair to assume that this socialist ideology was important to some sections of the Labour Party and its supporters. If not, why should it be included at all?

Winter has established a clear link between the WEC, the Webbs and Clause Four. What he has failed to do is explain how this related to the ideology of the new class-consciousness of the working class. Indeed, there is still no detailed study which examines the evolution of class consciousness in the First World War and explains why it was possible to offer Clause Four in 1918 and not in 1913. McKibbin's suggestion that it was there as a sop to the professional middle class, which had found socialism through the wartime experience, seems unconvincing.[13] One might note that Bernard Barker's attempt to explain why some prominent Liberal MPs, 'the 1918 Liberals', moved over to the Labour Party, suggested that they had many motives.[14] Some, like C.P. Trevelyan, were apparently won over to socialism. Others, like Cecil Wilson, hoped to do some good for the party they had joined. All seem to have concluded that the Liberal Party was a spent force. Such evidence hardly suggests the attractions of socialism were irresistible, but that the new ex-Liberal members were primarily concerned to join a growing party. This might also be the motivation behind the rising level of support for Labour emerging from the middle classes.

If Winter's explanation is still wanting, then why did Clause Four find its way into Labour's Constitution? McKibbin suggests that it served a useful purpose in sharpening the divide between the Labour and Liberal Parties, and offers a variety of reasons for this: the professional middle class were evidently enamoured of socialism, but socialism was of secondary importance to the issue of who controlled the Labour Party, and the trade unions were not much interested in it, and its vagueness and lack of rigour permitted it to unite a party where there was otherwise 'little doctrinal agreement'.[15] The first of these suggestions has already been dismissed. The second seems plausible, given that the trade-union movement, with its block vote, was the dominant force in the Labour Party and enhanced its control of the NEC under the 1918 Constitution. Yet it is the third, barely examined by McKibbin, which appears to offer the best answer.

It was the vagueness of Clause Four which permitted it to act as a unifying force within the Labour Party. The various Labour and socialist organisations which accreted to the Labour Party exhibited both pro-war and anti-war views. The WEC managed to unite these interests through the defence of living standards and via its Conscription of Riches campaign. Clause Four could be seen as an extension of this approach. It was detailed enough to distinguish Labour men from the Liberal Party but sufficiently vague to avoid serious conflict over the variety of socialist programmes on offer.

Indeed there is little evidence that Clause Four excited much interest at either the national or local level, beyond the recognition of the fact that, by accepting it, the Labour Party had formally declared its commitment to socialism. In the end, Clause Four proved a useful point of common agreement between socialists of all shades of opinion, but it should not be seen as more than an acceptable flag of convenience which helped to detach the Labour Party from the progressive end of the Liberal Party. The emergence of class politics and the war itself might also have had a more direct impact.

One must remember, however, that it was not just the Labour and Liberal parties that were faced with change and adjustment during the war. The Conservatives and Unionists faced such adaption. Indeed, on the eve of the Great War the Conservative Party was in some disarray, and it took its Unionist leader, Bonar Law, some effort to reorganise the party and revive its fortunes. Quite clearly the war allowed the natural patriotism of the Conservatives to surface, and it did well out of the tribulations of the Liberal Party in government. Nevertheless, according to John Stubbs, the Great War forced the Conservative Party to confront the issue of state control, Home Rule for Ireland and other issues. In effect, it forced it to confront the needs of the twentieth century and become the adaptable and dominant party of government that it was throughout the twentieth century (Document 6).

The First World War, Social Levelling and Industrial Protest

As Winter has stressed, the WEC fought to protect the standard of living of the working classes. It may have had some effect, because recent evidence suggests that the standard of living of the working classes, particularly the poorer sections, did improve substantially during the First World War. Bernard Waites, in *A Class Society at War: England 1914–1918*, suggests that there were improvements in class differences, but that the main social change was to consolidate the three main class groups in society. In effect, status groupings within class became less obvious, and it is possible that the working classes – the labour aristocracy and the rest – found that they were less different from one another than they had thought. When comparing the pre-war with the post-war experience it would appear that poverty, social deprivation, educational differences and other aspects of social difference were much reduced (Document 7). These views are broadly supported by J.M. Winter in his *The Great War and the British People*, which suggests that wage differentials did decrease: especially, manual workers found their wages and living standards much enhanced, semi-skilled and skilled workers less so, as a result of the fact that the poorest sections of the working class were now able to obtain continuous work rather than the sporadic employment of the pre-war years. Indeed, it is clear that throughout society there was a flattening of income differences, with most improvement occurring amongst the bottom 70 or 80 percent of society (Documents 13 and 14). There was also improvement in infant mortality levels, a sensitive indicator of social change (Documents 15). The working classes were also better fed (Document 8). Whilst the food intake of the nation fell, it was better distributed and nutritional standards were improved.

Red Clyde

Living standards and the preservation of the privileges of skill, related to industrial action, have provided the context to another debate. Most obviously the strike action of the skilled engineers of the Clydeside, where there was a rising demand for the production of munitions, has drawn the attention of a number of historians to its implication for the building of a Labour tradition

in Glasgow. It is clear that the skilled engineers and workers were under
pressure from a wartime government which wanted to introduce unskilled
and semi-skilled female labour, 'dilutees', into the industry. This provoked a
tremendous reaction from the workers – already sensitive to wage demands –
who looked to their shop stewards, rather than their unions, such as the
Amalgamated Society of Engineers (ASE), to protect their skilled privileges.
This led to a widespread strike threat on the Clyde, only defused by local
agreement and, eventually, the removal of some of the members of the organising Clyde Workers' Committee in 1916. The events that led to this have
given rise to the term, or legend, 'The Red Clyde'. James Hinton has suggested that this term is indeed fair, given that the privileged skilled workers'
protests led to a wider class movement which encouraged activists to move
into the ILP, the Labour Party and the Communist Party of Great Britain in
later years. This view has been rejected by Iain McLean in his *The Legend of
Red Clydeside* (1983), which suggests that the Clydeside engineers were a
sectional and isolated group which carried little support throughout its community, and whose concerns were barely related to issues such as housing and
rent which gave rise to Labour's growth in Glasgow and Scotland. Joseph
Melling, in a recent article, suggests that there is truth in both positions, and
that the struggles of a skilled group were not entirely divorced from the social
problems of Glasgow, and helped to explain the strong growth of the Labour
Party and socialist groups in that area in the 1920s (Document 9).

What is clear, however, is that the protest in the 'Red Clyde' was defeated
by the Government in 1916. In opposing the shop stewards, the Government
promoted the trade-union leadership, which had suspended trade-union
rights until the cessation of conflict. In return, the trade-union movement
gained the restoration of its rights, and jobs for its male members at the end
of the war (Document 17). In other words, the trade-union movement was
implicated in this process of controlling the shop stewards. And it is also clear
that there were other factors at play, such as the rent strike, which also provided the context for Labour's rapid growth on Clydeside after the war. In
other words, there was no straight line between the militancy on Clydeside in
1915 and 1916 and the growth of Glasgow as a Labour heartland after the war.

The Peace Movement

There is one other major issue that has attracted considerable attention in
this period: the extent to which their was opposition to the First World War.
The writings of Fenner Brockway, Siegfried Sassoon and others suggest that
there was some considerable opposition to the War. Indeed, there was opposition from religious groups, most obviously the Quakers, the ILP, whose

national position was to oppose the war but to allow individual conscience on the issue, various other socialist groups, and groups of socialists and Liberals who gathered together in various bodies such as the Union of Democratic Control (opposed to the loss of liberties) and the No-Conscription Fellowship. However, the question is how pervasive and significant this opposition was.

David Wright (Document 1) suggests that oppositional and pacifist groups were small and almost irrelevant. On the other hand, Cyril Pearce has recently argued that some communities, such as Huddersfield, exhibited strong anti-war tendencies (Document 10). In addition, there has been much questioning of the extent to which some organisations, such as the ILP, were anti-war and pacifist. The contemporary press and politicians often presented them in that fashion, but Keith Laybourn and Tony Jowitt, examining the ILP and the Labour movement in Bradford, deemed a centre of pacifism, throw doubt on this interpretation. In fact, few members of the Bradford ILP were pacifists, though many were anti-war, and the majority appear to have exercised individual conscience. As a result, a very large proportion of those in the Bradford ILP who could do so attested under the voluntary Derby Scheme to do their duty if so required (Document 11).

The fact is that the majority of the working class did well from the Great War, the trade-union movement saw its membership rise from about four millions to six millions, and most people seem to have supported the war effort. Nevertheless, there was a sense of war-weariness emerging by 1917, which led Philip Snowden and the ILP to mount the Peace Campaign, which Snowden carried into parliament as well as before the general public (Documents 19 and 20). It does not appear to have been particularly effective in ending the war, but may have been one of the factors, along with social unrest and rising expectations, which led the Government to form committees to examine post-war reconstruction and encourage political parties and David Lloyd George, the Prime Minister, to look to a better future (Document 18).

It is debatable whether or not women did quite as well out of the war as men did. In 1920, Millicent Garrett Fawcett, a leading suffragist, wrote that 'The war revolutionised the industrial position of women. It found them serfs and left them free.'[16] That view has been rejected by Gail Braybon, who produced two books, *Women and Workers in the First World War* in 1981 and *Out of the Cage* in 1987 with Penny Summerfield. Her general argument has been that women's war work was very much constricted, and constructed, by the needs and attitudes of male workers. More recently, Deborah Thom, in *Nice Girls and Rude Girls* (London, I.B. Tauris, 1994) (Document 12) has suggested that Braybon is right, although part of that constriction occurred by women themselves and shaped by their pre-war experiences in the trade-union movement. What appears clear is that despite women over thirty years of age gaining the vote in the 1918, regardless of their admission to a wider range of social and economic activities, and irrespective of their munitions and war work, there is little to suggest that there was a fundamental change in the position of women during the Great War.

Conclusion

Social change and industrial action saw the rising importance of the working classes, whose political importance was eventually recognised in the 1918 Franchise Act, which provided suffrage for men over twenty-one and women over thirty. These factors alone make the Great War a significant period of change. In the process, there was political change, with both the Conservative and Labour Parties adapting to the wartime developments in a way in which the Liberal Party was unable to do. Consequently, the changing political climate of pre-war Britain, particularly in progressive politics, was confirmed by the war. Nevertheless, the jury is still out on whether or not it was a 'useless slaughter'. There is sufficient evidence now to suggest that there was significant support for it amongst the British population, even if Haig, the British High Command and the politicians are still subject to intense scrutiny. Indeed, one cannot ignore the fact that after the horrific experiences of the war British politicians were reluctant to get involved in another. Appeasement has much of its appeal in the horrors of 1914–18.

Documents
SECONDARY SOURCES AND INTERPRETATIONS

1 – David Wright, *The Great War: A Useless Slaughter* (Huddersfield,
    University of Huddersfield, Pamphlets in History and Politics, 1991),
    pp 1, 3, 15, 20

Even though the Great War ended a lifetime ago, the Western Front remains deeply embedded in our culture. For the generation born before the Second World War, the Menin gate at Ypres, recording the names of 55,000 missing and dead, is one of the most sacred places on earth. The first day of the Battle of the Somme (1 July 1916), when the British suffered 60,000 casualties, including 20,000 dead, is the blackest day in our history…

    … the Somme has been seen as marking a fissure in British culture. As Philip Larkin wrote in his celebrated poem 'MCMXIV'

Never such innocence
Never before or since…
Never such innocence again.

Benign, humanitarian, liberal Englishmen, it is believed, lost this innocence at 7.30am on 1 July 1916. Scots, Welsh and Northern Irish are usually left unmentioned…

When the war came it brought death and bereavement on a massive scale. The 'Great War' is much more apt than 'The First World War', for as Sir Michael Howard has written: 'Only that mournful spondee, tolling like two strokes of a passing bell, can express all that the years 1914–1918 means for the peoples of Europe'. Above all what it means for the British. This is not to say that there was not grief in France and Germany and Austria; they too have their cemeteries and war memorials, Indeed, they lost more men that Britain (Germany c. 1.6 million, France c. 1.35 million, Britain c. 0.72)…

Yet the war administered the most profound shock to Britain, who had never before fielded a mass army in Europe. Even though France produced Henry Barbusse's *Under Fire* as early as 1917 and Germany Erich Maria Remarque's *All Quiet on the Western Front* in 1929, it was the British literary survivors of the war who went furthest in damning the war as futile slaughter; a war not worth fighting; a war where much blood was shed for a few yards of mud; a war where brave men were despatched to certain death by incompetent generals, urged on by unbalanced and uncomprehending civilians. We are all familiar with Wilfred Owen's poems and their memorable lines:

Was it for this the clay grey tall?
Oh what made the fatuous sunbeams toil
To break the earth's sleep at all?
The old Lie: Dulce et decorum est
Pro patria mori

Siegfried Sassoon's sardonic and bitter poems, as well as Robert Graves's *Goodbye to All That*, where the war is depicted as a pointless farce, have had a wide readership. Indeed, it is arguable that our view of the war has been created largely by such literature; a literature that was so very English since that of no other country went so far as to suggest that the war was utterly futile and not worth fighting. This attitude had a significant effect on British foreign policy in the 1930s… [There is then a discussion about the myths of the Great War.]

Historians since the 1960s, headed by John Terraine, have been busily chipping at the popular image of the Great War as a futile bloodbath inflicted by jingoistic politicians and inept generals on brave young men; at the image of the war as a useless slaughter, comprising, in the words of A.J.P. Taylor, 'brave, helpless soldiers; bungling incompetent generals, nothing achieved'. During the war itself, neither the soldiers at the front nor their families at home saw themselves as engaged in a futile exercise as opposed to participating in a noble crusade fought in defence of liberty and 'gallant little Belgium' against an aggressive expansionary 'Prussian militarism'. Disasters like the Somme and Passchendaele, it is argued, were the result of Britain suddenly being required after Verdun and French failures to field a mass ill-trained army against a superior, highly professional and well-entrenched enemy. Neither politicians, press nor public would permit Haig to sit tight on the defensive and wait for the Central Powers to collapse from the effects of blockade and relatively limited resources. Haig's offensive on the Somme, taken much against his inclination, was a forced move to placate the French and preserve the entente. Numerous scholars have argued that it is unfair to blame the horrific casualties on château- and desk-bound cavalry generals, given the overrapid expansion of the British army from a small gendarmerie designed to police Irish and colonial dissidents to a force of nearly 2 million on the Western front by 1918. As J.M. Bourne has acidly commented:

> Douglas Haig fulfilled the most important criterion of generalship. He won. The scale of his victories was the greatest in British military history. His countrymen have never forgiven him.

Other historians argue that Haig should not be forgiven, for neither he nor the generals proved able to adapt to modern technological warfare. British army emphasis on the offensive at all costs and of following a Napoleonic set-piece battle plan and breakthrough persisted, even when, by 1916, their bankruptcy was evident. Despite being relatively well-read and educated, Haig never developed his ideas beyond his 1896–97 Staff College even when planning the Somme and Passchendaele offensives. Moreover, he proved an introverted, uncommunicative, unapproachable warlord, with his GHQ largely isolated from Army and Corps commanders. Generals who persisted in seeing warfare as necessarily ordered and regulated failed to perceive the full implications of recent military technology and fire problems inherent in the mass armies of three great powers involved in a slogging match in a confined geographical area with little possibility of napoleonic outflanking movements or a devastating cavalry pursuit like that of Murat at Jena in 1806...

For many men on the Western Front the standard of food and pastoral care – the best of any of the Great Armies – was such that their living conditions were superior to the slums of Britain where many had been brought up, or rather survived. Despite the strain of fatalism and cynicism that became apparent among to the ranks by 1917, and revealed in soldiers songs, few appeared seriously to have echoed the complaints of the Royalist Earl of Berkshire in 1645: 'Noe body can tell what we have fought about all this whyle'. Perhaps the last word may be left to Emlyn Davies (17th Royal Welsh Fusiliers, writing in 1968:

Acceptance of the King's shilling brooked neither legitimate nor possible protest. So naturally and not unwillingly, we 'soldiered on'. Might I add 'happily too'. A new comradeship and unity blossomed into our young lives. So we just soldiered on. For God, For King and For Country, as we were each and all convinced.

2 – T. Wilson, *The Myriad Faces of War* (Cambridge, Polity Press, 1986), pp 850–2

One final question, then, remains. Had the war been for any worthwhile purpose, or was it simply a sustained exercise in futility?

A difference in attitude may be detected among historians towards the two great wars of this century. So the Second World War has been summed up by A.J.P. Taylor, in the concluding words of his book on that subject as 'a good war'. There are few historians who would say the same of the First World War. A.J.P. Taylor, for one, does not so judge it. The spirit of the Great War was to him epitomised by the song the British soldiers sang:

> We're here because we're here
> Because we're here
> Because we're here

'The War,' he writes, 'in fact was fought for its own sake. They fought because they fought because they fought because they fought. The war was not a great tribute to human wisdom.'

It is not surprising that the Great War excites these hostile judgements. For it was the first sustained demonstration of the monstrous powers for inflicting destruction that industrialisation had bestowed upon Western man...

Yet although it is necessary to record this judgement, to leave it without qualification would be misleading. Admittedly, in the case of Britain no large transformation for either good or ill was set in motion. Yet some changes were accomplished that, at the time or subsequently, appeared advantageous.

We have already noticed how war encouraged in Britain some acceleration of social reform and a rise in living standards of the poorest section. More agreeably for the imperially minded, it led to Britain gaining (for a while) an enhanced position in the Middle East...

Less tangible, but still of considerable note, the war had proved a striking vindication of the British way of life. Starting at a considerable disadvantage to other combatants, it had converted millions of untrained civilians into capable soldiers...

Nor can a discussion of the positive accomplishments of the war end there. For a question has many times suggested itself in these pages that can no longer be denied examination. The question can be expressed variously. If the destruction wrought by the war was great, were not the stakes also high? Was there, in fact, not much more at issue than fighting for the sake of fighting? Were not the Western Allies, notwithstanding much that was discreditable about them, upholding liberal democracy against a predatory military aristocracy? These inquiries may be summoned up in a single question: If the First World War, unlike the Second, could hardly be described as a 'good war', was it not also one of freedom's battles?

3 – Michael Bentley, *The Climax of Liberal Politics: British Liberalism in Theory and Practice 1868-1918* (London, Edward Arnold, 1987), p 148–9

The argument that the war had proved fatal had rested on propositions about party difficulties that the war threw up; they had not argued the case that the war *in itself* and by its very nature had instigated the disaster. This emphasis helped the 'Labour' case by allowing the period 1906–24 to be seen as a continuum and opening the possibility of comparing pre- and post-war condition (general elections, for example) without the feeling gaining ground that an exercise in which the war had been 'removed' rested on an absurdity. The present writer resisted this position, among others, in 1977 by arguing that the war did not function negatively by challenging Liberals' sense of principle but rather had a positive role in helping them decide what those principles were and in providing unique conditions in which the traditional broad-church understanding of Liberalism could no longer find living-space among the constricted reference-points of total war. From this perspective, 1916 became a very important year, not merely as the occasion of a party fissure but rather as the moment when two versions of true Liberalism parted company. That those two versions never reunited apart from a few weeks' rather farcical togetherness for the purpose of the 1923 election campaign, therefore became less of a surprise, as did the failure of Lloyd George ever to recapture the loyalty of traditional Liberals.

4 – J.M. Winter, *Socialism and the Challenge of War: Ideas and Politics in Britain, 1912–1918* (London, Routledge & Kegan Paul, 1974), pp 274, 275, 284–5

Why did the ideas of Sidney and Beatrice Webb in particular become the basis for Labour policy at the end of the First World War? The answer to this question must be sought not only in the experience of London in wartime but also in terms of Webbian socialism.

The Webbs' views were adopted out of necessity rather than out of choice or conviction. Neither Tawney nor Cole, nor any of their contemporaries had been able to present a viable alternative to Webbian socialism during the First World War, that is, at the very time the Labour movement most needed intellectual leadership.

It was precisely the ability to explain how institutions worked and developed over time which gave the Webbs their greatest advantage. The theories which Tawney and Cole advanced before the war avoided, perhaps deliberately, the central problems of comprehensive institutional change, a subject on which the Webbs were authorities. Other theories never explained adequately how a socialist society would actually work or how it might be brought about…

[Winter suggests that the policies of the Webbs were highly appropriate to the activities of the War Emergency Workers' National Committee, which were geared towards protecting the living standards of the workers and the Conscription of Riches campaign.] In this organisation, Sidney Webb put into effect with far-reaching consequences the institutional approach to political problems which he held (and in fact personified) throughout his life. Webb lived largely through committees and the work which he had done during the war suited him perfectly…

The First World War helped to push their [the Webbs] ideas even further to the organisational side of the argument, and to develop a view to socialism which received its most complete presentation in their *Soviet Communism: A New Civilisation*, published in November 1935. Their admiration of government from above, even at the price of authoritarianism, is apparent throughout their writings. Their illiberalism attains its ultimate expression in this massive defence of Stalin's dictatorship which appeared after the trial of Zinoviev and Kamenev, when the great purges had begun.

It is one of the ironies of British socialism, then, that the only school of thought which had a chance of political success was precisely the one least likely to realise the idealism which is at the centre of the socialist position. Here lies the ultimate importance of the theoretical writings of R.H. Tawney and G.D.H. Cole. They kept alive the socialist alternatives to the desiccated élitism of Sidney and Beatrice Webb.

At the same time, however, the inability of Tawney and Cole to deal effectively with the theoretical and practical problems of organising a political movement, let alone a modern industrial state of war, severely limited the impact of their critiques. Unlike the Webbs, their position lacked appeal largely because they did not speak to the most pressing problems of the day. The Webbs at least knew what matters needed immediate political attention.

In the first quarter of the twentieth century, then, British socialists were confronted with a difficult choice among three widely differing alternative political theories, none of which was fully adequate to the needs of the Labour movement. On the one side stood the bureaucratic approach of the

Webbs, rigid and unattractive, but, as they proved during the First World War, admittedly the most effective socialist position. Opposed to it were the more humane and much more utopian ideas of Tawney and Cole. There was no other option until the formation of the Communist Party in 1920.

5 – Ross McKibbin, *The Evolution of the Labour Party 1910–1924* (Oxford University Press, 1974), pp 91, 96

And yet, within a year, Henderson was out of the government, the Labour movement had agreed to meet German socialists in Stockholm, and the Labour Party had committed itself to the nationalisation of the means of production, distribution and exchange. How is this remarkable development to be explained? More particularly, how is clause IV, the socialist objective, to be explained? Part of the answer is to be found, not in clause IV itself, but in the circumstances in which the constitution was written and passed. It is easy to be overimpressed with the socialist objective and to be unconcerned with the corpus of the 1918 constitution, whose uncharacteristic adornment clause IV was. The constitution embodied not an ideology but a system by which power in the Labour Party was distributed...

Then how did Clause IV get there? Inevitably, for a number of reasons. The Party was committed to a 'programme', and clauses IV and V, though by no means prescriptions for political action, indicated the direction of the programme and offered the electorate a doctrine differentiated from that of other parties. Further, the socialist objective served the useful purpose, as Beer suggested, of sharpening the break between the Labour and Liberal Parties. Finally, clause IV, precisely because of its vagueness and lack of rigour paradoxically had an umbrella function: it was an acceptable formula in a Party where there otherwise little doctrinal agreement.

6 – John Stubbs, 'The Impact of the Great War on the Conservative Party' in Gillian Peele and Chris Cook (eds.), *The Politics of Reappraisal 1918–1939* (London, Macmillan, 1975), pp 17, 21, 31, 32, 35

With the outbreak of war in August 1914 the Unionists were faced with the necessity of redefining their role in the political system...

The war had a profound effect on the functions of the party organisation. The machinery of all political parties was put to work in the national interest. On 6 August 1914 the Executive Committee of the National Union accepted Steel-Maitland's recommendation to join with their Liberal counterparts in closing down publication of party leaflets, paying off some of the party speakers, and stopping all partisan public speaking...

The emergence of organised backbench opinion in the Conservative Party was an important development of the wartime period. A new pattern of relationship between the party leadership and the parliamentary rank-and-file was firmly established. This pattern was carried over to the 1922 Committee. The war years also saw important changes in the Unionist Party that did not relate so much to the dynamics of the structure of the party but rather to the meaning of Conservatism. The war knocked away the foundations of some cherished Conservative principles, hastened the advent of some articles of Conservative faith and raised a host of new problems that were to challenge inter-war Conservatism.

Unrelenting opposition to Home Rule had been one of the articles of faith of pre-war Unionists. Yet six weeks after the war began Home Rule was on the statute book balanced only by the vague assurances of an Amending Bill during the suspensory period. In the spring of 1916, following the Easter Rising in Dublin, the monolithic Unionist view of how to deal with the Irish question was shattered by the spectacle of Bonar Law and Carson joining forces to suggest a wartime Home Rule Settlement. Law supported Lloyd George's proposals for Ireland because they provided as fully for Ulster as had those the Unionists put forward at the time of the Buckingham Palace Conference in July 1914...

The war also moulded Conservative thinking on a number of important constitutional questions. One of the central issues that was resolved during the war was the matter of the franchise. Military and industrial service in the common cause by millions of citizens of the United Kingdom made it increasingly difficult for the Conservative party to continue supporting a franchise limited by property and rental qualification. Indeed, it was the Conservative party itself that was instrumental in making the franchise a political question during the war. This development occurred in the summer of 1916 because of the refusal of the Unionists and Liberals in the House of Lords to grant the government War Committees, aided by the Conservative-dominated 'Beach' Committee in the House of Lords, to grant the government a further extension of the life of Parliament unless a guarantee for the enfranchisement of the nation's servicemen was forthcoming. Ultimately the House of Commons refused to accept any registration legislation from the government. The impasse was resolved by the establishment of a Speaker's Conference on electoral reform and registration in October 1916. However, for the Conservatives to turn to the active consideration of universal manhood suffrage brought with it the reality of a massive unpropertied working class infusion into the electorate with the attendant fears of socialism...

The experience of war was fundamental in the evolution of the modern Conservative Party. War brought the party squarely into the twentieth century by both destroying many of the fundamental landmarks of pre-war

Conservatism and by creating a host of new challenges that could not be dealt with successfully by pre-war solutions. Ireland and the Welsh Church and the power of the House of Lords were essentially issues of the past; by 1918 the principles had been conceded if not *de jure* than at least *de facto*. The war raised the issue of the role of the state in society and the economy in such a way that Conservatives could no longer afford to ignore it. The other fundamental change in the Conservative Party brought about by the war was the permanent emergence of backbench politics. A pre-war unity based almost exclusively on opposition to Home Rule was destroyed by the strains of patriotic opposition and party coalitions discovered that they had power and that they were more than mere voting fodder. That power was exercised with brutal clarity in 1922 when the Conservative Party appeared to its adherents to have been taken away from the Conservatives.

7 – Bernard Waites, *A Class Society at War: England 1914–18* (Leamington Spa, Berg, 1987), pp 114, 279

Historians who have dwelt on the participation effect have linked it with a loosening of the class structure, implicitly assuming that there that there is a simple relationship between a narrowing of economic differentials and a tendency to 'classlessness'. In this argument, class structure is, in rather a facile way, elided with social stratification or hierarchical ranking. In my view, the empirical evidence will support another interpretation: society was certainly less steeply stratified, but narrowing of economic differentials took place primarily within the three basic social classes and encouraged the consolidation of each...

The argument of this study can be summarised as the contention that there took place between 1914 and 1924 a concatenation of changes in English society which altered the specific form of the class structure but did not fundamentally disturb those processes of social differentiation which are generic to a capitalist market society. In brief, these changes were an elimination of much of the poverty of prewar England, a redistribution of national income in favour of the salariat and manual workers, a narrowing of working-class wage differentials and middle-class salary differentials, a reduction of some of the large incomes derived from wealth and some redistribution of that wealth, an expansion of educational opportunities that led to white-collar employment and a strengthening of civic integration by the steps taken to include the working class and the Labour movement within a community of citizenship.

8 – J.M. Winter, *The Great War and the British People* (London, Macmillan, 1986, reprinted 1987), pp 3–4, 244, 305

The argument of this study is implicit in its structure. It is that the social and demographic impact of the war was the product of two distinctive processes: (i) the unprecedented recruitment and attrition of British manpower in uniform... and (ii) the mobilisation of a civilian war economy, the unintended and fortuitous benefits of which were the source of the disturbing paradox that the Great War was both an event of unparalleled carnage and suffering and the occasion of a significant improvement in the life expectancy of the civilian population, and especially of the worst-off sections of British society... It is argued that neither an improvement in medical care (which did not take place) nor an extension of public health service (which, to a certain extent, did take place) were primarily responsible for the decline in mortality rates in wartime. The fundamental cause of this phenomenon was an improved standard of living, and in particular, improved standards of nutrition among the urban and rural working class. Here is the key to the striking contrast between the demographic gains of the civilian population and the demographic losses of the generation that went off to war...

But overall, such evidence of war conditions leading to impaired health is overshadowed by many indications of the positive effects of the mobilisation of the industrial population after 1914. We have demonstrated that while food supplies were reduced, diets were maintained and, in some cases, actually improved in wartime. This was part of the function of the levelling up of low wages and a shift from traditionally poorly paid to better-paid jobs. It was also a reflection of wartime welfare policy, social subsidies, and of the redistribution of income and food within the working-class family.

In Britain during the First World War, underpaid and underemployed labourers were transformed within a few months of the outbreak of hostilities into full working partners in the war effort. The only way war-related production could have been expanded rapidly at a time of mass voluntary enlistment was by attracting workers to low-paid munitions factories by the promise of higher rates of pay, and this is precisely what the Ministry of War, and the later Ministry of Munitions, succeeded in doing. Furthermore, when a real challenge to working-class living standards arose in the form of increased rents in early 1915, the government acted with great haste to freeze the rents at pre-war level. What changed in wartime was both the enhancement of the market position of most grades of manual labour as well as a strengthening of the legal and moral entitlement of workers to exchange their labour for a living wage.

This is why even though *aggregate* food supply declined during the war, nutritional levels rose...

There was an unbridgeable existential divide in the experience of war. However, as we have tried to demonstrate in this book, there were other less terrifying 'meanings' of war to which a historian must attend. Among them is the paradox that because of the armed conflict, this country became a healthier place in which to live. But that phenomenon, however important in the long-term social history of the country, was bound to be eclipsed by the memory of the human cost of the conflict.

9 – Joseph Melling. 'Whatever Happened to Red Clydeside? Industrial Conflict and the Politics of Skill in the First World War', *International Review of Social History* Vol. XXXV (1990), Part 1, pp 6, 7, 29, 31, 32

[James] Hinton argued that the backbone of industrial militancy was formed amongst the engineering craftsmen threatened by new technologies and pro-voked into open resistance during the Government's dilution programme. The most familiar response of the labour aristocrat was to defend their craft privilege, but a specific section of the workforce recognised the need for fresh strategies. These rank-and-file radicals were led by a group of brilliant shop stewards opposed to the policies of moderate officials and ready to confront aggressive employers or government bureaucrats. Influenced by the Socialist Labour Party and similar bodies, this groups created the Clyde Workers' Committee (CWC) to coordinate resistance and formulate a radical policy of dilution which would secure workers' control. During the winter of 1915–1916, the socialist stewards challenged the authority of the British state until they were weakened by internal factions and finally crushed by a sinister alliance of employers, civil servants and politicians...

This interpretation of wartime conflict has been challenged in Iain McLean's *Legend of Red Clydeside*, which suggests that our understanding of Scottish society and politics has been badly distorted by the various mytho-logies of class struggle in the Clyde. McLean rejects Hinton's portrait of wartime conflict and concludes that the cadres of the Clyde Workers' Committee were isolated and confused in their dealing with a progressive government. Their own officials were attacked for betraying their mem-bers... The legacy of shop-floor unrest during the war years was not progressive politics but destructive sectionalism which inhibited the growth of the Labour Party. It was Labour's remarkable success in dealing with the housing question and religious sectarianism that enabled the Party to over-come the industrial squabbles of 1914–1919 to build a wide constituency of support in Glasgow. Whereas Hinton depicts the Ministry of Munitions as the largest arm of a Servile State intent on subordinating a restive labour movement to the political control of capitalism, McLean sees the Government department as dominated by progressive politicians and experienced civil servants – driven to repressive action during crises but generally seeking the co-operation of organised labour...

For Hinton it was the advances in technology and dilution which threatened the position of the skilled workers during the war, driving a majority into defensive craftism, and radicalising a minority of shop stewards... This interpretation of socialist politics is firmly rejected by historians such as McLean and Reid, who insist on the integrity of craft-union policies and their defence of the sectional interests of their members... [Socialism appears to have been encouraged by the issue of housing on Clydeside, although there may have been other factors. McLean feels that this was so because the conflict on the Clyde checked Labour's growth while Alistair Reid suggests that wartime controls convinced people of the viability of state socialism and thus further encouraged socialism. On the other hand, Melling suggests that the Great War destroyed the fragile political arrangements and that no straight line can be drawn between industrial militancy and the growth of post-war socialism on Clydeside.]

Union officials failed to protect their members against the aggression of the employers during the Munitions controversy and a crisis of confidence spread throughout the Clyde area. Different sections of the membership seized the opportunity to devise their own agreement. Despite the fierce criticism of the Parkhead stewards by left-wingers such as Gallacher, even the CWC was, in practice, seeking to secure the position of the skilled trades by shifting the basis of control from the craft society to the shop committees. This view challenges the argument that the real significance of the dilution struggle which lay in the polarisation of the tradesmen and a struggle between the militant shop stewards and union officials.

Nor can the unions be seen simply as [the representatives of] craftsmen. The lay tradesmen were trying to defend their autonomy in the face of female dilution, as were the Parkhead stewards. The friction with the full-time officials rose from the anxiety of the ASE executive to secure a binding national agreement and destroy the challenge of the CWC to the District. This challenge was a political threat to the fixed procedures of the war, but grew out of the practical experience of shop stewards rather than the political doctrine of local syndicalists.

[Melling notes that the state was not neutral when it came to industrial production and munitions.]

The political consequences of the industrial unrest were not immediately apparent. Many of the leading figures found their way to the Communist Party but numerous others remained in the ILP and the Labour Party. We cannot draw a straight line between workplace struggles and the wider politics of Scottish Labour. Campaigns on rents and housing also played a key part in the success of Labour politicians. But these were not discrete areas of activity, separate from the confrontation between skilled workers and the wartime state.

10 – Cyril Pearce, 'A Community of Resistance - the Anti-war Movement in Huddersfield 1914–1918', in Keith Dockray and Keith Laybourn (eds), *Representation and Reality of War: Essays in Honour of D.G. Wright* (Stroud, Sutton Publishing, 1999)

Since 1918, the general view of British attitudes to war has combined two unchanging assumptions: first, that it is possible to speak of a 'national' mood, and second, that the mood reflected the war's general popularity. The only significant way in which that view has been modified since it was first advanced is the acceptance that, by 1917, the war's popularity had begun to wane...

The question of anti-war sentiments in Huddersfield during the 1914–18 war was first raised publicly in 1915 by John Hunter Watts, a patriotic socialist and War Office recruiting agent. He warned his first public meeting in Huddersfield that '... the War Office informed him that the most serious opposition to recruiting came from this district...' Will Thorne spoke of Huddersfield as '... a hot-bed of pacifism', and Cunninghame Graham, another pro-war veteran of the Labour movement attacked Huddersfield's anti-war campaigners as '... skunks, scoundrels, neuters, neither men nor women...' Many years later, Wilfrid Whiteley, one of the 'skunks', confirmed the view that opposition to the war was stronger in Huddersfield than in other towns. He also maintained that it was more genuinely tolerated there than anywhere else he knew...

There was no great public show when the war was declared and few occasions during the war when Huddersfield demonstrated any real pro-war fervour... There were no anti-German riots and no sustained attempts to disrupt anti-war meetings...

[Thereafter there is a discussion of the general tolerance of anti-war sentiments within the Liberal elite in Huddersfield and amongst socialists, indicating that there was a broad-based commitment to anti-war views. There is also a detailed examination of the local Conscientious Objectors Clubs, such as Paddock Socialist Club, which acted as centres of resistance to conscription.]

In Huddersfield the opposition to war had numerous roots. For some it was a simple matter of international class loyalty; for others, the source was a deeper and less easily identified mix of ethical antipathies to violence and to the denial of individual freedoms which were to be seen inherent in war and militarism. These ethical positions grew from roots in the radical and non-conformist Christianity which were shared with local Liberalism...

[Local anti-war candidates do not seem to have been disadvantaged in the 1918 General Election.]

Where does all this put the Huddersfield experience and what might it have to say about the bigger picture? Should we regard it as eccentric to the general experience or symptomatic of something more widespread? On the other hand, perhaps the evidence here suggests that we ought to be asking different questions.

11 – Tony Jowitt and Keith Laybourn, 'War and Socialism: the Experience of the Bradford ILP 1914–1918', in David James, Tony Jowitt and Keith Laybourn (eds), *The Centennial History of the Independent Labour Party* (Halifax, Ryburn, 1992) pp 166, 167–8, 169, 170, 173

Contrary to the general impression given by the local Tory and Liberal press, there were very few members of the ILP who adopted an outright pacifist stand. At the national level the main advocates of pacifism were Bruce Glasier, Clifford Allen, Arthur Salter and Fenner Brockway, with Philip Snowden on the edge of this group though he was never a fully committed pacifist. There was a professional, middle-class, temper to this group which was composed largely of writers, journalists, academics and doctors. They took a pure pacifist line that all war was wrong, and some of them supplemented their hostility to war by forming the No-Conscription Fellowship and working with the Union of Democratic Control. Although there was some welling of support for this group when they managed to gain some measure of control at the national conference of the ILP in 1917, it was never a significant force in the politics of the Bradford ILP. Pacifism attracted only a few middle-class members of the ILP, most prominently the Quaker Arthur Priestman and William Leach...

The majority of the antiwar section of the Party appear to have followed the lead of Fred Jowett who was never an outright pacifist, but accepted the need for National Defence. Jowett, who had been returned as Bradford's first ILP MP in 1906, was the dominant figure in the Bradford Labour ranks during the First World War. Throughout the War he tried to articulate a viewpoint of what caused the War and how wars could be eradicated in the future. As he argued in his Chairman's speech to the 1915 ILP Conference at Norwich, 'Now is the time to speak and ensure that never again shall the witches' cauldron of secret diplomacy brew the broth of Hell for mankind'. In an important article in the *Bradford Pioneer* in June 1916 he explained that:

> I believe that the war would never have arisen if the government had carried out an open and honest foreign policy and disclosed to the people who had most to lose the relations between themselves and foreign governments with whom they were acting in collusion.

His constant theme throughout the war was that it had been caused by the secret treaties which had been arranged, though frequently denied, by the British Government. 'His fad', as the *Standard* said of Jowett, 'is the democratic control of foreign affairs'. In connection with this Jowett also demanded that the Government should specify its war aims and should be forced towards the negotiating table...

The fact is that a substantial proportion of the membership of the Bradford ILP was committed to the war effort either on the negative grounds of the need for National Defence or on the more positive grounds that Prussianism needed to be destroyed...

When the *Bradford Daily Telegraph* attacked the ILP's resistance to the war effort and their inability to 'raise a single finger to help the country to prosecute the war successfully', Jowett replied that 'In proportion to its membership the ILP has more adherents serving in the army and navy by far than either of the two other political parties'. Censuses of the Bradford ILP membership confirm this impression. A census in February 1916 indicated that of 461 young men in the local party membership of 1473, 113 were in the trenches, four had been killed, one was missing, nine had been wounded, three were prisoners of war, 118 were training in England, six were in the Navy and 207 were attested under the Derby scheme as necessary home workers. A similar survey in 1918 found that of the 492 members liable for service, 351 were serving in the forces whilst 48 were conscientious objectors or were on national work.

The emphasis placed upon the 'Peace' movement by the hostile Tory and Liberal press in Bradford has served to conceal the fact that there were substantial differences of opinion within the ILP and the Trades Council over the war issue. The press broadcast the view that Bradford was a hot bed of pacifism and anti-war feelings and that the Trades Council was at the centre of such activities. Prominent ex-Bradford ILP members added to the illusion by offering an informed tarring of all members of the ILP and Trades Council with the same brush. The leading ex-ILP critics of the Bradford ILP were Joseph Burgess and Edward R. Hartley. Joseph Burgess had had a long association with the ILP. It was his paper, the *Workman's Times*, which had called together delegates from the Labour societies to meet at the Bradford Conference in 1893. As an editor of Labour newspapers, and as a supporter of the Socialist Sunday School movement, he had established for himself great respect within the Labour movement. He worked in Lancashire and London for many years but came to live in Bradford before the First World

War, was editor of the *Bradford Pioneer* until the summer of 1915 and was elected President of the Bradford ILP in 1915. A critic of the war from the outset, proclaiming that 'We have no quarrel with Germany… Stand firm workers, in reaction to the seduction of those who would appeal to you in the name of patriotism', he had quickly changed his position by the summer of 1915. He joined the Socialist National Defence Committee in June 1915 and was threatening to stand as parliamentary candidate for the National Socialist Party for Blackburn at the next general election, although he never did so. The pages of the *Bradford Pioneer* are full of the letters of Burgess and the comments of the Bradford ILP in what one headline referred to as 'The Burgess Comedy'. The Bradford ILP was very sensitive to the antics of a man who had so recently been the centre of its activities.

12 – Deborah Thom, *Nice Girls and Rude Girls: Women Workers in World War I* (London, I.B. Tauris, 1998), pp 96, 207

Gail Braybon, in *Women Workers and the First World War*, has shown how the wartime admission of women to men's jobs was constricted, or constructed, by the needs and attitudes of male workers. I want to argue that part of that construction was made by women, as trade-union organisers, and the roots are to be found in the late nineteenth-century experience of women workers. Nor does the alternative conventional explanation for the changes in women's unionism quite work. In this socialist or labourist explanation, as in the books by Sheila Lewenhak and Sarah Boston, women represent a part of the 'forward march of labour'. They are organised late, and in specific forms, because of the force with which the tradition of the past weighed on the attitudes of the present. These historians attribute success to good leadership. The careers of two outstanding leaders show the processes and ideology of the organisation of women, Growth was as much to do with social change as heroic individual action. The argument is that the organisation of women was highly structured by ideological notions of the weakness of women at work and in society at large, and that in looking at such a formation, notions of patriarchy are inadequate and ignore the activities and ideas of women themselves. Women of whatever class did differ in their strategy and tactics of organisation, and this difference did matter and cannot be explained in class terms. In 1918 the historian of the Ministry of Munitions described women workers as they were seen in 1914 when their use in wartime factories was being discussed in government circles.

> Women were badly organised, prone to manipulation by employers, ignorant of workshop practices, in particular defensive, restrictive practices, and content to work in lowly positions for low pay. Women did not enjoy the protection of custom,

they were not organised in strong Trade Unions, nor could such organisations be built up in an emergency...

The question with which this book started was that of how far women had created a new world for themselves in the factories of the First World War. In the end, circumstances of war work were so circumscribed that although there was a change and women made a substantial contribution to the war the change did not endure, nor was it seen as changing women's nature as workers or as citizens. Some new models of women workers were created and given dramatic visibility by photographs, posters and demonstrations but they tended to show novelty, and disguise the limits of power obtained as a result of wartime administration. Workers were still being described either in relation to men – as Tommy's sister – or in relation to their moral economy, as nice or rude. These ascriptions could be exploited, and were, by organisations representing working women, but such an exploitation carried risks which became too evident in the labour market after the war. Profound cultural changes in the world of the women worker or the 'girl', the 'mother' or the woman citizen awaited the changes in society and economy of the next world war, expansion of education and the development of welfarist politics that could begin to create institutions in the interests of women.

PRIMARY EVIDENCE AND INFORMATION

13 – A.L. Bowley, *The Change in the Distribution of the National Income 1880–1913* (Oxford, Oxford University Press, 1920)

Distribution of Personal Incomes in the UK, 1910

Size of Income (£)	No. of incomes	% of no. of incomes	Aggregate vaue of incomes (£m)	% of total value of incomes
under 160	18,850,000	94.52	1,055	56.357
160–700	880,000	4.41	250	13.355
700–5000	200,000	1.00	415	22.167
5,000–10,000	8143	0.04	55.05	2.941
10,000–20,000	2903	0.0146	39.1	2.089
20,000–45,000	1026	0.005	29	1.549
45,000 and over	327	0.0016	28.9	1.543

14 – Board of Inland Revenues 64th Annual Report (1919–1920)

Distribution of Personal Incomes in the UK, 1919–20

Size of Income (£)	No. of incomes	% of no. of incomes	Aggregate vaue of incomes (£m)	% of total value of incomes
under 400	20,057,000	96.43	2546.044	70.98
400-1750	643,270	3.08	479.249	13.36
1,750-12,500	94,098	0.45	361,684	10.08
12,500-25,000	4247	0.02	74,749	2.08
25,000+	2385	0.01	125,749	3.50

15 – Infant Mortality Rates for England and Wales (1911–1913)

Based upon the Registrar-General's Annual Reports for England and Wales 1911–20 and indicating regional variations

Region	1911–13	1914	1915	1916	1917	1918	1919	1920
North	121	110	112	96	97	102	94	88
Midlands	101	86	92	76	77	78	74	64
South	93	80	89	71	77	78	68	59
Wales	110	99	101	83	85	86	83	55
England & Wales	100	95	95	82	87	87	80	72

16 – Wages and Conditions of Employment of Dock Labour, PP 1920 Cmd 936, p 32, 186–7, A.L. Bowley in conversation with Ernest Bevin

[Bowley felt that there might might be some resentment against the big wage claim being put in by the dockers and suggested that the dockers were well fed and well provided for.]

Bowley: … the recorded observations of working-class life show that this is the kind of food which, in fact, they have, and on which they can be, in fact, adequately fed… I do not think it is any serious hardship that there should not be two vegetables every day of the week. It is quite a common thing in middle-class families.

Bevin: But they have all sorts of food that the workers do not get?

Bowley: Not the middle class.

Bevin: What do you describe as 'middle class'?

Bowley: For example, the budget that was put in on your side by clerks and shop assistants.

Bevin: They are not middle class, are they? They are known as sweated
    workers because they are putting a Trade Board down for those trades.
    Take the shop assistant, whose budget was put in, living in three rooms at
    a rent of 6/-... You would not call him middle class, would you? I should
    class him as bottom dog.
Bowley: The middle class families I should have in mind would be the small
    professional or clerical families – civil servants, if you like, who have £400
    to £500 a year, and considerable expenses... I should very much doubt
    whether you find that two vegetables for every day of the week is all that
    common.
Bevin: Is not there a very great complaint of the tremendous economic
    pressure from the war profiteers on that class of people at the moment?
Bowley: There is.
Bevin: Do you suggest because the profiteers have succeeded in crushing the
    professional classes, that therefore a budget would be provided which
    admits the crushing of us as well?

17 – PRO MUN 5/63/322/22, Verbatim record of a conference with the ASE on the trade cards, 5 May 1917, Extract from the protestation of Christopher Addison, Minister of Munitions

... we have gone out of our way to take great risks to maintain the authority
of the Trade Unions... We have been besought by all kinds of deputations
from works and so on, but we have said, No, we cannot deal with you in that
way: we must deal with the orthodox Trade Union which represents the trade
collectively... This Ministry has consulted Trade Unions in season and out
of season more than any other Government Department has ever done... We
are entitled to ask your Union [ie the ASE]... to keep your Members in hand
as much as you can... the whole principle of Trade Union discipline and
order is at issue. There has been a determined and concerted attempt in different parts of the country to upset the authority of the established unions,
and we have stood in the breach and helped for all we were worth.

18 – David Lloyd George's widely quoted speech to Labour Party leaders in March 1917, reprinted in *The Times*, 7 March 1917

There is no doubt at all that the present war... presents an opportunity for
reconstruction of industrial and economic conditions of this country such as
has never been presented in the life of, probably, the world. The whole state
of society is more or less molten and you can stamp upon that molten mass

almost anything so long as you do it with firmness and determination... I firmly believe that what is known as the after the war settlement is the settlement that will direct the destinies of all classes for some generations to come. The country will be prepared for bigger things immediately after the war than it will be when it begins to resume the normal sort of clash of self-interests which always comes with the ordinary work-a-day business affairs and concerns of the world. I believe the country will be in a more enthusiastic mood, in a more exalted mood for the time being – in a greater mood for doing big things: and unless the opportunity is seized immediately after the war, believe it will pass away...

I hope that every class will not be hankering back to prewar conditions. I just drop that as a hint but I hope the working class will not be the class that will set such an example, because of every class insists upon getting back to prewar conditions, then God help this country! I say so in all solemnity.

19 – Philip Snowden, *A Plea for Peace* (Blackburn, Blackburn Labour Party, 1916) from Snowden's speech to the House of Commons, *Hansard*, 23 February 1916.

[This was the first major wartime speech to demand a negotiated settlement of the First World War.]

The Bill we are now asked to read a second time authorises a further expenditure of over £400,000,000 on the War, making a total of Votes for Credit of over £2,000,000,000. I do nor propose this afternoon to deal with the grave financial problems involved in these colossal figures. There will be other and early opportunities for doing so. But I think when the House of Commons is asked to vote such an enormous sum as this we are justified in asking whether there will be no alternative to this continued expenditure and whether it is not possible by some other means to bring this War to an end on terms and conditions which will realise the objects for which we are fighting. The Secretary of State for the Colonies, speaking in this House three months ago, in reply to a speech made by my Hon. friend and Members for Elland Division [C.P. Trevelyan], said it was absurd to say that any Member of the Government would not jump at the chance of bringing this War to an end, provided that it could be brought to an end on such terms as would realise our object. He said that everybody is anxious to bring the War to an end on conditions consistent with our national honour and security.

The Appalling Horror
That precisely explains my position this afternoon, and it is the justification for the proposal which we are putting forward...

The Time is Ripe
… I think it would be true to say that this country desires no other conclusion to this War than one that will give reparation for the wrong that has ever been done, and, as far as human judgement can secure it, guaranteed conditions against its repetition. The only difference between those of us who are opposed to it, is that while we are all equally anxious to see a speedy and successful termination of the War, we believe that this is more possible now than by the prolongation of the War in the hope that a decisive military victory will enable us to dictate terms to a vanquished foe…

Our Government's Responsibility
I am fully aware of the difficulty, but I was especially gratified by the tone and terms of a reply to a question which I addressed to the Prime Minister last December, in which he said the Allied Government would be willing to consider any serious proposals for peace which might come from belligerent or neutral counties.

One Step Further
The Prime Minister only needs to go one step further. He can give encouragement to offers of peace… There are many channels open to the Government through which negotiations may be opened up, and we have the right to demand that the Government shall state in much more definite and precise language the terms upon which they would be willing to consider peace.

20 – Philip Snowden, speaking in the House of Commons, *Hansard*, 13 February 1918

I know something of the state of feeling in the country. There is no enthusiasm for the war. There is an almost universal desire for peace. In a certain town in this country not long ago a rumour spread that peace had been declared. The population went wild for two or three hours, and then the rumour was found to be untrue. It occurred to somebody afterwards that never during the jubilation had a single person asked upon what terms the war had been settled. The people want peace; the soldiers want peace. One cannot travel in a railway train without knowing that. I was going down to South Wales about a fortnight ago and in the compartment were an Australian soldier, a Canadian soldier and two British soldiers. They talked freely. They were all, to use a very common expression, 'fed up'. I do not know if the Government know the state of feeling amongst the soldiers. It is not confined to the soldiers of our own army. We know it is the same in Germany; indeed, it is in all the armies… and I repeat it here, as bearing upon this point, that about three weeks or a month ago a soldier called to see me one evening. He had just returned from the front and he said he had been sent by his comrades to ask me how Alsace-Lorraine had come into the war. He said they had volunteered to fight for the liberation of Belgium and not to try to redress the result of a fifty-year-old quarrel. I warn the Government as the late President of the Board of Trade warned them, of this change in public opinion. The chairman of the Labour Party said that there was a real danger of revolution. There may be; there will be if the Government do not realise the state of feeling in the country and take steps to prevent it.

This amendment asks that the Government shall not rely merely upon the military weapon, that they should keep open the door of diplomacy, and that they should encourage instead of throwing cold water on every promising chance of promoting peace... The military situation to-day is no more hopeful than it was twelve months ago. If we go on for another twelve months it will be less hopeful than it is to-day. The Government could have made better peace terms six months ago, twelve months ago, two years ago than they can make to-day. The longer the war continues, the less prospect there is that they will be able to enforce their unreasonable terms. During the last twelve months, for no military advantage whatever, we have sacrificed in killed and wounded, according to the returns of the War Office, a million men... I am looking for the conclusion of this war by a union of the democracies of all belligerent nations. They have learned that lesson in common affliction and although one can hardly say that any good which may result from the war would be anything of a compensation for the stupendous evil which it has created, still it would be something if, as a result of this war, we had for ever a sweeping away of the power of those who have misused their powers in the past and have used them, not for the good of the people, but in order to satisfy their own Imperialist and selfish aims.

Notes on Chapter 3

1   J.M. Bourne, *Britain and the Great War 1914-1918* (London, Edward Arnold, 1989), rejects the 'tragic and futile' view; J.G. Fuller, *Troop Morale and Popular Culture in the British and Dominion Armies 1914–18* (Oxford University Press, 1991); S. Hynes, *A War Imagined* (London, Bodley Head, 1990); L. Macdonald, *1914–1918: Voices and Images of the Great War* (London, Michael Joseph, 1988); P. Simkins, *Kitchener's Army: The Raising of the New Armies 1914–16* (Manchester, Manchester University Press, 1988); T. Travers, *The Killing Ground: The British Army, The Western Front and the Emergence of Modern Warfare 1900–1918* (London, Unwin Hyman, 1987, pbk 1990).

2 Arthur Marwick, *Britain in the Century of Total War* (London, Macmillan, 1979 edn), p 84; Trevor Wilson, *The Downfall of the Liberal Party* (London, Collins, 1966 edn), p 29.

3 A. Marwick, *The Deluge* (London, Macmillan, 1975 edn); P. Abrams, 'The Failure of Social Reform, 1918–1920', *Past and Present* 24 (1963); R. Miliband, *Parliamentary Socialism* (London, Merlin, 1972 edn), R. McKibbin, *The Evolution of the Labour Party* (Oxford, Oxford University Press, 1974); J.M. Winter, *Socialism and the Challenge of War* (London, Routledge & Kegan Paul, 1974).

4 Thirteen of the 23 NEC members were directly elected by trade unionists.

5 J.M. Winter, *The Great War and the British People* (London, Macmillan, 1986) pp 103–4.

6 McKibbin, *The Evolution of the Labour Party*, p 91.

7 Miliband, *Parliamentary Socialism*; R. Harrison, 'The War Emergency Committee, 1914–1920', in A. Briggs and J. Saville (eds), *Essays in Labour History* (London, Macmillan, 1971), pp 211–59.

8 Winter, Socialism and the Challenge of War, p 184.

9 *Ibid.*, pp 187–8.

10 *Ibid.*, pp 214–15.

11 *Ibid.*, p 215.

12 Harrison, 'War Emergency Committee', p 256.

13 McKibbin, *The Evolution of the Labour Party*, p 97.

14 B. Barker, 'The Anatomy of Reform: The Social and Political Ideas of the Labour Leadership in Yorkshire', *International Review of Social History* XVIII (1973), pp 1–27.

15 McKibbin, *The Evolution of the Labour Party*, p 97.

16 M.G. Fawcett, *The Women's Victory and After* (1920), p 106.

Chapter 4

Britain on the Breadline: Slump, Poverty and the Politics of Realignment During the Inter-war Years 1918–39

Introduction

Unemployment was the dominating issue of British society during the inter-war years, creating social problems, determining the policies of government, and shaping the politics of the age. As a result of Britain's loss of export markets and her industrial decline in the staple industries, unemployment levels were rarely less than the 'intractable million', and reached about three million, more than 20 percent of the insured workforce, in 1931. Such horrendous levels of unemployment created difficulties at every level of society and influenced all aspects of life during the 'locust years' or the 'long weekend' when Britain, according to some, survived on the breadline. The attempted reconstruction of Britain between 1918 and 1921 had clearly failed.

The events of the inter-war years have produced several important debates. One concerns the extent of poverty and raises the question did poverty persist for a significant proportion of the community? A second concerns the related issue of health and asks whether Britain was healthy or hungry in the inter-war years. A third concerns the political implications of unemployment and broaches the question was the realignment of politics during the inter-war years a reflection of the economic and unemployment problems of the inter-war years, the continuous rise of class politics or the product of the Liberal Conservatives overestimating the true level of support for Labour? Arising out of this is the boost which the war and a divided progressive vote gave Stanley Baldwin and the Conservative Party. One should also note the stimulus given by the war to the development of the women's vote in the 1920s.

Unemployment and Health

Unemployment conditioned many aspects of working-class life, and none more so than issues of poverty and health. Until recently, historians have generally accepted that poverty diminished during the inter-war years. C.L. Mowat argued the point, as did Stevenson and Cook, who also add that the standard of living of the vast majority of people increased.[1] Few historians would now argue that poverty, for the whole nation, did not decline during the inter-war years. Nevertheless, such views tend to rest upon the evidence gathered by social investigators such as B.S. Rowntree, A.L. Bowley, M. Hogg and H. Llewelyn Smith.[2] Indeed, Seebohm Rowntree's suggestion (Document 15) that there was a rise of 30 percent in living standards generally in York, and in the rest of British society, seems a fair reflection of events, as does his suggestion that about 30 percent of the population of British towns were still living in poverty. Nevertheless, such national conclusions rest upon a relatively narrow range of material, and it is important to be aware of its limitations.

Keith Laybourn has examined some of these limitations, and has suggested that surveys varied in their statistical rigour, that there were very few detailed social investigations, and that there were few for the really depressed urban areas, as opposed to those areas less affected by unemployment such as York, London and Bristol (Document 3). Other historians have also thrown doubt upon the following level of poverty, sometimes in connection with the health issues of the period (Documents 5 and 6). They mention that up to 35 or 40 percent of the British population, half of the working class, probably experienced a decline in their living standards, or certainly no improvement.

Nevertheless, available national statistics suggest that this and the standard of living of society as a whole improved during the inter-war years, but that does not mean that a significant minority of the population did not continue to live in poverty or that even those who did were necessarily better off. Indeed, even in York more than half the children of the working classes were living in poverty (Document 15). It is also difficult to see how in such towns as Jarrow (Document 16), where three-quarters of the population were affected by unemployment in the mid 1930s, could have been better off in comparison to pre-war years when unemployment rarely reached 8 percent, even if there were now more state benefits available. Even these benefits were often subject to the Household Means Test introduced in the early 1930s (Document 16).

The scale of poverty might be open to question, but its major causes are not. Most surveys suggest that inadequate wages, the death of the husband, old age and illness continued to be important factors, but that the difference of the inter-war years was that unemployment of the chief wage-earner increased to become, averaged out over a number of surveys, the most important cause of poverty from a situation where it was generally a minor cause (Document 15).

Poverty obviously impacted upon health, and a second major debate has focused upon the extent to which health improved or deteriorated during the inter-war years. Traditionally, it has been argued that the health of the nation improved, a view more recently supported by D.H. Aldcroft, John Stevenson and Chris Cook (Documents 1 and 2) and, according to B.B. Gilbert, there was a growing commitment by the state to improve both the social and health provision of the nation as a whole (Document 4). These views have been challenged by Keith Laybourn, Margaret Mitchell and Charles Webster (Documents 3, 5 and 6), who argue that both problems, poverty and ill-health, were rooted in economic disadvantage. The thrust of these revisionist arguments, and particularly that presented by Webster, is that there is sufficient detailed research to question the view that health was improving across the board, and clear evidence that the biological statistics are not reliable. Mitchell points to increasing maternal mortality rates (Document 6), while Webster maintains that reliance placed upon the general fall in infant mortality blinded medical experts to what was really going on. In fact, whilst some statistics, such as infant mortality, may have improved, others, such as maternal mortality, worsened (Document 6). Even in the case of infant mortality, there was an enormous range of experiences. For instance, whilst infant mortality was 66 and 65 per thousand for England and Wales in 1931 and 1932, it was excess of 100 in Oldham and Warrington in 1931, 134 for children born into coal-mining families between 1930 and 1932, and was in excess of 134 on the new Mount Pleasant Estate in Stockton-on-Tees between 1928 and 1932.[3] Given this type of variation, Webster maintains that there are marked social distinctions in health according to class and occupation, region and precise location. In addition of this, he argues that health statistics are often subjective, as in the case of malnutrition, on which estimates could vary according to both the sex of the observer and the extent to which governments sought to massage or hide the health statistics. Indeed, John Boyd Orr's political bombshell, though hotly disputed, that during the mid-1930s up to half the population of Britain was undernourished strengthens the Webster argument (Document 14).

For the nation as a whole, poverty and ill-health were undoubtedly less pronounced during the inter-war yeas than they had been before 1914. Nevertheless, it is clear that in areas where there was high structural unemployment, and in all those areas where there was high cyclical unemployment in the early 1930s, poverty and ill-health were probably more rife than they were before 1914. In industrially depressed towns like Jarrow (Document 16) and Brynmawr, there can be no doubt that the conditions of working-class families were much worse that they had been in the pre-war years when unemployment was less pronounced; the hunger marches of the 1920s and 1930s were not vacuous statements of the plight of the unemployed. It is also clear that even in the generally more prosperous towns, which were subject to detailed investigation, that high levels of poverty and ill-health existed; there are no equivalent studies to that on York for the really depressed towns of Britain.

Politics

Unemployment also had a major impact upon British politics. Every general election during the inter-war years, with the possible exception of the 1918 one, was dominated by the concerns of British industry and unemployment. Indeed, the collapse of the Labour Government in 1931 had been brought about by the debate over cuts in unemployment benefit, consequent upon the need to curb public expenditure. The National Government also called a general election in October 1931 on the issue of the economy and the failure of the Labour Party in government to be prepared to address some of the economic and social consequences of government economic policy.

Certainly this period saw dramatic changes in the political position of parties. It saw the Labour Party rise and then falter under J. Ramsay MacDonald, the Liberal Party collapse even further, even with the return of David Lloyd George in 1923, and the Conservative Party become the dominant political party in Britain under the leadership of Stanley Baldwin. One major area of debate is the way in which the Labour Party emerged so rapidly in the early 1920s. Was this because it had captured the trade-union vote, as Ross McKibbin has suggested (see Chapter 2), or simply due to good fortune, in that the other political parties were not aware how weak it was, as Christopher Howard suggests (Document 9)? There has also been a major debate about the reasons for Ramsay MacDonald's decision to form a National Government in 1931. Was it due to MacDonald conspiring to betray the Labour Party/Government, or because the economic and political circumstances left him with little alternative? L. McNeill Weir suggests the former (Document 10), David Marquand and several other historians the latter (Document 11). As for the Liberal Party, there is still a debate here about its continued decline. Was this because its political mind was fixed, because of the divisive nature of David Lloyd George's leadership, or because it had lost the working-class vote to Labour (see Chapter 2 and Documents 7 and 8)? As for the Conservative Party, why did it emerge as the dominant political party? Was this because of Baldwin's leadership or because of a variety of factors, such as the collapse of Liberalism, that favoured its growth?

Obviously, the most dramatic development of the inter-war years was the replacement of the Liberal Party by the Labour Party as the second party in British politics. In 1918 the Liberal Party, though divided, was still the second parliamentary party in Britain. However, in 1922, and again in 1923, the Liberal Party had been dramatically overtaken by the Labour Party, although it did stage a minor recovery in 1929. In contrast, the Labour Party's growth appeared almost inexorable. Without examining the intense debates, and sub-debates, in detail, for they are touched upon in Chapter 2, it is clear that there has been a considerable change in progressive politics in Britain. Whilst Henry Pelling, Ross McKibbin and many others have stressed that emergence of trade-union support for the Labour Party ensured that it captured the working-class vote, more recent contributors, such as P.F. Clarke, Michael Bentley and Duncan Tanner, have maintained either that Labour came through to replace the Liberal Party because of its split in 1916, or that even then there was still a prospect that the Liberal Party could maintain its control of the progressive vote.[4] In fact the debate has moved on from that point with more recent contributors, such as Bill Lancaster, stressing the need to examine communities and regions in more detail.[5] For the inter-war years, however, the main issue is how far the degeneration of the Liberal Party had gone, and how deep-rooted was Labour's trade-union and working-class support. The issue is one of potential, for in 1918 the Liberals, divided between the supporters of Asquith and the supporters of Lloyd George, returned more MPs than the burgeoning Labour Party, which faced the Coalition Government of David Lloyd George. In this respect it is the second debate, promoted by the work of Christopher Howard which is more appropriate (Document 9).

Howard has questioned the effectiveness of Labour's organisation in the 1920s: 'The image of a vibrant expanding new party was an illusion. Labour was fortunate that its opponents were deceived.'[6] Yet Labour leaders would not have agreed with this assessment, even though the title of Howard's article, 'Expectation born to death', is drawn from MacDonald's comment, written in 1921, that 'the Labour party knocks the heart out of me and expectations are like babies born to death'.[7]

Exactly why the Labour Party grew so rapidly in the decade after the First World War has been a matter of considerable debate between those advocating the long-term growth of working-class support for the Labour Party and those stressing the division of the Liberal Party during the First World War. Almost unwittingly, Howard accepts the first of these arguments, for he notes that 'Widespread electoral support bore little resemblance to restricted party membership, however, and disappointments were common'.[8] Such a gap could only be explained by class voting, which took no note of party organisation and activity, if Howard's assumption of the weakness of Labour's political organisation is correct. But the issue is confused by the fact that he also asserts that both the Liberals and Conservatives would have been more successful had they seen through the illusion and perceived the real weakness of the Labour Party's organisation. Howard does not appear to have made his mind up whether it was class politics or the illusion of a rapidly organising Labour Party that accounts for Labour's electoral successes in the 1920s. He does not even consider the difficulties of a Liberal Party whose support was being squeezed both from the left and the right.

Nevertheless, the crux of his argument is that Labour's national and con- stituency activity failed to sustain much active support. The Labour leadership recognised this to be partly true, acknowledging that Labour failed to win the rural areas, that its national and local newspapers were always in a precarious financial position, and even the urban and industrial strongholds lacked faith when the Labour governments were unable to deliver the improved society it offered. Even in Aberavon, MacDonald's own constituency between 1922 and 1929, it was noted in 1926 that victory was not assured (Document 9).

A rather different picture is provided by Ross McKibbin and Bernard Barker[9] (Chapter 2). They feel that the Labour Party was making a deter- mined effort to improve both its national and local organisation, and that, by and large, they succeeded in doing so. But which view is correct? To what extent was the Labour Party well organised and effective throughout the 1920s?

It is clear that the Labour Party made great advances after the First World War. The National Executive Committee reorganised its activities, by appointing four standing sub-committees: organisation and elections; policy and programme; literature, research and publicity; and finance and general purposes. A star speaker system was introduced, permitting leading party figures to tour the country, and most constituencies had a local Labour Party, compared with about a quarter at the beginning the First World War. Local newspapers were produced to supplement the *Daily Herald*. There were deficiencies, but these developments were a vast improvement on what had previously existed. In addition, the trade-union connection with the Labour Party was firmer than ever before.

The Labour Party Constitution of 1918 allowed for the election of 13 of the 23 members of the new National Executive Committee and permitted trade unions to vote in the election of the rest. Throughout the 1920s, and particularly after 1926, the Joint Council of Labour, which brought together the Parliamentary Labour Party (PLP), the TUC and the Labour Party, became increasingly important in making the decisions for the 'constitutional' Labour movement. In 1934 it was renamed the National Council of Labour, and the TUC was the most important force on this body, in the shape of Ernest Bevin (from 1932) and Walter Citrine.

If the Labour Party had become the party of the working class, it had done so through the agency of the trade-union movement, and the price it had to pay was the restriction of its policies to a pale version of Clause Four, introduced gradually and selectively (see Chapter 2). Using the large block vote of the Transport and General Workers' Union, and other unions, Ernest Bevin was able to dominate the Labour Party annual conferences throughout the 1930s on issues such as the threat of fascism. Indeed, Bevin remarked that the Labour Party 'grew out of the bowels of the TUC'.[10] This is not to say that the Labour Party did not have the opportunity to do something to extend its socialist planning, for this often operated in a different sphere from trade unionism, although Bevin and the TUC Economic Planning Committee (1932) were part of the process.[11]

The relationship between the Labour Party and the trade unions was complex and not without major difficulties. Lewis Minkin, in a monumental work, has suggested that whilst the Labour Party and the trade unions are often seen as working closely together they often developed distinct policies and strategies, and operated in different spheres, which sometimes led to a contentious relationship. He argues that the metaphor that the Labour Party was the 'offspring of the TUC' is misleading because there has often been a disparity in the policies adopted by the two organisations.[12] Nevertheless, he maintains that the two bodies built up a common set of attitudes and rules between 1900 and 1948 – based upon loyalty and anti-communism – and that these operated effectively in a type of 'golden age' between 1948 and 1959 before becoming subject to increased strains and changes of recent times. For the inter-war years, then, there were difficulties as the ground rules were being built up, and it is not surprising that there should be some sharp disagreements in their relationships. The Labour Party's 1918 Constitution provided the potential for conflict between the broad socialist goals and the narrower base of trade-union objectives.

The closeness of the trade unions and the Labour Party clearly challenges the views of Howard, as do other factors (Document 9). Most obviously, the tendency of Liberal and Conservative parties to form 'anti-socialist' or 'citizens' alliances at local elections is a reflection of the fact that Labour was making a serious challenge to these parties at the local level.[13] By 1923, the message was clear: Labour was the party of the working class. It had built upon its pre-war and wartime roots and was not the fragile party that Howard suggests.

The results of Labour's increasing electoral support and organisational improvements came with the formation of the first Labour Government on

22 January 1924. It was a minority government led by Ramsay MacDonald, and it only survived because of Liberal Party support. So constrained, it achieved very little, other than the introduction of John Wheatley's Housing Act, which encouraged local authorities to build houses to rent to the working classes. Its attempt to reveal itself as a responsible Government, its dependence upon Liberals and its gradual approach meant that it was almost unable to further socialism, and it lasted a mere ten months.

The second Labour Government, also a minority one, offered little more to the furtherance of British socialism than the first. It came into power in May 1929 at a time when the economy was improving and unemployment falling, but was set back by the Wall Street Crash of November 1929 and its disastrous economic impact upon world trade. Faced with rising unemployment, increasing expenditure and financial imbalances, MacDonald's Government was forced to accept the all-party Sir George May Committee examination of the national finances in 1931 and the need to introduce massive public expenditure cuts. It was the MacDonald Government's attempt to balance the budget that raised the prospect of the ten (initially 20) percent cut in unemployment benefits, which divided the Labour Cabinet on the 23 and 24 August 1931, and paved the way for the formation of MacDonald's National Government.

The collapse of the second Labour Government has, of course, produced its own debate. From the 1930s it was normal to argue that MacDonald had betrayed the second Labour Government and carried out his 'long-thought-out plan'. L. MacNeill Weir captured the spirit of accusations levelled against MacDonald, maintaining that he was never a socialist, was an opportunist, that he schemed to ditch the Labour Government, and that he was guilty of betrayal (Document 10).

This explanation has been challenged by David Marquand and other writers. Marquand insists that there is little to suggest that MacDonald schemed to ditch the second Labour Government, and that MacDonald's only fault is that he held on to his nineteenth-century principles too long (Document 11). MacDonald's almost religious acceptance that the gold standard and free trade, plus his belief in the primacy of the state over party, ensured that he lacked the 'ability and willingness to jettison cherished assumptions in the face of changing realities'.[14]

The evidence suggests that Marquand is correct. MacDonald was as good a socialist as any of the early Labour leaders, writing for the Socialist Library, and was committed to the gradual extension of state powers over industry. He was an opportunist, but gave up his chairmanship of the Parliamentary Labour Party in 1914 in order to oppose the First World War. There is no specific evidence to suggest that MacDonald schemed to bring about the end of the second Labour Government, only innuendo and speculation. It is also obvious that, given the economic circumstances, it would have been difficult for MacDonald to have arranged the type of political scheming contemplated by his critics.[15] It was the need to cut expenditure in the drive to balance the budget and secure loans from abroad, in order to keep Britain on a gold standard and free trade system, that forced the Cabinet to agree, by 11 votes to 9, to reduce unemployment benefits by 10 percent. It was clear that the Cabinet was split, and that prompted MacDonald to take the resignation of his Cabinet to King George V. It was only a confluence of other events – including the support of the opposition leaders for a coalition Government headed by MacDonald and the appeal of the King – that led MacDonald to form the National Government.

MacDonald's action brought him the condemnation of the Labour Party and the trade unions. Indeed, when the financial crisis did occur, the issue was not the future of socialism but one of a conflict between the second Labour Government – committed to operating the gold standard and free trade, and thus faced with reducing government expenditure and unemployment benefits – and a TUC which felt that any such action would be a betrayal of the interests of the working classes. This was compounded by the general election of 1931, which saw the Labour Party reduced to 52 MPs from the 289 of 1929, and the National Government secured 556 seats, a majority of 497.

Labour reacted well to this defeat. It recognised that its organisation remained strong, its local parties recovered, and in November 1932 it made good some of the municipal losses it had incurred in November 1931. It also began to revitalise the party in 1932 with a 'Million New Member Campaign', which had increased individual membership by 100,000 within a year. In January 1933, it set up a Central By-Election Insurance Fund to help needy constituencies put forward candidates. But perhaps more important than such improvements in organisation was the decision to develop and re-examine its socialist policies and develop its position on public ownership. It almost tripled the number of seats it won at the 1935 general election.

In the meantime, the Conservative Party had regained the dominant political position it had lost in the 1905/6 general election. There is no real debate here, other than the examination of the reason for Conservative success. Was this due to the re-organisation of the party by Stanley Baldwin (Document 12), or to the fact that the Conservative Party was flexible, not hooked upon an ideology, and that the progressive political vote was divided. The balance of evidence has been focused upon the suggestion that, in some way, Stanley Baldwin changed the image of the Conservative Party, presenting it as a considerate and moderate party of English interests. There is certainly the view that Baldwin was a far more effective leader than he was presented as being by Winston Churchill and other political opponents. Whatever the reason, the Conservative Party, in the form of Conservative, Coalition or

National Governments, was in power between 1918 and 1924, 1924 and 1929, and between 1931 and the Second World War.

As far as the women's franchise is concerned, there is the suggestion that after the 1918 Franchise Act (see Chapter 3) the interest in women's suffrage declined. However, Cheryl Law, in *Suffrage and Power* (London, I.B. Tauris, 1997) (Document 13) suggests that that was anything but the case. The women's movement reorganised itself, tackled the issues of Britain's postwar reorganisation, extended its activities in the work of political parties, demanded equal rights and the extension of the franchise, which occurred in 1928 when women obtained the parliamentary vote on equal terms to those given to men. Law rejects the view, sometimes put forward by male writers, that the women's franchise and emancipation movement collapsed at the end of the First World War and indicates that there were numerous women's groups which networked in order to press for the extension of the women's franchise and women's issues throughout the 1920s. Other works, most particularly Pamela M. Graves, *Labour Women: Women in British Working-class Politics 1918-1939*,[16] endorse this approach. Indeed, Graves suggests that Labour Party unity was threatened in the 1920s as the 'women's question' came to the fore, although Labour's political debacle of 1931 led to the subsuming of the women's question in the quest for Labour Party unity. Indeed, in the 1920s there was a conflict within Labour ranks about the extent to which issues such as birth control should be raised. The Women's Labour League, which became the Women's Section of the Labour Party during the inter-war years, wished to work for the broad policies of the Labour Party, whilst the Women's Cooperative Guild wanted to encourage more overt action on behalf of women. The sum total of this and other recent research is to deny the assumption that the women's franchise movement all but disappeared in 1918.

Conclusion

In the final analysis, the inter-war years were ones of fundamental change. The economy moved from the old traditional industries to new ones, such as cars. Naturally, such change meant unemployment, and its consequences would dominate inter-war domestic events. There were serious social consequences of industrial change, and Webster and Mitchell's ideas seem fair, as far too many people lived in poverty, due increasingly to unemployment, for their plight to be swept away by some statistical average which might be subject to distortion. And even if the general health of the nation did improve, there were many areas where health conditions remained poor, often as a result of the economic depression and consequently high levels of unemployment.

This meant that the politics of the inter-war years were dominated by the issue of the economy and unemployment. All the major political parties saw its solution in terms of the gold standard and free trade in the 1920s, although Baldwin's brief flirtation with protectionism in the 1923 general election provided an alternative that was necessary. In the 1930s, however, following the economic and political debate of August 1931, the Conservative Party was able to push forward with its commitment to protectionist measures. It is clear that the flexibility of the Conservative Party, supporting both free trade and protectionism by twists and turns, benefitted it. Elsewhere, it is clear that the Liberal Party was declining and that Labour was developing rapidly in its place, benefiting from the support of the working class and organisational improvements, despite the reflections of Christopher Howard (Document 9). Nevertheless, there is no doubt that Labour's political fortunes were set back temporarily by the débâcle of 1931, although MacDonald was apparently driven by events rather than any intent to betray Labour.

The interwar years were thus ones of economic, social and political transition. Some sections of society did well, others suffered. For some, these were the 'locust years', for others, a 'long week-end'. British society was still as truly divided as at any stage in the twentieth century.

Documents
SECONDARY SOURCES AND INTERPRETATIONS

1 – D.H. Aldcroft, *The Interwar Economy: Britain, 1919–1939* (London, B.T. Batsford, 1970), p 375

… not only was there a significant increase in real incomes and real wages but, partly as a result of this improvement and together with the extension of community services, the nation generally was better fed and clothed, and was housed in better conditions than those prevailing before the war. The statistics again point to an improvement in the national health and physical well-being of the population. Death rates declined, children were on average fatter and healthier than their parents had been, and the worst forms of malnutritional diseases, such as rickets and scurvy, had all but disappeared by the second world war.

2 – John Stevenson and Chris Cook, *The Slump: Society and Politics During the Depression* (London, Jonathan Cape, 1977), pp 52–3

Similarly, in the field of public health, the findings of the social investigators were that there had been a broad general improvement in health which had continued into the 1930s. There were areas where improvement had not taken place, such as maternal mortality, and areas where the onset of the worst years of the depression had slowed down the rate of progress, as in the fields of infant mortality and tuberculosis. None the less, even these were beginning to show improvement in the years immediately before the war. Poverty, poor nutrition and bad health had been shown to be closely related factors. Even John Boyd Orr, who had produced some of the most damning evidence that the poorer income groups had a diet which was inadequate to maintain health, was moved to conclude that conditions were better than they had ever been before. Thus he wrote in the conclusion of *Food, Health and Income*, 'Bad as the picture is, however, it is better than any picture which could have been drawn in the past – much brighter than the picture of pre-war days'. As with the writers on poverty, the real complaint was that further improvements lay within reach. An improved level of public health depended upon a better diet, which in turn demanded higher incomes.

During the 1930s the issues of poverty, ill-health and bad housing were highly politicised. Many writers were critical of the complacency which they felt was representative of the government in the face of serious problems. In retrospect, however, it is plain that the truth lay somewhere between the claims of the major protagonists, so far as generalisation is possible. The official line on poverty and ill-health could often be regarded as complacent, but central government was almost entirely reliant upon the reports of local officials. One of the points which these debates made plain was the difficulty of obtaining objective criteria for poverty, malnutrition, overcrowding and so on… The concern to establish scientific criteria by which to study social conditions was a major part of their work and their findings were based upon a statistical appreciation of specific groups or areas. Rowntree, for example, based his information about York upon a detailed house-to-house survey of 16,362 families. The conclusions of these investigators could not easily be disregarded. Naturally, there were errors and difficulties of interpretation, but the conclusions of the inquiries of the 1930s pointed clearly to the survival of social problems.

3 – **Keith Laybourn**, *Britain on the Breadline: A Social and Political History of Britain 1918–1939* (Stroud, Sutton Publishing, 1990, 1998), pp 209, 210–11

Robert Graves and Alan Hodge do not do justice to the protracted nature of the problems of the inter-war years by light-heartedly suggesting that these years were a 'long weekend'. Many other epithets used to describe the inter-war years are more apposite. The fact is that from the view of the working class, whose members were likely to be in poverty or to be living a precarious existence within its vicinity, a breadline existence was a common and familiar experience in a period which might be regarded as 'wasted years'. But the problem of the inter-war years has always been one of perspective and emphasis. Did the improvements for those who were in constant employment – those members of the working class in the new expanding industries and the rapidly growing salaried middle class – outweigh the dire social conditions which were experienced by the traditional working class in the declining staple industries?...

Inevitably, the debates about the inter-war years have concerned these issues – seeking to measure the degree of change and improvement in the lives of the working classes. They pose many questions. Did poverty decline? Were the majority of the people healthier and better off than before the First World War? To what extent did society adjust to its economic problems? How much action was taken by governments to alleviate unemployment and poverty? In the final analysis the argument of this book has been less optimistic than those put forward by John Stevenson, Chris Cook and D.H. Aldcroft. It has argued five main points. It the first place it has stressed that governments simply failed to properly tackle the problem of unemployment because of their commitment to balanced budgets, regardless of whether they operated in a free trade or protectionist context. Though widely discussed by the 1930s, the expansionist and contractionist policies of J.M. Keynes' multiplier did not have a great influence upon the National governments. Secondly, it is maintained that the majority of the working class lived in poverty or near to poverty, with consequent ill-health – although the middle classes and better-off members of the working class ensured that about half the total British population were probably better off. One can debate forever the extent of poverty in these years but it should be remembered that few detailed poverty surveys actually dealt with the worst areas of unemployment where poverty was clearly a more acute problem than it had been before the First World War. Thirdly, it is argued that the depression of these years was not offset by the economic progress made in the Midlands and the south-eastern consumer industries – although the working classes in the regions were certainly prospering. Fourthly, it asserts that the association between the

working classes and the Labour Party was strongly enhanced by the economic
conditions of these years. Partly in consequence the Liberal Party plummeted
into political oblivion and Labour became the political alternative to the
Conservative Party in Britain's two-party political system. Labour was already
clearly identified with the working class by the end of the First World War
but the economic conditions of depression and unemployment strengthened
that link as never before. and possibly since. Fifthly, it appears that, despite
the social deprivation which persisted, a large proportion of the British population, and particularly those in the impoverished working class, were aware
of the international events and hostile to the threat of European fascism.
Amid acute deprivation, the majority of the working class identified with
those oppressed by fascism although, as with their own circumstances, they
were able to do little about the matter.

4 – Bentley B. Gilbert, British Social Policy 1914–1939 (London, B.T. Batsford, 1970), p vii

This study, then, is about the search for a new political consensus on what
had become the central issue of parliamentary contest, social policy.
Essentially, its argument is that in the two decades between the wars, while
labouring under a singular and huge economic handicap, Britain's political
leaders finally agreed, almost unconsciously, that society in some way or
another would have to find a means to support all its citizens at a decent level
of civilised life – in effect the national minimum. This understanding,
whether or not publicly accepted, was a private political consensus by the end
of the 1930s.

Hence, 1939 provides a reasonable terminal date. The social planning
that occurred during the Second World War was not an out-growth of
national attempts to find a social policy. Rather it was the reflection of the
conviction at which the nation had already arrived. The Beveridge Report
and the White Papers on National Insurance and the National Health Service,
children's allowances, and the announcement of a policy of full employment
were all products of wartime experience. But, more important, they represented attempts to find solutions to problems of peace. The questions they
raised turned on matters of administration not on matters of principle. The
principle had already been agreed upon. Out of the twenties and thirties a
commitment had evolved. The destruction of wealth between 1939 and 1945
made action more immediately necessary, but the war itself did not bring the
welfare state.

5 – Charles Webster, 'Healthy or Hungry Thirties', *History Workshop* 13, 1982, pp 123–4

What conclusions can be drawn from the various categories of medical evidence relating to standards of health during the interwar period? Much of the above analysis casts doubt on the judgements contained in the official sources... The mortality averages seem to offer unquestionable evidence supporting an optimistic interpretation of trends in health during the interwar period: on the basis of national averages, infant and maternal mortality rates were in 1939 higher than ever before. Closer attention relating to the data relating to infant mortality, however, suggests a more diverse and less flattering picture than is sketched in the official reports. In 1921 the infant mortality rate in England and Wales stood at 83; in 1931 it was 66; in 1941, 60; and in 1946, 43. In this story of advance, the '30s emerge as a drag in the downward trend in infant mortality. The most rapid rate of decline was reached with 28% between 1918 and 1923, and this rate was equalled again between 1941 and 1946. During the '30s this momentum was reduced by more than 50%, enough for England and Wales to fall decisively behind other western nations with respect to most of the components of infant mortality. Similarly, if maternal mortality is taken as the yard-stick of prevailing levels of health, it is difficult to support an optimistic conclusion from averages which rose during the interwar period to reach a peak in the mid '30s.

The most acute problem with respect to mortality rates relates to the fallacies inherent in averages. The average is an abstraction, the value of which depends on the pattern of dispersion of the class of phenomenon under consideration. Because of the wide dispersion characteristics of mortality rates, the average underestimates the advances in health enjoyed by some sections of the community, and it overestimates the position with respect to a substantial minority. The latter, the economists' decreasing 'submerged fraction' should not be regarded as a virtually extinct residuum, since it embraces major sections of the populations of Scotland, Wales, Northern Ireland, and the north of England, as well as majorities within many English cities in other regions.

For these communities, the improvement in mortality rates during the interwar period was real but small in extent; while class inequalities remained largely unchanged...

With respect to morbidity, the absence of sound data especially for the period before 1930 renders it difficult to draw conclusions about interwar trends. Even for the '30s the evidence is fragmentary. Nevertheless, three points seem clear; first, levels of ill-health were much higher than suggested in the official statistics; secondly, class, occupational and regional differentials were of precisely the same order as those outlined with respect to mortality;

thirdly, as in the case of mortality, the basic explanation for excess morbidity lies firmly in the sphere of economic disadvantage...

The fact of morbidity raises the question of the degree of benefits derived by the lower social classes from the expansion of social welfare during the interwar period. Economic historians attach great weight to the value of this form of subsidy to the families of low wage earners and the unemployed. Less is said concerning the ineligibility of the long-term unemployed and their dependants for medical care under the National Health Insurance. The application of welfare benefits was very uneven, and their operation was not inevitably to the advantage of the most needy. For women, contact with ante-natal and child welfare clinics was much lower than the official statistics suggested, while post-natal clinics were rarely available. Some health authorities disapproved of free milk schemes because this type of benefit was thought to weaken the resolve of mothers...

The most optimistic construction of the states of health during the inter-war period derives from the general infant mortality rates for England and Wales. A radically different perspective results from finer analysis of mortality data, together with proper appreciation of the importance of data relating to morbidity. Fuller exploitation of the available demographic and epidemio-logical evidence suggests that the persistence of gross disparities between the sexes, or between social and occupational groups constitute the dominant feature of the inter-war pattern of health. For those substantial sections of the population in a position of disadvantage it is difficult to maintain that the interwar period was marked by any meaningful improvement in health. Advances in one direction were likely to be offset by deterioration in another. In view of the impressive body of evidence suggesting that the health prob-lems experienced during the '30s were rooted in economic disadvantage, it is perverse to argue that the interwar economic depression was free from adverse repercussions on standards of health. The depression must be regarded as a significant exacerbating factor, tending to worsen still further prevailing low levels of health, and so contributing towards a crisis of subsistence and health different in kind but similar in gravity to the crises known to students of pre-industrial society.

6 – Margaret Mitchell, 'The Effects of Unemployment on the Social Conditions of Women and Children in the 1930s', *History Workshop* no. 19, Spring 1985, pp 105–22

The enduring image of the 1930s is that of the unemployed man – on hunger marches; on street corners; in the dole queue. But, as the Pilgrim Trust made clear, beyond the man in the queue we should always be aware of those two or three at home who he has to support. They calculated that the 250,000 long-term unemployed were responsible for 170,000 wives and 270,000 young children. Within this submerged section of the population the health of, and ultimately the survival rates for, the most vulnerable groups, women in childbirth and their infants – provided a sensitive barometer of the standard of living of the unemployed as a whole and highlighted the extent to which the policies of national and local government recognised selective social responsibility…

In 1979 J.M. Winter concluded that 'On the basis [of examination of the data available on infant and maternal mortality]… no direct correlation can be made between economic insecurity and the mortality experience of a particularly vulnerable section of the British population… such deprivation as undoubtedly existed did affect adversely the life expectation of the infant and maternal population'…

The impressive decline in infant mortality (Table 1) during the first half of the twentieth century reveals that: from 1900–1910 the rate fell by 44; from 1910–1920 the rate fell by 26; from 1920–1930 the rate fell by 20; from 1930–1940 the rate fell by 4; from 1940–1950 the rate fell by 26.

The exceptionally poor rate of decline for the decade 1930–1940 suggests that a connection between infant mortality and economic crisis is, at the very least, a possibility. J.M. Winter emphasises the fact that the survival rates for infants in 1939 were 'higher than they had ever been before'. Whilst this statement is perfectly true, it is also true that they should have been a great deal higher still.

As social investigators of the time pointed out, infant mortality in Britain (which included the appallingly high figures for Scotland) was substantially higher than most other European countries, even those with a lower per capita income…

Class differentials in infant mortality rates appears to be endemic in British society. Titmuss drew attention to the 'widening of the gap' between classes in relation to both mortality and the incidence of disease, during the 1930s, and, forty years after the advent of the Welfare State, it remains a dominant factor…

In 1936 the maternal mortality rate for S.E. England was 2.57 but in Wales it was 5.17 and in the North 4.36. That these persistently high and increasing rates should occur after the introduction of the Maternity and Child Welfare Act was particularly surprising and clearly points to a worsening of the economic situation in specific areas…

Within the limitations of this study, the demographic evidence I have examined supports Webster's thesis that the health problem (and indeed the very survival) of a particular sensitive section of the population were 'rooted in economic disadvantage' which was caused to a great extent by unemployment.

To conclude that the 1930s can be seen as a 'period of major improvement of the health of mothers and infants in Britain' without differentiating between socio-economic groups, is to perpetuate the contemporary official presentation of the evidence, influenced as it was by the particular political, economic and cultural ideology of the time. The undoubted improvements in conditions for the majority of working-class women and children due to improvements in medical knowledge and provision, education in Maternal and Child Welfare Clinics, and a rising standard of living for those in employment, masks the existence of the severe and increasing deprivation of the substantial numbers of women and children affected by long term unemployment. Dependence on diverse, pragmatic and often totally inadequate public provision, exacted a heavy toll in human terms. The impressionistic evidence quoted from social inquiries, and personal accounts of the period, serves to reinforce this conclusion.

7 – John Campbell, 'The Renewal of Liberalism: Liberalism Without Liberals', in Gillian Peele and Chris Cook, *The Politics of Reappraisal 1918–1939* (London, Macmillan, 1975), p 88

The history of the Liberal Party between the wars is in most respects a melancholy record. The party declined from strength to insignificance in twenty years: a governing party of 260 MPs when the armistice was signed in 1918, it had dwindled by the declaration of war in 1939 to a mere parliamentary pressure group of eighteen members. It may be that the social upheaval of 1914–18 and the extension of the suffrage to the mass electorate spelled inevitably the doom of the Liberal Party and the rise of Labour in its place. Nevertheless, its own internal divisions gratuitously hastened the party's fall: the Asquith-Lloyd George split kept the party divided in the crucial years 1918–24 when Labour, to its own surprise, advanced to government; while the further three-way split – Samuel-Simon-Lloyd George – in 1931 shattered it finally at the very moment when Labour's débâcle might have offered it fresh hope. The story is one of discord, bitter recrimination, and, at first sight, total failure.

8 – Chris Cook, *The Age of Alignment: Electoral Politics in Britain 1922–1929* (London, Macmillan, 1975), p 343

The conclusion from this thesis is that there was not a single date when the Liberal Party declined. Rather, it was a long-term phenomenon which varied, both in item and degree, from area to area. In such regions as industrial Scotland, East Lancashire or London the Liberals were in serious difficulties before 1914. Yet in such areas as rural Cheshire, North Wales and rural Scotland, the real challenge of Labour was not significant until 1924 or even 1929. The Liberal decline resembled the pictures of a kaleidoscope, changing from constituency to constituency, with all the complexity of a Seurat landscape.

By 1923, despite the collapse of so much constituency organisation, the process of decline had not reached the stage when recovery was impossible. A year later, it was difficult to deny that the Liberal decline had passed the point of no return. Ten months had witnessed, if not the destruction of a party, at least a débâcle that made total recovery almost an impossibility.

In this sense the tariff election, the advent of a Labour Government and the general election of 1924 marked a great divide in British politics. The Labour Party had tasted power, however briefly, for the first time. The Liberal Party had ensured that almost certainly it would never assume power in its own right again. For these reasons, the political spectrum was different in kind and in degree in October 1924 than in November 1922. These two years constituted a period of alignment in British politics in which the position of the Liberal Party had changed so that it was never again to succeed in winning power.

9 – Christopher Howard, 'Expectation Born to Death: Local Labour Party Expansion in the 1920s' in J. Winter (ed.), *Working Class in Modern British History: Essays in Honour of Henry Pelling* (Cambridge, Cambridge University Press, 1983), p 74

… with unemployment rising and short-time working now widespread, rank-and-file criticism of the leadership was growing. The future was no longer assured, and at the next election 'JRM will have to work very hard otherwise the seat is lost'…

MacDonald was no doubt relieved to leave all this behind and move to the safer and cheaper seat of Seaham Harbour in 1928. MacDonald may well have said that Aberavon finally asked too much of him, but it might be as well to ask whether the leadership expected too much of the local parties. Despite the heady success of the immediate post-war period… and the nostalgic testimony of many who battled through the period, the picture gained from local party records does not suggest that this was the golden age of working-class politics.

10 – L. MacNeill Weir, *The Tragedy of Ramsay MacDonald* (London, Secker & Warburg, 1938), pp xi, 383, 384

MacDonald was always the most accommodating of Socialists. His Socialism was of a kind that Sir William Harcourt meant when he said on a famous occasion 'We are all Socialists now'. His socialism is that far off Never Never land born of vague aspirations and described by him in picturesque generalities. It is a Turner landscape of beautiful colours and glorious indefiniteness. He saw it not with a telescope but with a kaleidoscope... Anyone can believe in it without sacrifice or even inconvenience.

It is evident that MacDonald never really accepted the Socialist faith of a classless world, based on unselfish service.

The members of the Labour Cabinet naturally assumed on that Sunday night, 23 August [1931] that Mr Baldwin would be asked to form a government. But it is significant that MacDonald had something quite different in view. Without a word of consultation with his Cabinet colleagues, without even informing them of his intentions to set up a National Government with himself as Prime Minister, he proceeded to carry out his long-thought-out plan.

Snowden throws a side-light on MacDonald's attitude at this time: 'When the Labour Cabinet as a whole declined to agree to a reduction of unemployment pay, Mr MacDonald assumed too hurriedly that this involved the resignation of his Government. He neither showed nor expressed any grief at this regrettable development. On the contrary he set about the formation of the National Government with an enthusiasm which showed that the adventure was highly agreeable to him.'

It was therefore amazing to them when the Cabinet assembled the next morning. MacDonald came in and announced to them that a new government had been formed – in short that he was in and they were out...

The impression left on the minds of those who had heard that speech... was that the whole thing had been arranged long before and that, while in Cabinet and Committee they had been making panic stricken efforts to balance the Budget, the whole business had been humbug and make-believe.

11 – David Marquand, *Ramsay MacDonald* (London, Jonathan Cape, 1977), pp xiii–xiv, 624, 628, 635, 636

I have tried to depict MacDonald as a man of his own time, facing the problems of his own time and applying or failing to apply the solutions of his own time, and not as an exemplar or a warning for ours. I believe that when he is looked at in this way, without the hindsight which seems to me to mar many interpretations of the period, he emerges as a greater and, at the same time, as a more attractive man than he has generally been thought to be; the hostile view of him which became almost universal, at any rate in the Labour movement, after the split in 1931 seems to me to emerge as myth rather than history. But although I have tried to avoid the trap of hindsight, I have also tried to avoid the opposite trap of apologia, and to 'portray him warts and all'...

All his life, MacDonald fought against a class view of politics, and for the primacy of political action as against industrial action; for him, the logical corollary was that the party must be prepared, when necessary, to subordinate the sectional class of the unions to its own conception of the national interest...

If the crash was to be avoided, the Government had either to make more cost cuts immediately or to leave office immediately. And it was now clear for the first time that if it left office it would be up to MacDonald to decide whether it would be followed by a Conservative-Liberal coalition or by the National Government under his leadership.

For more than a generation, Labour men and women were to take it for granted, not only that MacDonald had betrayed the Labour Party in forming the National Government, but that he had been indecently eager to betray it. No such eagerness can be detected in his behaviour during the critical weekend of August 21–23rd. Chamberlain and Samuel made their offer [to join MacDonald in a National Government] on Friday night. So far from accepting it, MacDonald spent most of Saturday and Sunday in a long-drawn-out attempt to persuade his colleagues to stay in office and make the extra economies themselves... [The Cabinet refused; and Snowden and Thomas asked that their dissent should be recorded in the minutes. MacDonald and Snowden were to go to the opposition leaders to check whether another £20 million cut would satisfy them. MacDonald's communication with his children suggested that he intended to resign as matters came to a head on 23 and 24 August 1931.]

The next thirteen hours were the most critical in MacDonald's career, and among the most critical in recent British history. Before the Cabinet meeting he had expected to leave office with his colleagues, and to support the cut in unemployment benefit from the Opposition benches. Though the evidence is scanty and inconclusive, there is some reason to believe that it was after his next meeting with the King that second thoughts began to creep in. When he arrived at the Palace – looking 'scared and unbalanced', as Wigram put it later – he told the King that he had no alternative but to tender the Cabinet's resignation. According to Wigram, the King 'impressed upon the Prime Minister that he was the only man to lead the country through the crisis and hoped that he would reconsider the situation'... [This led to a variety of hurried discussions.]

On the whole, then, it seems probable that when MacDonald went to bed on August 23rd, he was no longer certain that he would leave office next day and was beginning to toy with the notion that he might take the King's advice after all...

[After discussions with the King and the Opposition leaders matters came to a head.] By 10.35 [on the morning of 24 August] it had been agreed that Baldwin and Samuel would serve under MacDonald in a National Government.

12 – Robert Blake, *The Conservative Party* (London, Eyre and Spottiswood, 1970) writing of Baldwin's political abilities, pp 216–17, 244

If he evaded realities, the nation was glad to follow. To the public he seemed to embody the English spirit and his speeches to sound the authentic note of the English character which they so much admired and so seldom resembled. Pipe-smoking, phlegmatic, honest, kind, commonsensical, fond of pigs, the classics and the country, he represented to Englishmen an idealised and enlarged version of themselves. While the political climate remained clear they venerated, almost worshipped him. His tragedy was that the weather changed and in the end his worshippers, like some primitive people, sought to beat the tribal god whom they had ordained... He was a decent and honourable man. He was modest. He had a high sense of duty...

The truth was that the Conservative party under Baldwin had managed to recover a large area of the middle ground in politics which is the key to electoral success and which they lost in 1906, after being in possession for nearly twenty years before that. By the mid 1920s they no longer had the harsh appearance that they had displayed in the immediate pre-war years. From 1906 to 1914 they had seemed too often to be the party of rich men reluctant to pay taxes, of Englishmen determined to retain control over the 'Celtic fringe', of Ulstermen ready to rend the fabric of the constitution and subvert the loyalty of the army in order to uphold the Protestant ascendancy. The Conservatives seemed to lack compassion.

Under Baldwin the picture was different. Their social composition did not, it is true, greatly change. The movement of the business men, bankers, industrialists into the party, which had begun well before the turn of the century, continued – a reflection of a general process of absorption and amalgamation which had been affecting the governing class for the last thirty years. The Conservatives were still the rich man's party. But there was a new awareness of social problems, a new consciousness of poverty and unemployment. The party no doubt contained its quota of 'hard faced business men who looked as if they had done well out of the war', but it was significant that their leader should have been the man who coined the phrase. Obliged to choose between a Liberal party torn by strife, a Labour party incapable of governing, and a Conservative party which appeared reliable and reasonably humane, the electorate not surprisingly voted for the latter [sic]. Under Baldwin the Conservatives did not seem to lack compassion.

13 – Cheryl Law, *Suffrage and Power: The Women's Movement 1918–1928* (London, I.B. Tauris, 1997), pp 218–20, 225–8

Why did successive governments not have the political will to complete the enfranchisement of women before 1928? In response to such determined opposition and repeated postponements, why did the women's movement not return to threatened militancy? Was it only as a result of the movement's tenacity and manipulation of every small advantage that the franchise extension was achieved in 1928 or was there an agreed ten-year waiting period which parliament was determined would be enforced?...

In terms of credit, the NUSEC [National Union of Societies for Equal Citizenship] displayed its usual confidence in believing itself to have been primarily responsible for the 1928 success. The NUSEC believed its tactics of inexorable pressure had been the political lever it needed to press the claim home.

> If the National Union had yielded to either section in 1922 we should not have obtained from Mr Bonar Law... his declaration of personal belief in equal franchise, which is said to have considerably influenced the present Government... If we had not again pressed the question on all three Parties at the general Election of 1924 we should not have obtained from the present Prime Minister [Stanley Baldwin] his now famous promise of 'equal political rights'.

By contrast, the SPG [Six Point Group] had never put faith in such pledges. If it had been a larger organisation it might well have revived the militancy which it so frequently discussed...

As it was the first to recognise, the movement had progressed a long way since the war. Even with the limited franchise, women were in quite a different position from that of the pre-war militant years. They now had something to lose; they were now inside the establishment, and militancy against the establishment would, strictly speaking, have been militancy against themselves...

No sooner had their key objective finally been accomplished than the many organisations which comprised the movement began the process of planning for the future, realigning their aims in the light of their full citizenship and potential parliamentary power. Similar to the review process of 1918, when the movement's agenda had been scrutinised with a view to future campaigning, the feeling endured that the movement was still very much only at the beginning of its journey towards equality. In the words of the WFL [Women's Freedom League]:

> To have won equal voting rights for women and men is a great victory, but it will
> have been an infinitely greater achievement when we have succeeded in abolish-
> ing for ever the 'woman's sphere', 'women's work' and a 'woman's wage', and have
> decided that the whole wide world and all its opportunities is just as much the
> sphere of women, as of men...

This is an achievement yet to be realised...

Turning to the findings of this research, the contention has been made and demonstrated that sustaining suffrage and women's right agitation throughout the First World War were essential to the evolution of the move-ment. Without such wartime activity, there would have been insufficient pressure available to take advantage of the constitutional loophole whereby women's suffrage amendments were forced on to the legislative agenda in 1916. To use Mrs Fawcett's analogy of the progress of the movement:

> Sometimes the pace was fairly rapid; sometimes it was very slow, but it was
> constant and always in one direction. I have compared it to a glacier; but like a
> glacier, it was ceaseless and irresistible... it always moved in the direction of the
> removal of the statutory and social disabilities of women.

Rather than losing its impetus, despite the exhaustion of the war years, the movement gained new vigour from its franchise success, and went to entrench its position by constructing an extended network. Utilising the accumulated skill of the previous 50 years the need was to consolidate its gains, extend its sphere of operation, effect further legislative change and fight the continued pressure to restrict women's lives...

Far from the proliferation of organisations duplicating effort and diluting effectiveness, this network [of women's organisations] was essential to cope with the enormity of the task in hand which concerned itself with every aspect of women's lives. Women were responding to and recognising the truth of the maxim of industrial and political groups, that strength lies in organisation and co-operation. [Martin] Pugh has dismissed the period stating that 'No historian, of either sex, has felt moved to characterise the inter-war decades as the "Age of Women"'. On the contrary, we might want to contend that the decade 1918–1928 was the movement's most democratic so far, especially when considering the high number of women who 'surged into the Labour Party and the Co-operative Movement as if they had been waiting for doors to open, together with the success of the non-party Women's Citizens' Association (WCAs) which blanketed the country...'

In the face of sustained resistance, the women's movement stood firm. It pushed its demands, lobbied politicians, strengthened and educated its membership using its political campaign weaponry for developing the strategic electioneering tactics, whilst targeting its message at press, public and politi-cians. Apart from the successes detailed in the preceding chapters, mecha-nisms had been established for effecting reforms, and women themselves had changed irrevocably. By 1925 there were 14,000 women enrolled on diploma and degree course; half a million clerical workers and approximately 1300 qualified women doctors; the first women were allowed to sit for the administrative class of the civil service, and by 1927 the struggle for women police had resulted in an increase to 142 women employed with the same powers as male officers...

The feminist movement was largely sustained by 'professional' women's rights workers, large numbers of whom worked through from the movement's earliest years to the 1920s and beyond. The belief that the majority of the experienced suffrage workers gave up the struggle in 1918 is quickly dispelled by the most cursory reading of suffrage periodicals and annual reports. On the contrary, it is the continuity of personnel which reveals the level or commitment of these activists who made the emancipation of women their life's work. Tenacity was one of their biggest assets.

PRIMARY EVIDENCE AND INFORMATION

14 – John Boyd Orr, *Food, Health and Income: Report on a Survey of Adequacy of Diet in Relation to Income* (London, Macmillan, 1936), pp 7, 20–1, 49–50

Foreword

The state of nutrition of the people of this country is surveyed here on a broad scale and from a new angle. Instead of discussing minimum requirements about which there had been so much controversy, this survey considers optimum requirements. Optimum requirements are based on the physiological ideal, which we define as 'a state of well-being such that no improvement can be effected by a change of the diet'. The standard of adequacy of diet adopted is one which will maintain the standard of perfect nutrition.

The average diet of each of six groups into which the population has been divided according to income are compared with these requirements for perfect nutrition. The health of the population is reviewed to see to what extent inadequacy of diet is reflected in ill-health and poor physique.

It is difficult in the present state of knowledge to lay down precise and detailed criteria of perfect nutrition. The basis of comparison taken for health is, therefore, the state of health and physique of those groups of population who can choose their diets freely, without any economic consideration seriously affecting their choice... the state of nutrition of the higher income groups, whose diet is not limited by income, can be taken as a standard which can be attained with the present dietary habits of the people of this country.

The tentative conclusion reached, is that a diet completely adequate for health, according to modern standards, is reached at an income level above that of 50 percent of the population. This means that 50 percent of the population are living at a level of nutrition so high that, on the average, no improvement can be effected by increased consumption.

The important aspect of the survey, however, is the inadequacy of the diets of the lower income groups, and the markedly lower standard of health of the people, and especially of the children in these groups, compared with that of the higher income groups...

Distribution of National Income and Food Expenditure at Different Income Levels

Table VI   Classification of the population by income groups and average food expenditure per head in each group

Group	Income per head per week	Estimated average expenditure on food	Estimated population of group Numbers	Percentage
I	Up to 10s	4s	4,500,000	10
II	10s to 15s	6s	9,000,000	20
III	15s to 20s	8s	9,000,000	20
IV	20s to 30s	10s	9,000,000	20
V	30s to 45s	12s	9,000,000	20
VI	Over 45s	14s	4,500,000	10
Average	30s	9s		

Summary and Conclusion
The food position of the country has been investigated to show the average consumption of the main foodstuffs at different income levels. The standard of food requirements and the standard of health adopted are not the present average but the optimum, ie, the physiological standard, which, though ideal, is attainable in practice with the national food supply sufficient to provide a diet adequate for health for any member of the community. The main findings may be summarised as follows...

II The consumption of bread and potatoes is practically uniform throughout the different income level groups. Consumption of milk, eggs, fruit, vegetables, meat and fish rises with income. Thus, in the poorest group the average consumption of milk, including tinned milk, is equivalent to 1.8 pints per head per week; in the wealthiest group 5.5 pints. The poorest group consume 1.5 eggs per head per week; the wealthiest 4.5. The poorest spend 2.4d on fruit; the wealthiest 1s 8d.

III An examination of the composition of the diets of the different groups shows that the degree of adequacy of health increases as incomes rise. The average diet of the poorest group, comprising 4.4 million people, is, by the standard adopted, deficient in every constituent examined. The second group, comprising 9 million people, is adequate in protein, fat and carbohydrates, but deficient in all the vitamins and minerals considered. The third group, comprising another 9 million, is deficient in several of the important vitamins and minerals. Complete adequacy is almost reached in groups IV, and in the still wealthier groups the diet has a surplus of all constituents considered.

IV A review of the state of health of the people of the different groups suggests that, as income increases, disease and death-rate decrease, children grow more quickly, adult stature is greater and general health and physique improve.

V The result of tests on children show that improvement of diet in the lower groups is accompanied by improvement in health and increased rate of growth, which approximates to that of children in the higher income groups.

VI To make the diet of the poorer groups the same as that of the first group whose diet is adequate for full health, ie group IV, would involved increases in consumption of a number of the more expensive foodstuffs, viz., milk, eggs, butter, fruit, vegetables and meat, varying from 12 to 25 percent.

If these findings be accepted as sufficiently accurate to form a working hypothesis, they raise important economic and political problems. Consideration of these is outwith the scope of investigation... This new knowledge of nutrition, which shows that there can be an enormous improvement in the health and physique of the nation, coming at the same time as the greatly increased powers of producing food, has created an entirely new situation which demands economic statesmanship.

15 – B. Seebohm Rowntree, *Poverty and Progress: A Second Social Survey of York* (London, Longman, Green & Co., 1941), pp 451, 452, 456, 457, 459, 460, 461, 476

Summary and Conclusion
In 1899 of the working-class population 15.46 per cent (7230 persons) were living in primary poverty... In 1936 6.8 per cent of the working population (3767) were living in primary poverty. In other words the proportion of the working-class population living in abject poverty had been reduced by more than one half...

In 1899 the average wages of the male heads of families was 27s 5d, equal to 47s 6d at 1936 prices. In 1936 it was 63s 0d, an increase of 32.6 per cent. The corresponding increase in the wages of female heads of families was from 12s 1.5d (equal to 20s 11.5d in 1936) to 32s 8d, an increase of 55.9 per cent...

The substantial increase in real wages occurred notwithstanding the fact that hours of work were greatly reduced...

It will be remembered that I have taken the standard of living attainable by a family of man, wife and three dependent children with an available income of 43s 6d a week after paying rent, as the minimum. Families whose incomes do not enable then to live up to this standard are classified as below the poverty line. This poverty line has no relation whatever to the primary poverty line adopted in the 1899 survey, which only provided 30s 7d (at 1936 prices) for a family of five persons.

A family of five with 43s 6d after paying rent can, if they lay out their money with great economy, buy food sufficient for physical efficiency and clothing sufficient for warmth and respectability...

Our inquiry showed that 31.1 per cent of the working-class population were in receipt of insufficient income to enable then to live in accordance with the above standard, and so are classified as living under the poverty line; 18.9 per cent belong to families with incomes of less than 10s a week above the minimum figure; 13.9 per cent to those with incomes between 10s to 20s above it, and 36.1 per cent to families with incomes of not less than 20s a week above...

Three-quarters of the poverty is due to three causes; 28.6 per cent is due to unemployment, 32.8 per cent to the fact that workers in regular work are not receiving wages sufficiently high to enable then to live above the poverty line, and 14.7 per cent are in poverty on account of old age...

The Three Periods of Economic Distress
The period of greatest economic stress in a workingman's life is when he has young children to support, and perhaps the most disconcerting fact revealed by this investigation is that of the working-class children under one year of age 52.5 per cent were found to be living below the poverty line; that 47 per cent would probably remain in poverty for five years or more and 31.5 per cent for ten years or more. It must, of course, be remembered that not only they but the whole of the families concerned would remain in poverty for these periods. Thus working-class people are liable to be in poverty during childhood and women are liable to be in poverty during the time that they are bearing children. The seriousness of this from the standpoint of the national physique can hardly be overstated. Many are liable to be in poverty again in old age...

The 1899 'Poverty Line' Quite Different from that of 1936
In this survey I have made no attempt to measure the amount of 'secondary' poverty by direct observation, partly because the methods of doing this adopted in 1899 appear to me now as being too rough and ready to give reliable results...

The facts that in 1899 only 33.39 per cent of the working class was regarded as living in poverty, either primary or secondary, whereas in 1936

31.1 per cent are living below the minimum through lack of income, and an unknown further proportion, possibly 7 to 10 per cent, are living in 'secondary' poverty, have therefore no relation to each other.

The only figures that are absolutely comparable are those for primary poverty and as we have seen the proportion of the working-class population living in primary poverty in 1936 was 6.8 per cent, whereas in 1899 it was 15.46 per cent...

Conclusion

... The economic conditions of the workers is better by 30 per cent than in 1899, though working hours are shorter. Housing is immeasurably better, health is better, education is better...

It is gratifying that so much progress has been achieved, but if instead of looking backward we look forward. Then we see how far the standard of living of many workers falls short of any standard which could be regarded, even for the time being as satisfactory. Great though the progress made during the last forty years has been, there is no cause for satisfaction in the fact that in a country so rich as England, over 30 per cent of the workers in a typical provincial city should have incomes so small that it is beyond their means to live even at the stringently economical level adopted as a minimum in this survey, nor in the fact that almost half the children of working-class parents spend the first five years of their lies in poverty and that almost a third of them live below the poverty line for ten years or more...

16 – Ellen Wilkinson, *The Town That Was Murdered* (London, Gollancz, Left Book Club, 1939),[17] p 236, 237, 238–9

Bad housing, overcrowding, underfeeding, low wages for any work that is going, household incomes cut to the limit by public assistance, or Means Test or whatever is the cutting machine of the time... these mean disease and pre-mature death. No goodwill speeches, no glowing perorations about 'the patience of our people under misfortune' alter the plain fact that if people have to live and bear and bring up children in bad houses on too little food, their resistance to disease is lowered and they die before they should. Their babies die, too, at an unnecessary and easily-preventable high rate...

The census of 1921 gave a much higher rate of overcrowding, 42.32 per cent on a slightly lower population figure... What this appallingly high figure meant in human lives is shown by the vital statistics. The general death rate in Jarrow in 1921 was 17.29 per thousand as compared with the average for England and Wales of 12.1. The rate of grouped towns the same size as Jarrow was 11.7. The infantile death rates was 116 per thousand as compared with the general rate for the country of 83.

The deaths from tuberculosis and respiratory diseases was 39 per cent of the total, an extraordinary high figure. 1921 was not a 'bad' year like 1919, when the infantile mortality rate for Jarrow reached 153 per thousand. Yet the medical officer of health points out: 'Had the Jarrow death rate been on the same level as for England and Wales, there would have been only 438 deaths instead of 626'. Which is to say that in the condition of 1921, 188 people died for the reason that they lived in Jarrow.

In 1923 the medical officer reports that the conditions of overcrowding remain unaltered. 'Of the total population of 36,000,' he adds, '6000 are drawing the dole, and another 23,000 are receiving poor law relief'. Under such conditions the Conservative Housing Act of 1923, which aimed at 'stimulating building by private enterprise' was of no value in meeting the problem. More advantage might be taken of the Wheatley Act with its £9 per house for forty years, had the Town Council of the period with its moderate majority really taken energetic action.

Seven years after the war the evil remained as bad as ever. A comparison of the different wards showed as usual the enormous discrepancy between the Grange Ward, where are situated most of the good houses that Jarrow had then, and the crowded East, Central and North Wards.

Ward	Death rate per 1000
East	20.57
Central	19.38
North	19.27
West	14.66
South	12.44
Grange	9.12
Borough Average	15.5

Notes on Chapter 4

1   C.L. Mowat, *Britain Between the Wars, 1918–1940* (London, Methuen, 1968); J. Stevenson and C. Cook, *The Slump* (London, Jonathan Cape, 1977), pp 31–53.
2   B.S. Rowntree, *Poverty: A Study of Town Life* (London, Longman, 1901); B.S. Rowntree, *Progress and Poverty: A Second Social Survey of York* (London, Longman, 1941); A.L. Bowley and Burnett-Hurst, *Livelihood and Poverty* (1915); H. Llewellyn Smith (ed.), *The New Survey of London Life and Labour* (London, P.S. King, 1934), 3 vols; A.L. Bowley and M. Hogg, *Has Poverty Diminished?* (London, P.S. King, 1925).
3   Keith Laybourn, *Britain on the Breadline* (Stroud, Suttons, 1990, 1998) pp 54–8.
4   Henry Pelling, *The Origins of the Labour Party* (London, Macmillan 1954); Ross

McKibbin, *The Evolution of the Labour Party 1910–1924* (Oxford, Oxford University Press, 1974); P.F. Clarke, *Lancashire and the New Liberalism* (Cambridge, Cambridge University Press, 1971); M. Bentley, *The Climax of Liberal Politics: British Liberalism in Theory and Practice 1868–1918* (London, Edward Arnold, 1987); D. Tanner, *Political Change and the Labour Party* (Cambridge: Cambridge University Press, 1991).

5   Bill Lancaster, *Radicalism, Cooperation and Socialism: Leicester Working-class Politics 1860–1906* (Leicester, Leicester University Press, 1987).

6   Christopher Howard, 'Expectations Born to Death: Local Labour Party Expenditure in the 1920s' in J. Winter (ed.), *Working Class in Modern British History: Essays in Honour of Henry Pelling* (Cambridge, Cambridge University Press, 1983), p 81.

7   *Ibid.*, p 65.

8   *Ibid.*, p 78.

9   McKibbin, *The Evolution of the Labour Party 1910–1924*; B. Barker, 'Anatomy of Reform: The Social and Political Leadership of the Labour Leadership of Yorkshire', *International Review of Social History* Vol. 18, 1973, pp 1–27.

10 *Labour Party Conference Report*, 1935 (London, Labour Party, 1935), p 179.

11 A. Booth, *British Economic Policy 1931–1949: Was There a Keynesian Revolution?* (London, Harvester Wheatsheaf, 1989); S. Glynn and A. Booth, *The Road to Full Employment* (London, Allen & Unwin, 1987).

12 Lewis Minkin, *The Contentious Alliance: Trade Unions and the Labour Party* (Edinburgh, Edinburgh University Press), 1991, p 1.

13 Jack Reynolds and Keith Laybourn, *Labour Heartland: A History of the Labour Party in West Yorkshire During the Inter-War Years 1918–1939* (Bradford, Bradford University Press, 1987), pp 58–61, 158–161.

14 David Marquand, *Ramsay MacDonald* (London, Jonathan Cape, 1977), p 795.

15 Keith Laybourn, *The Rise of Labour* (London, Edward Arnold, 1998), pp 76–83.

16 Pamela M. Graves, *Labour Women: Women in British Working Class Politics, 1918–1939* (Cambridge, Cambridge University Press, 1994).

17 Gollancz have no detailed information on copyright, and requested that I should state that all attempts at tracing the copyright holder were unsuccessful.

Chapter 5

Industrial Relations and the General Strike 1919–39

Introduction

The First World War was a turning-point in British industrial relations. Whilst there was industrial unrest between 1910 and 1921, the war saw the Government intervene in industrial relations, on a scale never seen before, through DORA (the Defence of the Realm Act), the Munitions of War Acts and the Military Service Acts. The wartime situation made it imperative that both trade unions and employers work together in running industry for the purpose of increasing industrial output. In some industries, Whitley Councils – named after J.H. Whitley, the Speaker of the House of Commons who produced the Whitley Report on industrial relations in 1917 – were set up in order to regulate industrial relations. This level of government intervention continued in the immediate post-war years, especially after the large number of industrial disputes that occurred at the end of 1918 and 1919. Faced with this situation, and concerns at the possible collapse of the social structure in Britain, the National Industrial Conference was called for 27 February 1919, bringing together employers, trade unions and industrial councils. It formed a Provisional Joint Committee, which first met in March, to advise the government on industrial relations and to encourage the formation of a permanent Industrial Council. Such developments reflected a pre-war propensity to avoid industrial militancy if at all possible (Document 1).

Government direct cooperation did not last long, and governments were rarely involved with employers' organisations and trade unions in industrial discussions. Governments preferred to leave industries to get on with their own industrial negotiations, except in the case of the coal miners' strike and the General Strike of 1926. This policy changed in only minor ways in the 1930s. Nevertheless, governments were never able to ignore industrial relations again as they had done before 1914.

Industrial relations in this period was complex. They were about welfare provision as well as industrial relations (Document 2), and there were also marked variations between different industries. During the inter-war years, the old declining staple industries often faced major industrial conflict as wages were reduced, whilst the new consumer-oriented industries often experienced better industrial relations because the trade unions were less powerful or because economic conditions were better. Yet even here there is a variable pattern. In the case of the staple steel industry there was a loss of demand from railways and shipbuilding but gains in the electrical, motor car and aircraft industries, and industrial relations remained generally good. Also, in some of the new industries such as cars, and particularly at Morris Motors, industrial relations were conditioned by high wages and the hostility of employers towards trade unionism (Document 3). There were also changes in the size of the industrial unit. Mergers of firms led to the development of a more professional management approach, which was usually less paternalistic than the old family firm arrangements that had emerged in the nineteenth century. At the same time, there was serious economic depression during the inter-war years which led to more centralisation within trade unions, and a greater willingness to work with employers and the state. There was also a greater interest in replacing the self-help approach in industrial relations with the idea of state welfare benefits and the social wage in a situation of weak inter-war trade unionism (Document 2). Industrial relations and trade-union conflict was thus a contentious area for debate during the inter-war years.

This chapter focuses upon various issues, debates and events of the inter-war years. In the first place it examines the pattern of industrial conflict generally and reveals how governments responded to it: did governments avoid involvement as far as possible and focus upon more general ways of helping the economy? Secondly, the vast majority of the chapter deals with the General Strike of 1926, the major industrial conflict in twentieth-century British industrial history. Thirdly, some attention will be given to the trade-union movement in the 1930s: to what extent did the trade-union movement recover its position in the 1930s, and how did this affect the pattern of industrial relations?

...ustrial Relations and the General Strike of 1926

The years 1918 to 1920 saw something of a post-war economic boom which permitted trade unions to improve working conditions and wages. Trade union membership, as a result, reached over eight million by 1920. However, with the end of the boom David Lloyd George's Coalition Government was anxious to divest itself of both ownership and direct involvement in industry and industrial relations.

Governments of the early inter-war years were directly involved in industrial relations through their control of coal mining and the railways. Reluctantly they operated as one of the major employers of the state, though they quickly divested themselves of these industries. Indeed, the strategy adopted by the dominant Conservative Party in government was that industries should be returned to and/or operated by employers, and that industrial relations and industrial direction should be dealt with by governments only at a distance. The steel industry, indeed, adopted this policy and enjoyed very good industrial relations throughout the 1920s, without the need for government intervention. This was not the case more generally, though, for in national disputes governments were inevitably drawn in. Indeed, in the national wool strike/lockout in 1925, Arthur Steel-Maitland, the Minister of Labour, was drawn into arranging a settlement and a Court of Inquiry to offer arbitration in the dispute. The involvement of government was even more marked in the General Strike of 1926.

The General Strike of 3–12 May 1926 was the most important industrial conflicts in British history. It saw upwards of one and three-quarter million workers come out in support of about one million miners who had been locked out for rejecting wage reductions. It was a bitter dispute which divided the nation along sharp class lines. It was also a pivotal moment for the development of British industrial relations and a turning point in the relationship between the Communist Party of Great Britain (CPGB) and the TUC. In other words, its immediate impact upon British society and labour politics was pervasive, even if it barely changed the long-term pattern of events.

It began as a result of the coal owners' lock-out of miners who had refused to accept lower wages following the ending of the Government's nine-month subsidy, agreed on 31 July 1925, 'Red Friday'. The decision to support the miners had been accepted by the TUC at a meeting on 1 May 1926. The TUC set up a negotiating committee to deal with the dispute, which agreed to call off the dispute on 12 May without any guarantees. At first glance, it appears that the most dramatic example of class loyalty in British history had ended in ignominious defeat for the whole trade-union movement.

Naturally, the General Strike has produced many debates and a huge historiography. Whilst the Government presented it as being some type of revolutionary plot, fuelled by communists, it is clear that the TUC saw it as an attempt to defend the wages of miners. The CPGB considered it a revolutionary opportunity. The organised working class gave its whole-hearted support to the strike, the middle classes gave their support to the Government, some through the voluntary Organisation for the Maintenance of Supplies (OMS).

At this juncture three points will be made. The first is that the General Strike was the product of an interplay of circumstances whereby industrial tensions in the coal industry became inflamed at a time when both the Government and the TUC were moving on a collision course over industrial relations. Secondly, it is clear that the General Strike was remarkably well organised by the TUC, despite the lateness of the preparations. There is no doubt that the Government was in control, and that it was able to make great play of the constitutional challenge that the General Strike presented, but the TUC performed well in a difficult situation. In the end, the TUC was forced to call off the dispute, without any guarantees, and lost much support. Nonetheless, there is a third point, which is that the General Strike was not the disaster often portrayed. Trade unions lost members and industrial passivity followed, but such developments were occurring before 1926, and the movement regained its balance within a decade.

The reasons for the conflict have divided historians. Essentially, there have been five major explanations offered. Two – that it was the culmination of industrial militancy and the efforts of the Communists – can be dismissed. In the first case, strike activity was declining during the early 1920s (Document 10), and there is ample evidence that the employers and trade unionists were actively involved in reducing the levels of industrial conflict from about 1916 onwards.[1] Also, the CPGB's influence appears to have been casual rather than causal, for it carried little influence throughout the country, other than in one or two communities, such as Battersea, which had a Communist MP and some communist representation on the local strike committee. The other three explanations have focused upon the problems of the coal industry, the determination of Baldwin's Conservative Government to reduce wages and the commitment of the TUC to defend the wages of all workers.

The General Strike had its immediate origins in the miners' lockout of 1926 and the long-term events which put its position back to that of the First World War, during which the coal industry fell under the control of the wartime Coalition Government. After the Great War, the Lloyd George Coalition Government set up the Sankey Commission to determine whether or not the coal industry should be retained by the state or returned to the coal-owners. Once the Majority Report of the Sankey Commission, set up to examine that issue in 1919, had declared that it was in favour of nationalisation, the issue became politically sensitive as the Government rejected this advice, despite having previously declared its willingness to accept a majority verdict. Having reneged upon this promise, the Government faced industrial conflict in July 1919 and a very serious industrial threat when the coal mines were formally handed back to the coal owners on 31 March 1921. The seriousness of the resulting miners' strike was much reduced when the National Union of Railwaymen and the National Transport Workers failed to support the miners, via the 'Triple Alliance', on 15 April 1921, a day better known since as 'Black Friday'.

'Black Friday' conditioned the attitude of the General Council of the TUC when it was committed to supporting the miners in their dispute over wage reduction in July 1925. That support forced the Baldwin Conservative Government to intervene with a nine-month subsidy for the mining industry and the formation of a royal commission to investigate coal mining, in order to avoid widespread conflict. Poor industrial relations in the mining industry sparked the General Strike, but the conflict between the policies of the Government and the TUC provided the context out of which a wider dispute could emerge.

All post-war governments were committed to returning to the gold standard, and were prepared to deflate the economy to strengthen the pound before that return in 1925. The end-product was deflation, an increase in unemployment, the reduction of costs and the decline of monetary wage levels. Indeed, Stanley Baldwin announced that wages would have to fall, and one newspaper commented,

> Wages, said Mr Baldwin, have to be brought down. This is not simply an incautious and inconsidered statement by Mr Baldwin, a slip of the tongue: it is the settled and deliberate policy of the governing class, who have entered upon a course of action which has for its object the deliberate intensification of unemployment as a method of forcing down wages.[2]

Government economic policy was strongly geared towards confrontation with the trade unions. The Government rejection of the Sankey Report and the events of 'Black Friday' merely confirmed this, and demonstrated how the Defence of the Realm Act (DORA) had provided Government with a battery of controls to regulate industrial relations. Indeed, in February 1919 a Cabinet committee on industrial unrest was set up. It was later extended, and became known as the Strike Committee in September 1919, during the transport strike. In October 1919, it became the Supply and Transport Committee under Sir Eric Geddes, the Chief Civil Commissioner. Responsible to the Cabinet, it created special divisional offices in the regions, and worked with public and voluntary bodies. In addition, it operated within the Emergency Powers Act, introduced at the time of the miners' strike in October 1920. It gave power to the executive, on the declaration of an emergency, to introduce temporary, but legally binding, regulations by order in council to preserve peace and to maintain essential supplies. The Supply and Transport Committee was revived in May 1923 by Stanley Baldwin as part of the Government's anti-strike organisation.[3] It was this Government body that the TUC faced during the General Strike in 1926.

The falling wages and rising unemployment of the early 1920s put the TUC on the defensive and ensured that it was on collision course with the Government. After the collapse of the Triple Alliance and 'Black Friday', it formed the General Council as its executive body in place of its more industrially limited Parliamentary Committee. Endorsed at the 1921 TUC conference, the General Council intervened in inter-union disputes, attempted to improve trade-union organisation and sought to co-ordinate industrial action by the unions and 'to assist any union which is attacked on any vital question of Trade Union principle'.[4] The real purpose of the General Council was, therefore, to establish trade-union unity and to intervene in major industrial disputes in a way which it had not been able to do before. In 1922, the TUC set up a Joint Defence Committee, later known as the Committee for Co-ordination of Trade Union Effort, to accomplish this aim. Yet it was not until the Hull TUC Conference of 1924 that the General Council was given the powers it needed. The General Council established contact with the trades councils through a Joint Consultative Committee, with the aim of converting them to local publicity agencies and, for the first time, mediated in industrial disputes which involved shipbuilding workers, dockers, builders and railwaymen.[5]

A strengthened General Council came into conflict with the economic policies of the Conservative Government in July 1925 over the threat to reduce miners' wages. Faced with this situation, the TUC gave the miners the support the Triple Alliance had denied them in April 1921, and eventually the Government stepped in with its nine-month coal subsidy on Friday 31 July 1925, Red Friday.

The scene was set for attempts to avoid conflict. The Royal Commission on the Coal Industry (1925–6), better known as the Samuel Commission, was set up to examine the situation in the coal industry, and suggested that there was a need to amalgamate existing mines, to nationalise mining royalties and to improve industrial relations. It was felt that the last objective could be achieved by a cocktail of measures, including the development of profit-sharing schemes, the formation of pit committees, and the maintenance of national wage agreements, albeit with some regional variations. The Commission acknowledged that such changes would take years, and suggested that the immediate way forward was not to continue with a subsidy but to reduce the minimum wages of the miners.[6] However, there was little inclination to accept the Samuel Commission in full. The Government considered the nationalisation of mining royalties too expensive; the miners refused to accept the recommended wage reductions, and the employers opposed the continuance of national wage settlements and were reluctant to consider the rationalisation of mines. Only the TUC, looking for some escape from conflict, seems to have pinned any hope on the Samuel Commission as a solution to the potential conflict. This proved to be a forlorn hope.

The Government prepared for the conflict by strengthening its counter-strike measures, and the Home Secretary submitted a report on 7 August 1925 which led to the expansion of specialised staff, the recruitment of employers' representatives in ports, the stockpiling of resources and the establishment of contacts with local authorities and voluntary bodies.[7] Many towns developed their voluntary organisations. Haulage, in the hands of voluntary bodies, was organised into 150 committees. In November 1925, the Government arranged to have full access to broadcasting facilities, and the Ministry of Health sent out 'Circular 636' to local authorities, instructing them of their responsibilities under its emergency provisions. By February 1926, the Home Secretary was able to inform the Cabinet that 'little remained to be done' in respect of the threatened strike.[8]

In contrast, the TUC and the trade-union movement did little to prepare, in case their actions were taken to be provocative. Walter Citrine, Acting Secretary of the TUC, was all too aware of the need to take action. The difficulty was that the trade unions were reluctant to give the TUC power to control events, and the General Council did not receive its power to run the General Strike until 1 May 1926. The limited nature and lateness of the TUC preparations was later referred to by Ernest Bevin at a Conference of Executives (of unions) in January 1927 (Document 18).

In the final analysis, the Government had prepared for action whilst the TUC had not. Indeed, the TUC pinned its hopes on the Samuel Commission's recommendations, but there was little prospect that they would be accepted by the Government, the employers or the coal miners. The General Strike was about to occur.

A second debate revolves around the strike and its overall effectiveness before it was called off. The local organisation of the strike was chaotic.[9] Yet, at the end of the dispute the majority of workers who had been brought out still remained loyal to it. So how effective was the trade-union response to the General Strike? This is not as straightforward a question as it might at first appear, for there are several obvious supplementary questions. How effective was the TUC in organising the strike? How effective were the Government preparations in thwarting their efforts? How seriously did the Government take the constitutional threat posed by the dispute? How efficient and responsive was local organisation of the dispute?

The national situation is rather easier to examine than the local one, and evidence suggests that the General Council developed a modestly effective administrative machinery – performing quite impressively despite its lack of communication and the consequent confusion that arose over the role of trades councils, strike committees and transport committees, even though there was no serious challenge to Government control (Document 11). Local events are more difficult to assess because the local studies that have been published are partial, and often deal with areas that were relatively well organised during the dispute.

The General Council called about 1,750,000 workers out in support of the miners one minute before midnight on Monday 3 May, the vast majority of whom stayed out for the nine days. Most of these were first-line workers employed in transport, printing, iron and steel, power stations, building and chemical industries. The second-line workers, employed in industries such as engineering, shipbuilding and textiles, were held in reserve. Of these, only the engineers and shipbuilding workers were called out from 12 May, the day the strike ended. To call out so many workers was a major feat of organisation, and from the start the General Council attempted to create an administrative structure commensurate with the task it faced. Ernest Bevin organised the Ways and Means Committee, soon to become the Power and Orders Committee, co-ordinated the activities of the various unions, and the Food and Essential Services Committee was formed to make arrangements for the distribution of food and the maintenance of health services. There was also a Publicity Committee to counter Government propaganda. This moderate success owed a great deal to Bevin, who exercised overall responsibility for the conduct of the dispute. Although his control of the situation was somewhat febrile at the beginning, it gradually extended throughout many essential industries connected with the issue of permits to move food and essential supplies.

The TUC presented its side of the dispute through the *British Worker*, which went into production on 5 May 1926 and was distributed by print workers through trade unions. The circulation of the London edition rose to around 500,000, but did not meet demand, and so other editions were produced in Glasgow, Cardiff, Newcastle, Sunderland, Leicester and Leeds in an effort to make good the deficiency.[10] It also published circulars to stress that it was merely fighting an industrial dispute to support the miners, not a political dispute to defeat the Baldwin Government (Document 13).

Despite these efforts, the TUC was never likely to be fully effective. It was not able to stop the operation of many London power stations, the majority of provincial power stations or the main ports.[11] In addition, electricity supply was often maintained by the workers themselves, as long as no attempt was made by local bus and tram companies to run a service. Ports such as Liverpool and Dover were also kept going by volunteer labour.

The Government was quite clearly in control of the situation. Faced with a strike designed to force it to provide some type of extended subsidy to the mining industry, it refused to negotiate with the TUC until the dispute was called off. It was committed to ensuring that food supplies, vital services and law and order were maintained, and its emergency activities, particularly the railways companies, proved to be impressively smooth (Document 16). Most areas had 20,000 or more volunteers, far more than was required for the crisis, and in London, where 114,000 men had come forward, by 11 May only 9500 had been given work.[12] The OMS and other voluntary bodies supplying the Government with labour was hardly called upon for help. The fact is that the Government was able to maintain the operation of road transport because the haulage committees were able to rely upon their regular drivers.[13]

The Government, and particularly the Prime Minister, played upon the political fear of the dispute to gain public support (Document 12). Its case was well presented because of its dominance of the media. It took over the printing presses of the *Morning Post*, with Winston Churchill as editor, and he 'took the line that the strike threatened the Constitution, and at times his language became somewhat intemperate'.[14] The *British Gazette* increased its circulation rapidly from 232,000 on 5 May to 2,209,000 by the 12 May.[15] It had access to facilities and paper not readily available to the workers' press. The Government also dominated the airwaves, as the BBC only permitted Baldwin, Government ministers and those favourable to the Government position the opportunity to broadcast to the nation. This ensured that views contrary to those of the Government were not broadcast, and that the Government was able to emphasise the constitutional challenge the General Strike posed without much contradiction.

The Government also kept in close contact with the railway companies, both in order to keep a check on the movement of food and to inform the public of the available train services (Document 16). All the railway companies held their daily meetings of managers, line meetings, railway police meetings, and the like, and met the Minister of Transport or his representatives. Their day-to-day position was announced by BBC broadcasts.[16]

The Government was clearly able to control the national situation, and was far more prepared for the dispute. But how effective were the local authorities and the trade unions at the local level? This is not at all clear. There were upwards of 500 councils of action, or similar bodies, formed on the workers' side, although Emile Burns was only able to obtain 190 replies, 131 of a detailed nature, for his Labour Research Department survey of their activities in 1926.[17] Burns's assessment was that the trades councils and councils of action were 'suddenly asked to take a new and urgent task, without any but the vaguest suggestion of how they should carry it out and that viewed as a whole it was carried out effectively'.[18]

Indeed, the trades councils and councils of action formed numerous sub-committees, issued local permits, distributed relief, organised pickets, made local arrangements with sympathetic co-operative societies, published bulletins, arranged speakers for open-air meetings and covered a wide range of activities. The Labour Research Department indicates that between 70 and 72 of the 140 councils of action or trades councils who replied on the matter issued local strike publications, including the *Preston Strike News*, *Brighton Bulletin*, *Westminster Worker*, *Newcastle Workers' Chronicle*, *Northern Light*, and *Bulletin of the Blaydon and Chopwell District Council of Action*.[19] The publication of such newsheets exceeded the orders of the TUC, which felt that no local comment should be made, and ordered, unsuccessfully, the cessation of all strike bulletins on 10 May.

Yet such a vast array of activity does not indicate the level of effectiveness of the strike, although it may convey a high level of commitment by the working classes. Clearly, the TUC had some problems, emanating from its late preparations. It had to deal with 465 trades councils or councils of action in Britain, as well as a similar number of transport committees, instead of being able to work with 11 districts organisations (London and ten other divisions), as the Government was able to do.[20] Notwithstanding such problems, a number of regional district organisations were formed, such as the Merseyside Council of Action, which covered Birkenhead, Bootle, Liverpool and Wallasay. There were also county federations of councils of action in Lanarkshire and east Glamorgan, and a shadowy body known as the North West Area Strike Council, based on Manchester.[21]

There were many administrative failings as well as successes in the attempts to make the General Strike effective at the local level. Many councils of action had no bulletins, and some, such as Middlesbrough, Sheffield and St Albans, were fragmented. There was also much confusion between the trades councils/councils of action and the local transport committees (of the transport unions) about who was allowed to issue permits. Yet recent work tends, on the whole, to be more favourable than contemporary opinion allowed, pointing to the way in which the trades councils and councils of action prepared for the conflict and were reasonably effective.

It would appear that the rank-and-file responded well to the strike call. There were about 40,000 workers directly participating in the dispute in Leeds, about 7000 in York, 100,000 on Merseyside.[22] Most of the railway workers came out and, on average, more than eighty percent of the railway workers of the Great Western Railway, more or less everybody except the clerical and supervisory staff, were out on strike for the nine days and beyond[23] (Document 14). The Plebs League's survey of the response, published in *A Worker's History of the Great Strike* also suggests that in the vast majority of cases most of the front-line workers came out.[24] It is difficult to gain a complete picture of the rank-and-file support, but it does appear to have been extensive: most of the front-line workers came out and the railwaymen were solid.

The vast majority of strike committees and councils of action abided by the instructions of the General Council, constantly reiterated in the *British Worker*, that they must 'stand firm and keep order'.[25] This was accepted even when the General Council sought to reduce the number of permits, and when mass picketing occurred. Consequently, serious violence was rare. Indeed, the General Council noted that 'Despite the presence of armed police and the military, the workers have preserved a quiet orderliness and dignity, which the General Council urges them to maintain…',[26] although there were disturbances on London, Edinburgh, Glasgow, Plymouth, Middlesborough, Newcastle and many other towns; and the derailing of the 'Flying Scotsman', the Edinburgh-to-London express, near Newcastle on 10 May.

Nevertheless, as was the case with the Government, the local authorities were generally able to maintain some control of essential services and food-stuffs, except perhaps in some of the mining areas. Most towns appointed officers and committees to keep food and coal supplies flowing, normally drawn from their existing administrative structure. They had many volunteers to draw upon but, as previously suggested, rarely used them, either because they did not need them or because they feared the conflict that they might encourage.

The General Strike, by its very diversity and local and regional variation, presents difficulties of assessment. The Tory press raged against the revolution and the Government played upon such fears.[27] Yet there was no revolutionary threat as such, and whilst violence and conflict occurred it did not assume the seriousness so often associated with European disturbances. The fact is that the Government and the local authorities felt that they kept matters well under control while allowing the strike committees some local successes in closing down the railways and other forms of transport. They, in fact, did not need to use the large number of volunteers or make much use of military presence. For nine days Britain experienced a significant shutdown of its normal life without the Government losing control of the situation. Indeed, as the dispute continued the Government became more confident of its position, just as the TUC began to fear for the trade-union movement. In the final analysis, however, it did not matter that workers responded magnificently to the strike call, because it was a small coterie of trade-union leaders, and not the rank-and-file, who determined the outcome of the dispute.

A.J. Cook wrote of the General Strike that 'The workers acted as one. Splendid discipline. Splendid loyalty!' He then asked, 'Why was the strike called off?'[28] It is a question that has occupied the minds of historians and contemporaries alike. Cook's answer was that Jimmy Thomas and the right-wing leaders of the TUC were opposed to the strike, and sought to end it with indecent haste.[29] The Communist Party also attacked the General Council by suggesting that the calling off of the dispute was 'the greatest crime that has ever been permitted'.[30] Others have expressed similar views, encouraged partly by Jimmy Thomas's comments in the House of Commons that the strike had to be called off before 'it got out of hand'.[31] Whilst the fine detail might vary, the gist of the argument is that the General Council sought a pretext to end the dispute at the earliest opportunity. Unlike the Government, it welcomed the offer of help from Sir Herbert Samuel as the route to an honourable settlement. It negotiated with him on 7 and 8 May, and helped to produce the first version of the 'Samuel Memorandum' (Document 15), which advocated the re-organisation of the coal industry and a wage reduction for a year, but included the added device of an impartial National Wages Board to maintain a watch over the reorganisation of the industry and local wage agreements. This was shown to the miners on the following day and rejected by them in a meeting with the TUC on the 10 May, despite some suggested alterations.[32] After another fruitless meeting between the General Council and the miners on 11 May, the General Council asked Walter Citrine to contact the Prime Minister, and arranged to meet at 10 Downing Street at 12 noon the next day.[33] By 12.20pm, the strike had been called off.

This famous meeting saw the representatives of the General Council enter 10 Downing Street only on the proviso that the General Strike had been called off and without any guarantees. Baldwin talked vaguely about the 'Samuel Memorandum', and made no mention at all of the end of victimisation. Arthur Pugh and Walter Citrine, upon their return to TUC headquarters in Eccleston Square, sent telegrams to the trade unions instructing them to order the resumption of work. In a later letter, they circulated the details of the Samuel Memorandum. It was held to represent 'sufficient assurances... as to the lines upon which a settlement could be reached to justify them terminating the General Strike', a decision taken to enable negotiations to continue. The General Council later justified its position, in June, by suggesting that 'The strike was terminated for one sufficient reason only, namely that in view of the attitude of the Miners' Federation its continuance would have rendered its purpose futile'.[34]

The General Strike had come to a swift and unsatisfactory conclusion largely because the General Council believed that it could not win. It was barely committed to the dispute from the start, did not like the way in which its actions were challenging the Constitution, believed that the dispute could bleed the finances of trade unions dry, and felt that the coal miners would not compromise. It looked for an escape route, and the Samuel Memorandum seemed to provide an opportunity for an orderly retreat from conflict. When the Memorandum was not accepted by the Government, Arthur Pugh complained to Samuel that he had been misled, and Ernest Bevin and other members of the General Council felt the same, despite the fact that Samuel had made it quite clear that he was not acting on behalf of the Government, but using his good offices to help settle the dispute.[35] Obviously, the calling off of the General Strike was a disaster for the General Council, but it did not mean that the trade-union movement was set back a generation. Indeed, the trade-union movement was remarkably more successful after 1926 than it had been before.

There is no doubt that the collapse of the General Strike and the capitulation of the miners in the coal lock-out in November 1926 were devastating to the British trade-union movement, earning the General Council obloquy. The prestige of the trade-union movement certainly suffered in the short term. Yet the trade unions were not destroyed, and were still able to mount an effective check to the employers.

The main criticism of the General Council came from the communists , who maintained that the decision to call off the General Strike 'is the greatest crime that has ever been permitted, not only against the miners but against the working class of Great Britain and the whole world'.[36] A.J. Cook, the miners' leader, was similarly critical of the strike being called off without any guarantees.[37] Three points began to emerge in these criticisms: that the General Council betrayed the miners, which is debatable, that the TUC leadership was not committed to the struggle, which is correct, and that the strike was winnable, which was clearly wrong. Conflated, they imply that the General Strike was, in some way, a turning point in British trade-union history.

Martin Jacques suggests the 'watershed' or 'turning point' thesis, a view that has also been supported by Alan Bullock and Patrick Renshaw[38] (Documents 6, 7 and 8). The General Strike is seen as the last moment of a period of trade-union militancy, after which the trade unions adopted a more cautious approach to strike action as their membership declined. These views do not accord with those of Gordon Phillips, Hugh Clegg and Keith Laybourn, who maintain that the trajectory of trade union history did not change after 1926, that employers and trade unionists continued much as they had done before, and that more peaceable industrial relations had been developing before 1926 (Documents 4, 5 and 9). Indeed, strike levels had been falling from the early 1920s, and trade-union membership did begin to increase from 1933 onwards, which throws doubt on 1926 being some type of major watershed.

Notwithstanding such an assessment, it is clear that in the short run there were consequences. There was, for instance, a major debate throughout 1926 and 1927, during which the TUC attempted to stifle criticism of its actions and to produce its definitive explanation of the events leading to it calling, conducting and ending the strike (Document 17). The General Council attempted to maintain a rule of silence, although there was some comment on the democratic nature of the trade-union movement and general support for the miners at the TUC Conference at Bournemouth, 6–11 September 1926. Eventually, it rebutted the various charges made against it at a Conference of Trade Union Executives on 20 and 21 January 1927.[39] Most particularly, it suggested that it had the full powers needed to make all the decisions in the dispute, and that the miners effectively made consultation with them futile, since they would not agree to negotiations, and that the Government would have had to accept the Samuel Memorandum had the miners accepted it. Such suggestions are debatable, but the whole issue was less vitriolic than it might have been, given that it took place within the context of Government declaring its intention to take action to curb trade-union power.

The Baldwin Government also pressed forward the Trades Disputes and Trade Union Act, which came into force on 29 July 1927. It was kaleidoscopic in the interests which it brought together, and lacked real direction and coherence in its eight main clauses, three of which prohibited sympathetic strike action, demanded that trade unionists opt into paying the political levy, rather than opt out, and prevented some trade unions being connected with the TUC. Yet the impact of the 1927 Act was limited. It provoked only one or two cases in connection with sympathetic strike action before it was withdrawn in 1946, although it did reduce the number of trade unionists paying the levy for the Labour Party from 3,200,000 in 1927 to 2,000,000 in 1929.[40]

It is difficult to sustain the view that the General Strike was a turning-point in British industrial relations, even though it had some short-term consequences for the trade-union movement. The fact is that trade-union membership was falling before the strike and continued to fall, at a slower rate, until the mid-1930s. The TUC lost some credibility, but soon recovered, and the Government was not able to effect any significant ban upon sympathetic strike action.

The General Strike of 1926, the most important conflict in British industrial history, was the product of economic and social tensions in British society which saw the TUC attempting to defend the wages of its members at a time when the Government was aiming to rationalise British industry and to reduce wage costs. The conflict could have occurred at any time, but what determined that the action would take place in May 1926 were the conditions within the British coal industry.

The General Council of the TUC was reluctant to become too deeply involved in supporting the miners against wage cuts in 1925 and 1926 but, faced with the fact that it could not allow the trade-union movement to let the miners down as it had done in April 1921, it was committed to a course of action which is did not believe in. It deluded itself into thinking that its action in calling a General Strike was simply industrial action to support the miners, when in fact it was also a direct challenge to the Government and the British Constitution. The Government and the

Communist Party saw the implications of the TUC's actions even if the TUC did not. (Document 5).

The Government was well prepared for the strike, and had created an administrative structure to deal with it. Yet it soon realised that there was no revolutionary intent behind the actions of the General Council. It therefore waited for the General Council to call off the dispute, realising that without the approval of the miners the Samuel Memorandum would not provide the TUC with an escape route from conflict, nor force the Government to extend the coal-mining subsidy.

The Government's faith in the lack of commitment of the General Council was well founded. The General Council organised the strike remarkably well, given the lateness of the preparations. Yet the local organisation was not important because the decision to call off the strike was taken at the national, not the local, level. It was an action which brought upon the General Council the criticism of the trade-union movement and the Labour left, but the damage was not permanent. Trade unions lost membership and the Government introduced restrictive legislation, but by the early 1930s the trade-union movement was advancing, not retreating, and the General Strike appears to have slowed down the attack of the employers upon wages rather than speeded it up.

The General Strike may have been the subject of many marvellous myths, but the reality is that it changed little. If anything, it revealed to the General Council the limits of the trade-union movement and encouraged it also to seek more effective representation through the Labour Party. There had not been a strike of this type before, and there has not been one since. Never before or since has there been such an obvious social conflict within British society.

1927 Onwards

For whatever reason, whether or not it was the stabilisation of the economy or the fact that employers were reluctant to become embroiled in further major disputes, the number of strikes fell, as did the number of strike days lost in the late 1920s (Document 10). There were fluctuations in the level of strike activity throughout the 1930s, but at a much lower level than had previously been the case. Trade-union membership also began to increase, from 4.4 million in 1933 to 6.3 million in 1939. Trade unions also began to diversify, increasingly, under Ernest Bevin's lead, dominating the Labour Party conferences and decision-making processes in the 1930s. Doubt has been thrown upon the extent to which the trade-union movement improved its position, but there is no doubt about the recovery of the trade-union movement, even if many of its demands were aspiration rather than achievement. And in some areas, such as the securing of 'holidays with pay' in 1938, some social aspects of employment were achieved.

Conclusion

Industrial decline and unemployment were major problems for the British trade-union movement. They led to reductions in wages and major industrial conflicts, such as the General Strike, and to a major weakening of the movement. Nevertheless, one should not see the General Strike of 1926 as some type of turning point in industrial relations. It is true that trade unions were weakened by the events, and that the intensified depression of 1929–1932 did not help matters. Nonetheless, trade unions did recover, did win some social concessions in their employment rights, and were on an even keel by the late 1930s. There was also a consistency of trade-union policies throughout, with trade unions continuing to encourage negotiations with employers both before and after 1926. In a sense, one should see the inter-war years as a period when trade-union policies gradually evolved. Far from bringing the denouement of the inter-war trade-union movement, the General Strike reaffirmed, in the fullest form possible, the potential power of trade unionism within the capitalist system. By the late 1930s, the British trade-union movement was probably as powerful, industrially and politically, as it had ever been, and was firmly in control of its membership.

Documents
SECONDARY SOURCES AND INTERPRETATIONS

1 – C. Wrigley, 'Trade Unionists, Employers and the Cause of Industrial Unity and Peace, 1916–1921' in C. Wrigley and J. Shepherd (eds), *On the Move: Essays in Labour and Transport History presented to Philip Bagwell* (London, Hambledon Press, 1991), p 155

Among a significant number of trade unionists the experience of wartime cooperation with employers, combined with a distaste for the new militancy, reinforced a pre-war taste for joint committees and in the settling of industrial differences within industries without recourse to Whitehall. This tendency also revealed itself in the participation of many trade unionists, nationally and locally, in forming alliances with employers' organisations in order to propagate the cause of industrial peace and cooperation. During the period of maximum industrial and social unrest bodies such as the National Alliance of Employers and Employed [NAEE] and the Industrial League campaigned vigorously in many of Britain's industrial centres. While the trade unionists of national standing who busied themselves in these organisations were often of second or third-rate importance, leading Party figures – notably J.R. Clynes and Arthur Henderson – did bless the organisations with their efforts.

2 – Noel Whiteside, 'Social Welfare and Industrial Relations 1914–1939' in C.J. Wrigley (ed.), *A History of British Industrial Relations, Volume II: 1914–1939* (Brighton, Harvester Press, 1987), pp 233–6

The nature and strength of collective bargaining in particular industries and trades provided the foundations for varying union attitudes towards the extension of public welfare. The association between wages and welfare also influenced the development of state social policies - notably during the First World War and its immediate aftermath – thereby throwing into question the traditional assumptions about the proper demarcation between 'political' and 'industrial' spheres of activity. In other words, the division between public provision and wage bargaining became less distinct. In the post-Armistice period, both sides of industry were generally willing to broaden the sphere of industrial bargaining and to dismantle central controls, while the Coalition government, disturbed by continuing evidence of extensive social and industrial unrest sought to appease labour through the introduction of legislative solutions to their social discontents. Industrial recession and rising unemployment reversed this trend. As bargaining power diminished, so labour leaders turned increasingly to the state in order to safeguard their members' interests. Social security became established as an issue of public policy, rather than one of individual private responsibility. Within the labour movement itself, this development was reflected in increasing acceptance of central regulation at the expense of local autonomy and in rising support for political – rather than industrial – measures to protect workers' living standards. This trend therefore implied a redefinition – indeed a diminution – in the scope of industrial bargaining and a much greater desire by both sides of industry to influence the development of policies inside Whitehall. [Yet it is acknowledged that employers did not like the burden of social welfare on business.]

   The effect of interwar recession on union organisation and politics was very marked. The period saw a decline in union autonomy and the scope of collective actions and support, alongside a growing recognition that state provision was essential to protect workers' material needs. This change of policy noted by a number of historians, coincided with a drop in political mobilisation and rank-and-file militancy and the emergence of central union leadership dedicated less to the politics of industrial conflict than to cooperation between organised labour, employers and the state. This shift from the industrial to the public sphere was, however, born of union weakness not of strength and, in the longer terms, industrial impotence became reflected in political ineffectiveness. Although concessions made during the 1920s conferred substantial material benefit on working people, the hallmark of the politics of Citrine and Bevin during the 1930s was its spectacular lack of success. The TUC failed to break the hold of economic orthodoxy over the second Labour government, failed to secure the introduction of retirement pensions or the raising of the school-leaving age, failed to protect benefit rates or to promote any union policies designed to alleviate unemployment and promote industrial recovery. Even so, the importance of the 'social wage' in safeguarding working-class welfare was, by the 1930s paramount. The TUC, following the tradition established by general labour and industrial unions, was drawn into closer cooperation with the Labour Party; this alliance provided the political foundations for the programme of social reforms in the late 1940s. Union support for Beveridge's social insurance proposals must therefore be understood in terms of the changing sphere of industrial relations and the general decline in union bargaining power.

These changes signified a fundamental alteration in the ideological foundations of British trade unionism. [The article goes on to argue that the change was from working-class self-help to support for state welfare.]

3 – Steven Tolliday, 'The Failure of Mass Production Unionism in the Motor Industry, 1914–1939' in C.J. Wrigley (ed.), *A History of British Industrial Relations, Volume II: 1914–1939* (Brighton, Harvester, 1987), pp 292–5, 317–18

Conditions in the motor industry presented many problems for union recruitment. The combination of managerial hostility, high earnings and insecurity of employment made it a daunting task. Most of the unions concerned concentrated on defending their existing limited membership by traditional methods, which were often inappropriate or proved counterproductive. The AEU and the NUVB focused their demands on issues of workplace control. But these were the areas where employers were most intensely jealous of their hard-won freedom of action, and it was hard for them to defend their existing positions, let alone extend them. When the revival of union activity came in the late 1930s it centred on active piecework bargaining in the shops, accepting the rules of the game but bargaining for a bigger share of the cake. It was when the unions began to show that they could deliver the goods in the workplace that opportunities for rapid development began to open up. Once the TGWU began to make inroads on these lines inter-union rivalry acted as a powerful spur to other unions to change their approaches.

4 – Gordon Phillips, *The General Strike* (London, Weidenfeld and Nicolson, 1976), pp 293–5

Only in a very modest and unspectacular fashion, therefore, did the General Strike alter the ideas or behaviour of the union movement. It reinforced a trend towards industrial peace that was already under way, and it confirmed a long-established faith in a regulated system of voluntary collective bargaining. Its chief effect, however, was simply to change the movement's rhetorical style, the tone of its public discourse. This means that to some extent the unions presented a different and more acceptable image to the outside world. It also entailed an adjustment, more significant but more difficult to assess, in the relations of the union leadership to the rank and file...

In the end the General Strike merits historical study less for what it changed in the labour movement, than for what it revealed was unchanging. It was the product of a trade unionism which, though it seemed to contain many inconsistent features, was still too stable a compound to be transformed by so short a process. The union movement was durable in its make-up, as it revealed on this occasion, because it was predominantly defensive in its objectives, disinclined to state its purpose in ideological terms, concerned primarily with the achievement of an effective organisation and internal discipline, not with a long-term programme of social and political reconstruction. Not only was the General Strike justified by reference to these relatively unambitious standards in the first instance; it could be reckoned subsequently, on the same basis, by no means a total failure. The relations of the unions with the social system of which they were part were similarly difficult to disturb... Moreover the crisis of 1926 served to indicate how far the leaders and the members of these institutions shared, especially in the political sphere, the values of their fellow-citizens, the belief in the constitutional modes of government, in the virtues of legality and conciliatory approach to potentially disruptive social issues. Neither the grievances which had brought about the General Strike, nor the inhibitions which had limited its scope and shortened its course, were much affected by the experience of it; one or two generations later they were scarcely in evidence.

5 – Keith Laybourn, *The General Strike of 1926* (Manchester, Manchester University Press, 1993), pp 118–121

The General Strike of 1926, the most important conflict in British industrial history was a product of the economic and social tensions which had been building up in British society in the early 1920s. Although there were many factors which contributed to this conflict it is clear that it was the product of an interplay of circumstances whereby the industrial tensions in the coal industry became inflamed at a time when both the Government and the TUC were moving on a collision course over industrial policies. Whilst governments of the early 1920s were generally geared towards improving industrial relations they harboured the underlying objective of reducing wage levels, especially so after the return to the Gold Standard and the reflation of the pound in April 1925. A reluctant and conservative TUC also wished to avoid conflict but found the circumstances of the mining industry… drove it into a conflict which most of its leading figures… strove to avoid…

Once committed to supporting the miners the General Council had, however reluctantly, to face the fact that its industrial action raised political issues… The General Strike was more than simply sympathetic strike action, more than an alliance between unions directed at the coal owners, it was an attack upon the whole of British society and inevitably challenged the authority of the Baldwin Government. Circumstances beyond their control had pushed the General Council of the TUC in a direction in which it did not want to go and which it knew it could not sustain. In the end the heart of the trade union movement overruled the reservations of its leaders.

The Conservative Government saw the General Strike in constitutional terms and recognised that it could not back away from the conflict if it was to maintain any credibility. It prepared for the worst, entertaining the need for significant military involvement but soon scaled down its actions when it realised, after four or five days, that there was no revolutionary intent on the part of the General Council even if the consequences of a trade-union victory might have fundamentally altered the pattern of political control in Britain. It soon realised that its preparations were sufficient and that it was able to control the events even if transport and railways in particular had come to a complete halt. Nevertheless, given the scale of the dispute there was relatively little violence and the Government was prepared to bide its time and let the trade unions take the decision to retreat in the full knowledge that the Negotiating Committee of the TUC was progressing the Samuel Memorandum in the hope of an end to the dispute. Given that the miners were unlikely to accept it, or the Samuel Report, there was little danger that the Government would be forced to stump up another coal subsidy as it had done in July 1925…

Given the scale of the defeat and humiliation of the General Council of the TUC in 1926 it is difficult not to believe that the British trade union was not damaged by it. Certainly there was some immediate loss of support, its funds were depleted and its leaders under suspicion. Nonetheless, it recovered quickly. The trade union movement does not appear to have been less militant, even if the level of industrial conflict did fall in 1927 and 1928. The fact is that the General Council had been seeking alternatives to industrial conflict well before 1926 and its objective of industrial peace through a unified movement continued, even though it had come to accept the limitations of an industrial alliance after 1926. Thus, it is difficult to view the General Strike as a watershed in British industrial relations.

6 – M. Jacques, 'Consequences of the General Strike' in J. Skelley (ed.),
The General Strike, May 1926 **(London, Lawrence and Wishart, 1976),**
p 375

These tendencies did not, however, become decisive until after the General Strike. Thus between 1921 and 1926 the mood of key sections of industrial workers remained militant, combative and cohesive. At the same time, the trade union movement was, within limits, willing and prepared to fight. Thus while the appearance of mass unemployment had an important impact on the trade union movement it did not itself mark a decisive turning point.

7 – Alan Bullock, *The Life and Times of Ernest Bevin, Volume I: Trade Union Leader 1881–1940* **(London, Heinemann, 1960), p 345**

The events of 1926 showed Bevin and the other union leaders that there were limits not only to their power but also to the use they could make of it unless they were prepared to risk being carried much further than they meant to go. Industrial action on a national scale was bound to have political implications whether intended or not. [In essence, Bullock's view is that the unions did not abandon the strike weapon but used it more cautiously.]

8 – Patrick Renshaw, *The General Strike* **(London, Eyre Methuen, 1975),**
p 250

[The General Strike was a dividing point between] the turbulent class politics of the immediate post-war period and the relative quiescent acceptance by Labour of mass unemployment in the late 1920s and the 1930s.

9 – **Hugh A. Clegg,** *A History of British Trade Unions since 1889, Volume II: 1911–1933* (Oxford, Oxford University Press, 1985), pp 421, 528

In 1925 the unions had feared a general attack by the employers on their wages and conditions. The aftermath of the general strike might have given the employers a convenient opportunity to carry through such an attack; but it did not happen. No considerable groups of workers, apart from the miners, suffered an extension of agreed working hours either in 1926 or 1927. The major reduction in wages outside coalmining in 1926 was in railways, due to adjustments under the cost-of-living sliding scale. In 1927 coalmining wages fell again as district minimum percentage additions were reduced under the agreements signed at the end of the lockout… Without the changes in miners' pay, the overall index of wage rates would have remained almost stable through 1926 and 1927.

Stability in wages was due to general economic stability. The employers did not attack because they did not have to attack…

Most firms in most industries were not facing disastrous losses, nor even the prospect of disastrous losses. The worst hit firms might decide that they must have a reduction in pay in order to stay in business. Their colleagues, or enough of them, might agree that a reduction in labour costs would improve their prospects too, so that negotiations with the unions could begin. However, when the unions proved reluctant to make concessions, the employers would have to consider the possibility of a lockout. Those who were not hard pressed and in no immediate danger of running at a considerable loss might have no strong incentive to vote in favour of a course which threatened them with heavy losses in the immediate future. The conditions of 1930–3 were unfavourable to unity among employers.

PRIMARY EVIDENCE AND INFORMATION

10 – Number of strikes (or lock-outs), strikers and days lost as a result of strikes in the United Kingdom, 1918–39 (various sources)

Year	Number of Strikes	Number of Strikers	Number of Days Lost
1918	1,165	1,116,000	5,875,000
1919	1,352	2,591,000	34,969,000
1920	1,607	1,932,000	26,568,000
1921	763	1,801,000	85,872.000
1922	576	552,000	19,850,000
1923	628	405,000	10,672,000
1924	710	613,000	8,424,000
1925	604	441,000	7,952,000
1926	323	2,734,000	162,233,000
1927	308	108,000	1,174,000
1928	302	124,000	1,388,000
1929	431	533,000	8,287,000
1930	422	307,000	4,399,000
1931	420	490,000	6,983,000
1932	389	379,000	6,488,000
1933	357	136,000	1,072,000
1934	471	134,000	959,000
1935	553	271,000	1,955,000
1936	818	316,000	1,829,000
1937	1129	597,000	3,413,000
1938	875	275,000	1,334,000
1939	94	337,000	1,356,000

11 – General Council of the TUC 'Proposal for Co-ordinated Action', put to the trade unions on 30 April and adopted 1 May, TUC General Council, *The Mining Crisis and the National Strike* (London, TUC, June 1926)

1. Scope

The Trades Union Congress General Council and the Miners' Federation of Great Britain having been unable to obtain a satisfactory settlement of the matters in dispute in the coalmining industry, and the Government and the mineowners having forced a lockout, the General Council, in view of the need for co-ordinated action on the part of the affiliated unions in defence of the policy laid down by the General Council of the Trades Union Congress directs as follows:

Trades and undertakings to cease work

Except as hereinafter provided, the following trades and undertakings shall cease work as and when required by the General Council:

Transport, including all affiliated unions connected with Transport ie railways, sea transport...

Printing trades, including the Press.

Productive industries. (a) Iron and steel. (b) Metal and heavy chemical group. Including all metal workers and other workers who are engaged, or may be engaged, in installing alternative plant to take the place of coal.

Building trade. All workers engaged on building, except such as are employed definitely in housing and hospital work... shall cease work.

Electricity and gas... Trade unions connected with the supply of electricity and gas shall co-operate with the object of ceasing to supply power. The Council request that the Executives of the Trade Unions concerned shall meet at once with a view to formulating common policy.

Sanitary services. The General Council direct that sanitary services be continued.

Health and food services. The General Council recommend that there should be no interference in regard to these, and that the Trade Union concerned should do everything in their power to organise the distribution of milk and food for the whole population.

With regard to hospitals, clinics, convalescent homes, sanatoria, infant welfare centres, maternity homes, nursing homes, schools, the General Council direct that every affiliated union take every opportunity to ensure that food, milk, medical and surgical supplies shall be efficiently provided.

2. Trade Union discipline

... (b) The General Council recommend that the actual calling out of the workers shall be left to the unions, and instructions should only be issued by the accredited representatives of the unions participating in the dispute.

3. Trades Councils

The work of the Trades Councils, in conjunction with the local officers of the trade unions actually participating in the dispute, shall be to assist in carrying out the foregoing provisions (ie stoppage of work in various trades and undertakings, and the exceptions thereto), and they shall be charged with the responsibility of organising the trade unionists in dispute in the most effective manner for the preservation of peace and order...

6. Procedures

(a) These proposals shall be immediately considered by the Executive of the Trade Unions concerned in the stoppage, who will at once report as to whether they will place their powers in the hands of the General Council and carry out the instructions which the General Council may issue from time to time concerning the necessary action and the conduct of the dispute.

(b) And, further, that the Executive of all other affiliated unions are asked to report at once as to whether they will place their powers in the hands of the General Council and carry out the instructions of the General Council from time to time, both regarding the conduct of the dispute and financial assistance.

A. Pugh, Chairman
Walter M. Citrine, Acting Secretary

12 – The BBC broadcast of Prime Minister Baldwin, Saturday 8 May 1926, as reported in the *Daily Express*, 10 May 1926

What it the issue for which the Government is fighting? It is fighting because while the negotiations were still in progress the TUC ordered a general strike, presumably to force Parliament and the community to heed its will.

With that object the TUC has declared that the railways shall not move and that the unloading of ships shall stop, and that no news shall reach the public. The supply of electricity, the transportation of food supplies of the people have been interrupted.

The TUC declare that this is merely an industrial dispute, but their method of helping the miners is to affect the community.

Can there be a more direct attack upon the community than that a body not elected by the voters of the country, without consulting even trade unionists, and in order to impose conditions never yet defined should disrupt the life of the nation and try to starve it into submission?

I wish to make it as clear as I can that the Government is not fighting to lower the standard of living of the miners or any other class of workers.

My whole desire is to maintain the standard of living of every worker, and I am ready to press the employers to make every sacrifice to this end, consistent with keeping industry in its proper working order.

This is the Government's position. The general strike must be called off absolutely and without reserve. The mining dispute can then be settled...

I am a man of peace. I am longing and working and praying for peace. But I will not surrender the safety and security of the British Constitution.

You have placed me in power eighteen months ago by the largest majority afforded to any party for many years.

Have I done anything to forfeit that confidence? Cannot you trust me to ensure a square deal for the parties and secure even justice between man and man?

13 – The TUC, 'Where We Stand', *British Worker*, 10 May 1926

It is being persistently stated that Mr Ramsay MacDonald, Mr Herbert Samuel, Mr Arthur Cook and other Trade Union leaders have been engaged in an attempt to re-open negotiations with a view to ending the General Stoppage.

The General Council wish it to be clearly understood that there is no truth in this assertion.

No official or unofficial overtures have been made to the Government by any individual or group of individuals, either with or without the sanction of the General Council. Complete control of all negotiations is vested in the General Council, who have had no direct communication with the Government since they sent their emphatic letter of protest against the Cabinet's wanton action in wrecking the peace discussions that were proceeding.

The position of the General Council may be stated in simple and unequivocal terms. They are ready at a moment to enter into preliminary discussions regarding the withdrawal of the lock-out notices and ending in the General Stoppages and the resumption of negotiations for an honourable settlement of the Mining Dispute. These preliminary discussions must be free from any condition.

The Government must remember, and the public are asked to remember, that the General Stoppages took place as a result of the action of the Cabinet in breaking off peace discussions and issuing their ultimatum, using as their excuse the unauthorised action of the printing staff of a London newspaper. The responsibility of the present grave situation rests entirely upon the Cabinet. Even the newspapers concerned admit it to be true 'that when the negotiations broke down the trade union representatives knew nothing of the stoppage of the *Daily Mail*'.

It is therefore merely fantastic for the Prime Minister to pretend that the Trade Unions are engaged in an attack upon the Constitution of the Country. Every instruction issued by the General Council is evidence of their determination to maintain the struggle strictly on the basis of an industrial dispute. They have ordered every member taking part to be exemplary in his conduct and not to give any cause for police interference.

The General Council struggled hard for peace. They are anxious that an honourable peace shall be secured as soon as possible.

They are not attacking the Constitution. They are not fighting the community. They are defending the mine workers against the mine owners.

14 – National Union of Railwaymen, *General Strike News Bulletin*, **11 May 1926, a copy of which is in the National Museum of Labour History, NMLH/GS/SCB/006**

[It begins with an appeal, from C.T. Cramp, for union members to remain steadfast, then lists brief reports from 116 centres, a few of which are indicated.]

To the Branch and Strike Committee Secretaries.

A telegraphic message in the following terms was circulated to all Branches and Strike Committees this morning.

'EVERYTHING GOING WELL IN SPITE OF ALL ATTEMPTS TO MISLEAD. IGNORE ANY INSTRUCTIONS OTHER THAN FROM THIS OFFICE. REMAIN SOLID. ALL OUR MEMBERS WILL RESOLUTELY REFUSE TO BE ASSOCIATED WITH ANY ACTS OF WRECKAGE AND DESTRUCTION'

We have now entered on the second week of the Strike, and we are stronger today than ever we were; stronger not only by experience of the loyalty of our members, but by the fact that not a single instance of deviation by any centre can be found.

The reports that so many thousands of Railwaymen are at work should be entirely ignored. Those who are at work belong to the Administrative Staff and not to the Rank and File. Those who belong to the Railway Trade Unions have ceased work practically to a man, and can be relied to remain solid to the end, notwithstanding the efforts being made by the Railway Companies to induce the men to return to work. Personal letters have been addressed to members of staff, and these have, in a number of instances, been followed up by telegrams of mysterious origin, instructing them to report for duty at a certain time. This indicates the efforts being made to mislead our men.

Rumours have also been circulated to the effect that no members of the Supervisory and Clerical Staffs will be reinstated until sanctioned by the General manager. This is obviously another attempt to mislead the men and coerce them to return to work. IT CANNOT BE TOO STRONGLY EMPHASISED THAT THESE RUMOURS SHOULD BE TREATED WITH THE CONTEMPT THEY DESERVE.

THE FORCES AGAINST YOU ARE DISPLAYING WEAKNESS BY THESE INSIDIOUS ATTEMPTS TO DECEIVE. IGNORE THEM, AND REMAIN FIRM AND LOYAL TO YOUR UNIONS.

'KEEP STEADFAST'

C.T. Cramp (signed)

Branch	Nature of Letter or Telegram
Slades Green	All solid.
Merthyr Tydfil	Position very firm – complete stoppage.
Cudworth	Still firm and in good heart.
Immingham	We are OK here.
Wymondham	Solidarity maintained
South Milford	Position firmer than eve. Members solid.
Halifax	Position unchanged – position solid. Unparalleled enthusiasm.
Manchester	Manchester 12 maintaining 100% solidarity.
Tyne Dock 1	Stoppage 100%.
Garforth	Every member of branch out.
Newport (Mon.)	All solid and quiet.
Wakefield	All men standing firm.

[and many others]

15 – The 'Samuel Memorandum' and related correspondence, in the TUC Archives and many local trade union collections, and the *British Worker*, 13 May 1926; also in the National Museum of Labour History, NMLH/GS/SC13/003

A. Pugh
President, General Council
Trades Union Congress   May 12th, 1926

Dear Mr Pugh,

At the outcome of the conversations which I have had with your Committee, I attach a memorandum embodying the conclusions that have been reached.

I have made it clear to your Committee from the outset that I have been acting entirely on my own initiative, have received no authority from the Government, and can give no assurance on their behalf.

I am of opinion that the proposals embodied in the Memorandum are suitable for adoption and are likely to promote a settlement of the differences in the Coal Industry.

I shall strongly recommend their acceptance by the Government when the negotiations are renewed.

Yours sincerely,

Herbert Samuel (signed)

Sir Herbert Samuel
London   12 May 1926

Dear Sir,

The General Council have carefully considered your letter of to-day and the memorandum attached to it, concurred in your opinion that it offers a basis on which the negotiations upon the conditions of the Coal Industry can be renewed.

They are taking the necessary measures to terminate the General Strike, relying upon public assurances of the Prime Minister as to the steps that we should follow. They assume that during the resumed negotiations the subsidy will be renewed and that the lockout notices to the Miners will be immediately withdrawn.

Yours faithfully

Arthur Pugh, Chairman (signed)   Walter Citrine, Acting Secretary (signed)

Memorandum

1. The negotiations upon the conditions of the coal industry should be resumed, the subsidy being renewed for such reasonable period as may be required for that purpose.

2. Any negotiations are unlikely to be successful unless they provide the means of settling disputes in the industry other than conferences between the mine-owners and they alone. A National Wages board should, therefore, be established which would include representatives of the two parties with a neutral element and an independent Chairman. The proposals in this direction tentatively made in the Report of the Royal Commission should be pressed and the powers of the proposed Board enlarged.

3. The parties of the Board should be entitled to raise before it any points they consider relevant to the issues under discussion.

4. There should be no revision of the previous wage rates unless there are sufficient assurances that the measures of reorganisation proposed by the Commission will be effectively adopted. A Committee should be established as proposed by the Prime Minister on which representatives of the men should be included, whose duty it should be to co-operate with the Government in the preparation of the legislative and administrative measures that are required. The same Committee, or alternatively, the National Wages Board, should assure itself that the necessary steps, so far as they relate to matters within the industry, are not neglected or unduly postponed.

5. After these points have been agreed and the Mines National Wages Board has considered every practicable means of meeting such immediate financial difficulties as exist, it may, if that course is to be found to be absolutely necessary, proceed to the preparation of a wage agreement.

6. Any such agreement should

(i)   if practicable, be on simpler lines than those hitherto followed.

(ii) not adversely affect in any way the wages of the lowest paid men.

(iii) fix reasonable wages below which the wage of no class of labour, for a normal customary week's work, should be reduced in any circumstance.

7. Measures should be adopted to prevent the recruitment of new workers, over the age of 18 years, into the industry if unemployed miners are available.

8. Workers who are displaced as a consequence of the closing of uneconomic collieries should be provided for by

(a) The transfer of such men as may be mobile, with the Government assistance that may be required, as recommended in the Report of the Royal Commission.

(b) The maintenance, for such period as may be fixed, of those who cannot be transferred, and for whom alternative employment cannot be found, this maintenance to compose in addition to the existing rate of unemployment paid under the Unemployment Insurance Act, of such an amount as may be agreed. A contribution should be made by treasury to cover the additional sums so disbursed.

(c) The rapid construction of new houses to accommodate transferred workers. The Trades Union Congress will facilitate this by consultation and co-operation with all those concerned.

16 – Labour Report of the Great Western Railway to the Board from Sir Felix Pole, 21 May 1926, PRO, RAIL 786, 6

[The report indicated that 81 percent of Great Western staff were on strike throughout the General Strike, that 5620 staff were enrolled at Paddington and that 2234 were used, with 2200 special constables used throughout the system. From the first day of the strike volunteers were also trained as signalmen being given two three-hour lectures.]

A text book specifically prepared for such an emergency was used.

Altogether 252 volunteers were passed in effect to take charge of signal boxes and over 200 were sent to different boxes.

The London and North Eastern Railway Company indicated that they were seriously short of signalmen and 28 of the men trained in Great Western classes were supplied.

All volunteer signalmen performed their duties satisfactorily...

Seven special trains were arranged for the conveyance of ocean passenger traffic and moved between London and Plymouth and all requirements were satisfactorily made.

Special scheduled milk trains were run to London each day and the return of empty churns to the provinces was satisfactorily dealt with. Prior to the strike an assurance was given to the Government that the company would do everything possible to handle milk traffic for London but, as an additional safeguard, the Government arranged for a large number of lorries to be sent into the country so as to be available in the event of any failure. It was soon demonstrated that the motor lorries were not required and they were kept back and utilised for other work...

Freight Trains

24 hours to 9 pm	Number of Trains	Total Mileage	% of Normal Mileage
4 May	101	4035	6.00
5 May	8	275	0.38
6 May	17	573	0.79
7 May	30	1216	1.67
8 May	47	2099	2.88
9 May	53	1569	14.33
10 May	93	3321	5.35
11 May	134	4677	6.41
12 May	128	4226	5.79
13 May	138	4385	6.01
14 May	157	5652	7.74

17 – General Council, *Report of the Conference of Executives of Affiliated Unions*, 25 June 1926 (London, TUC, 1926)

[The TUC defended itself against charges of failure and betrayal. It blamed the failure upon the intransigence of the leaders of the MFGB.]

The General Council could not follow the Miners' Executive in the policy of mere negation. Such a course would have been to permit the splendid response of the sympathetic strike to evaporate by a process of attrition, which would have brought the unions to a position of bankruptcy, would have undermined the morale of the membership, and thus have destroyed their capacity to resist attempts that might be made to impose adverse conditions and general discrimination against the active membership when the industries directly engaged in the strike resumed their operations.

The Council were satisfied that, however long they continued the strike, they would still be in the same position so far as the attitude of the Miners' Executive were concerned, and consequently the Council was not justified in permitting the unions to continue their sacrifice for another day.

The strike was terminated for one sufficient reason only, namely that in view of the attitude of the Miners' Federation its continuance would have rendered its purpose futile.

18 – TUC General Council, *Report of Proceedings at a Special Conference of Executives,* **20 January 1927, statement by Ernest Bevin**

With regard to the preparation for the strike, there was no preparation until April, 27 (1926), and I do not want anyone to go away from this conference under the impression that the General Council had any particular plan to run the movement. In fact the General Council did not sit down to draft the plans until they were called together on April 27th, and it is better for everybody to know the task was thrown upon us from April 27th to May 1st, and when that task is understood you will be able to appreciate not the little difficulties but the wonderful response and organisation we had.

Notes on Chapter 5

1 C. Wrigley, 'Trade Unionists, Employers and the Cause of Industrial Unity and Peace, 1916-1921', in C. Wrigley and J. Shepherd (eds), *On the Move: Essays in Labour and Transport History Presented to Philip Bagwell* (London, Hambledon Press, 1991).

2 *Yorkshire Factory Times,* 13 August 1925.

3 R.R. James, *Memoirs of a Conservative: J.C.C. Davidson Memoirs and Papers 1910–1937* (London, Weidenfeld and Nicolson, 1969), ch. 8.

4 TUC, Standing Orders, 1921.

5 TUC , Report, 1924.

6 *Report on the Royal Commission on the Coal Industry 1925* (London, HMSO, Cmd 2600, 1926), p xi, 232–7.

7 A. Mason, 'The Government and the General Strike', *International Review of Social History* 14, 1968.

8 Public Record Office, Cabinet Papers, Cab 81 (26).

9 Emile Burns, *The General Strike, May 1926: Trades Council in Action* (London, Labour Research Department, 1926).

10 On 11 May 500,000 copies were produced in London, 40,000 in Cardiff, 30,000 in Glasgow and 70,000 in Manchester.

11 Interview with Mr Skinner, a retired power worker who worked at a power station in Barnsley during the General Strike, conducted by Keith Laybourn in 1979; *Illustrated London News,* 15 May 1926.

12 Public Record Office, Cab 29/260 ST (24) 23rd Meeting, 14, Cab 27/331 S.T. Bull, 10 May 1926.

13 *Illustrated London News,* 8 May 1926; *The Sphere,* 8 May 1926.

14 James, *Memoirs of a Conservative,* p 242, quoting from J.C.C. Davidson's draft memoirs.

15 *British Gazette,* 13 May 1926.

16 Public Record Office, RAIL 786, 6.

17 Burns, *The General Strike, May 1926.*

18 *Ibid.*, ch. 4.
19 *Ibid.*, ch. 4.
20 *Ibid.*, p 76.
21 *Ibid.*, p 76; J. Maclean, 'The 1926 General Strike in Lanarkshire' (London, Pamphlet 65, Our History, CPGB), p 10. The Lanarkshire Joint Committee of the Council of Action had contact with 23 councils of action in Lanarkshire and was connected with the General Council of the Scottish Trades Union Congress, which had overall control of the General Strike in Scotland.
22 Hills, York, p 14; Baines and Bean, 'Merseyside', pp 248–51.
23 J.H. Porter, 'Devon and the General Strike, 1926', *International Review of Social History* 23, 3, 1978, p 355; PRO, RAIL 786, 6 and 7 indicates this in the General Managers' reports and the Great Western Railway Bulletin.
24 R.W. Postgate, Ellen Wilkinson and J.F. Horrabin (eds), *A Workers' History of the Great Strike* (London, Blackfriars Press, 1927), pp 28–32.
25 *British Worker*, 5 May 1926.
26 *Ibid.*
27 *British Gazette*, 6 May 1926; *Daily Express*, 10 May 1926.
28 Cook, *The Nine Days*, pp 17–18.
29 *Ibid.*, pp 18–24.
30 *Workers' Bulletin*, 13 May 1926.
31 *Hansard*, 13 May 1926.
32 Citrine, *Men and Work*, pp 144–5; General Council, *Mining Dispute*, (London, TUC, 1927), p 21.
33 Citrine, 'Mining Crisis and the National Strike, 11 May 1926'; Citrine, *Men at Work*, pp 200–1.
34 TUC General Council, *Report to the Conference of the Executive of Affiliated Unions*, June 25, 1926 (London, TUC, 1926), p 26.
35 Samuel Papers (House of Lords Record Office) A /66, Pugh to Samuel, 18 May 1926; *Observer*, 23 May 1926.
36 *Workers' Bulletin*, 13 May 1926.
37 Cook, *Nine Days*, p 23.
38 M. Jacques, 'Consequences of the General Strike' in J. Skelley (ed.), *The General Strike, 1926* (London, Lawrence and Wishart, 1976), pp 375–7; A. Bullock, *The Life and Times of Ernest Bevin, Vol. I: Trade Union Leader 1881–1940* (London, Heinemann, 1960), p 345; P. Renshaw, *The General Strike* (London, Eyre Methuen, 1975), p 250.
39 TUC General Council, *Report of the Proceedings at a Special Conference of Trade Union*, 20–21 January 1927 (London, TUC, 1927), pp 4–5, 21–7, 42–3, 45.
40 Labour Party Conference, *Annual Report 1929* (London, Labour Party, 1929), p 92.

Chapter 6

The Reaction to Fascism at Home and Abroad in the 1930s and the Politics of Appeasement 1938–9

Introduction

Hitler's assumption of power in Germany in January 1933 sent political reverberations throughout the world. Harry Pollitt, of the Communist Party of Great Britain (CPGB), put it bluntly when he stated that 'The proletariat suffered a terrific defeat as a result of the triumph of Fascism in Germany'.[1] The Comintern (or Third International) declared national and international communist organisations would work with other reformist socialist parties, who they previously referred to as 'social fascists', in order to form a united front against fascism. This was turned into a popular front against fascism, involving non-socialist parties in 1935. Mussolini's invasion of Ethiopia in the mid-1930s and the invasion of Spain by General Franco and fascist organisations on 19 July 1936 heightened further the fear that fascism would provoke war. This eventually came about as Hitler expanded eastward into Austria, Czechoslovakia and Poland in 1938 and 1939, forcing Britain to declare war on Germany on 3 September 1939.

There are therefore three major debates associated with the rise of fascism in Britain and Europe in the 1930s, as well as numerous sub-debates. The first focuses upon the British Union of Fascists (BUF), and asks why it failed to become a mass party? The second deals with the Spanish Civil War and poses the question why did the British do so little about the Spanish Civil War? The third concerns the policy of appeasement and asks the twin questions why did Chamberlain adopt appeasement and why did it fail to prevent war?

The BUF was formed in October 1932, but it is difficult to see how it would have attracted any attention had it not been for the support of Sir Oswald Mosley. A prominent politician in both the Conservative and Labour Parties in the 1920s, Mosley had formed the New Party *en route* to forming the BUF. Invariably, fascist movements have taken on the characteristics of their leaders. Indeed, it was Mosley who gave the BUF ideas, and focused its activities on the economic renaissance of Britain, Empire and increased social unity through public service related to the perceived needs of the British nation (Documents 10–15). His ideas in these areas had first emerged at the 1918 general election (Document 10), were developed further in the mid-1920s (Documents 11 and 12), and were distilled in the Mosley Memorandum of 1930 and the Mosley Manifesto which appeared at the end of the year – with their battery of social policies to reduce unemployment and increase economic demand (Document 12). Mosley lectured about 200 times a year for the BUF between 1933 and 1937, including being the main speaker at the infamous Olympia meeting on 7 June 1934, in which there was conflict between the BUF on the one hand, and on the other the CPGB, the Jewish community and other anti-fascists (Document 3, 16, 17 and 18). Indeed, without Mosley, who sought to be its great authoritarian leader, if not dictator, there would have been no fascist movement of any significance in Britain. When he became less active in the movement, from 1937 onwards, its limited impact began to wane. But was the failure of British fascism simply a product of a failed leadership?

Many explanations have been offered as to why British fascism failed when contrasted with its European counterparts. John Stevenson and Chris Cook suggest that it was because of the stability of British society and the reaction to the violence associated with conflict between the CPGB and the BUF (Document 1). Others have suggested it was because the movement was alien to British society, that it emerged into an improving, not a worsening, economic situation and because it was unable to tap into a working-class support already very much tied up by the Labour Party and the trade unions. There certainly seems to have been no obvious niche for fascism, and its membership seems to have been drawn thinly from across a wide range of social backgrounds, although there was a strong middle-class and military presence in the leadership (Documents 2 and 19). It may have been its anti-semitism which made the difference, although opinion is varied about whether or not such views won or lost it support (Document 2). As it is, Mosley claimed not to be antisemitic in his autobiography, *My Life* (1967), although there is evidence that he did take an anti-semitic stance between 1934 and 1937, and that he permitted into the party such figures as William Joyce (later Lord Haw Haw) and Mick Clarke, who were determinedly so (Documents 16 and 18). Indeed, the fascists and the Jews clashed violently, most obviously at Olympia on 7 June 1934 and in the Battle of Cable Street, in the East End of London, in early October 1936, after which the Public Order Act was passed, imposing controls upon marches and public demonstrations (Documents 3, 17 and 18).

Whatever the reasons for the failure of British fascism – whether it be one of leadership, circumstances or policies – it is clear that certain factors cannot be ignored. Most obviously, the party did come late, and was thrust into a stable political situation where the National Government had been returned with 529 MPs out of a possible 625 in the October 1931 general election. There was no serious challenge to the National Government, and the economic situation was improving by the mid-1930s. Mosley himself felt that the 1936 Public Order Act was the decisive factor, since it banned the wearing of military or semi-military uniforms, and that the Second World War made it impossible for his fascist organisation to continue. One might also reflect that Mosley lacked the sticking power required to do well in British politics, moving from one political party to another. A.J.P. Taylor assessed him memorably when he wrote that

> Mosley was, in fact, a highly gifted playboy. From the moment he modelled himself on Mussolini he resembled nothing so much as an actor touring the provinces in a play which someone else had made a success in London. Watching newsreels of Mosley on the march through the East End recalls the memory of another Londoner. Oswald Mosley aspired to be The Great Dictator. Sir Charles Chaplin played the role better.[2]

The Spanish Civil War was obviously vital in all these developments, but has raised its own questions about the British reaction. Why did the British Labour movement not give fuller support? Why was the National Government able to ignore the plight of the Republican Government of Spain? And what was the attitude of the British public? Evidence suggests that the support for the Spanish Republican Government far outweighed that for Franco and the Spanish Fascists amongst the British public at large. The Spanish Aid Committee, the relief of Basques refugees, the widespread showing of films favouring the Republican perspective, the provision of medical relief all testify to the support for the Republican Government being far in excess of that for the Fascists. Nevertheless, historians have divided as to the extent of that commitment. Jim Fyrth, in his *The Signal was Spain* and K.W. Watkins, in *Britain Divided*, suggest that there was strong public support and rank-and file sympathy for the Spanish Republican side, although Watkins does note the deep right-left split. This contrasts with George Orwell's pessimistic assumption, in *Homage to Catalonia* (1938) that the British working class let their brethren in Spain die without offering them any significant support.

Both extreme views – overwhelming support and a marked lack of interest – tend to exaggerate the reality of war in their own particular directions. The former exaggerates the power of a Labour movement in a political environ-ment overwhelmingly dominated by Stanley Baldwin, Neville Chamberlain and a National Government with a very substantial political majority. In such as situation it suited the National Government to support a non-intervention policy for the international community, ignoring the blatant disregard of it by some countries, particularly as Chamberlain had no wish to support the socialist and communist Republican Government of Spain. The fact that the Labour Party accepted non-intervention for the first year also allowed it to ignore some of the sensitive differences of opinion to subside (Document 4). The latter view ignores the immense humanitarian aid that was given, and underestimates the problems faced by the British Labour movement. Indeed, it is clear that there were pressing reasons why the British Labour Party and the trade unions were hesitant to become too involved.

One reason for this is that the Labour Party did not wish to associate itself with the CPGB, which it felt wished to use it to gain access to mass support for the united and popular fronts. This had been Labour's policy throughout the inter-war years. They therefore opposed the formation of the British Battalion of the International Brigade by the CPGB.

For the trade unions, the issue was rather more complex. The fact is that in some key unions, such as Ernest Bevin's Transport and General Workers' Union, there was a significant problem, in that the Liverpool dockers were Catholic and opposed to the rumoured murders of Catholic priests in Spain (Document 4). The union would have been deeply divided had Bevin's union done more than offer about £1000 of humanitarian aid. The details of this are presented in recent work by Tom Buchanan (Documents 4). Neverthe-less, many unions and trades councils appear to have spoken in favour of the Republican Government in Spain (Document 20). Yet in the end, the Spanish Civil War proved to be something of a political *cul de sac*, sidelined by the non-intervention policy of the British and French Governments, and ending with victory for Franco and the fascists at the beginning of April 1939.[3]

Yet Hitler's ambitions culminated in the Second World War. With the expansionist policy of 'Lebensraum' (the creation of living space in Europe for the German people), Hitler looked to the east to expand in Austria, Czechoslovakia and Poland. Emphasising the strong German presence in Austria, and following the Austrian President's order not to oppose the Germans, Hitler was able to announce the *Anschluss* on 13 March 1938, when Germany absorbed Austria into the 'Greater Germany'. Neville Chamberlain, the British Prime Minister, does not seem to have been overly perturbed at this development, but was concerned about German claims in Czechoslovakia. Britain had promised France that she would protect the borders of Czechoslovakia, but Hitler demanded that the large German com-munity, particularly in the Sudetan areas, would be allowed to vote on whether or not to join Germany or to remain within Czechoslovakia. He announced a deadline of 1 October 1938 for agreement on this. Chamberlain, after a round a meetings which saw him make three trips to see Hitler in September 1938, eventually conceded to Hitler's demands, at the end of September 1938, in the infamous Munich Agreement. A year later, however, in September 1939, Britain declared war on Germany because of the German invasion of Poland.

The great concern of British politicians was how to deal with Hitler's expansionist activities. The British armed forces were weak, and it did not seem likely that the League of Nations would be able to act in concert to restrain Hitler. Indeed, it had blatantly failed to prevent Italy's invasion of Abyssinia.

Realistically, there were only three alternative actions that might maintain peace: to seek collective security through the League of Nations, to form an alliance with powers opposed to the German and fascists states, or to pursue appeasement. The first was instantly rejected. Indeed Neville Chamberlain asked the question, in March 1938: 'What country in Europe today if threatened by a large Power can rely upon the League of Nations for protection?' His answer was 'None'.[4] The second seemed unlikely for, whilst Britain had an alliance with France, Chamberlain was unwilling to develop an Anglo-Soviet alliance (Document 5). That left appeasement.

Chamberlain's pursuit of appeasement has, of course, been subject to detailed scrutiny. At one time, it was suggested by Michael Foot and the other authors of *The Guilty Men* (London, 1940), that Chamberlain had stumbled into war because he naively believed that Hitler could be appeased. Instead of facing up to Hitler, he gave him everything he asked for and thus, ironically, hastened the onset of war. Keith Feiling attempted a modest defence of Chamberlain from such accusations in *The Life of Neville Chamberlain* (1946). Since then, there have been mixed responses to Chamberlain. Martin Gilbert and Richard Gott were critical of his action in *The Appeasers* (1963),[5] but in a later book, *The Roots of Appeasement*,[6] Gilbert was more considerate of his 'honourable quest' to maintain peace (Document 8). Indeed, since the late 1960s the availability of new records has led to the defence of Chamberlain, suggesting that he was far from being naive and cowardly, that appeasement was the only realistic policy available to him and that it was widely supported by the British public.[7] David Dilks has been foremost in defending Chamberlain's reputation in this respect (Document 9) suggesting that he did the best possible, given that Britain needed time to build up a defence capability, and that he was prepared to give an undertaking to defend Poland.

More recently, however, these revisionist view have been challenged. Ian Colvin, for instance, has suggested that Chamberlain was naive in his personal diplomacy (Document 7). His problem is that in pursuing appeasement he ignored the other alternatives that might have prevented war. Richard Cockett goes even further, and suggests that Chamberlain manipulated the 'free press' in such a way as to give the impression that both the Government and the nation were united in support of appeasement, when neither was (Document 6). R.A.C. Parker has gone even further in suggesting that Chamberlain ruled out alternatives to appeasement that might have secured peace (Document 5).

No doubt the debate about Chamberlain's actions and motives will continue. What seems more certain is that British fascism failed to develop, largely because the political and economic situation it faced in the 1930s did not provide the type of political instability which had given rise to fascism in Italy, Germany and Spain. What seems equally certain is that the National Government run by Baldwin and Chamberlain marginalised the Spanish Civil War, and that even a generally supportive British Labour movement was hampered by internal divisions which did not allow it to go much beyond providing a limited amount of humanitarian aid. Indeed, Orwell is perhaps correct in suggesting that the British Labour movement did not help their brethren in Spain with so much as a single strike, even if they were generally supportive of the Spanish Republican Government.

Documents
SECONDARY SOURCES AND INTERPRETATIONS

1 – John Stevenson and Chris Cook, *The Slump* (London, Jonathan Cape, 1977), pp 216–17

The history of the BUF requires some analysis of its central figure. It is difficult to conceive of a fascist movement of any significance at all in Britain without Mosley's leadership. He provided it with drive, intelligence and powerful oratorical skill. But his weaknesses contributed to the failures of the movement. Impulsive, arrogant and ambitious, he was unable to play the waiting game which proved so successful to some of the Continental dictators in their search for power. His action in founding the New Party showed his failure to appreciate the resilience of British institutions and political allegiances in the face of depression. His shift to an openly fascist stance reaped some dividends but also lost him valuable support...

British fascism was almost a non-starter. Anti-semitism had only a minor appeal to the British electorate and the pre-conditions for a breakdown of normal government were absent. British fascism was not only killed by the war, it was weakening both in the provinces and in the capital by the late thirties. Mosley could still command a sizeable audience and retained some popularity as an orator and an unconventional politician, but these attributes were besides the point. Neither through parliamentary means nor through less conventional methods could the fascists achieve success in 1939. Nor at any point had it been very likely that they would.

2 – Robert Skidelsky, *Oswald Mosley* (London, Macmillan, 1975, 1981, 1990 edn), pp 317, 318, 333, 335

We really know very little about British fascism. Certain aspects have been covered with varying degrees of accuracy and insight; its organisation, its anti-semitism, the violent abuse to which it gave rise. However, we know next to nothing about its mass support...

Mosley's appeal to youth broke through the class barriers from the start. However, among the middle- and upper-class recruits certain types predominated. They were typically ex-soldiers, marginal professional men dissatisfied with what life had to offer, and sportsmen. These, of course, are not discrete categories. Of a leadership sample of 103 selected by W.F. Mandle, 62 had served in the armed forces... not just in the war, but as career soldiers...

British fascism was not ruined, as some have alleged, by its violence which offended British decency. Anti-semitism probably gained more support than it alienated. However, in an indirect way the BUF's disreputableness did hinder its progress. From about 1936 onwards Mosley's propaganda outlets started drying up, which may well have reduced his support to below its maximum in the given conditions. This can be put another way by saying that Mosley never solved the tactical problems posed by the violent Communist opposition...

Unlike European communist movements, fascist movements have always taken on the personality of their leaders. Leadership was, of course, the central concept in their fascist theory of politics: Mosley was unusual among fascists in introducing an element of economic determinism into his plan for winning power. It is quite possible to imagine a fascist movement in England of the 1930s without Mosley. But it would have been very different: much nastier, and probably less effective.

What, then, was his contribution? We have already mentioned policy and money. In addition, Mosley was the BUF's chief, and most remarkable, propagandist. He carried a crippling load of speaking, more than any British politicians has ever done. From 1933 to 1937 he made about 200 speeches a year...

3 –   Richard Thurlow, *Fascism in Britain: A History 1918–1985* (Oxford, Basil Blackwell, 1987, pp 101, 109, 116

It was, however, after Mosley's Olympia meeting on 7 June 1934 that public opinion in general began to harden significantly against the BUF. Although the meeting led to an immediate increase in recruitment, the BUF lost the propaganda war concerning responsibility for the violence associated with the occasion, and in this respect it marked a turning-point in the fortunes of the movement...

The forces of government, the working-class organisations and Jewish establishments wished initially to ignore Mosley and the fascists in the hope that it would deny them publicity and defuse the potentially explosive situation. However, some members of the Communist party and the Jewish community were increasingly concerned about fascist expansionism in Europe, Hitler's anti-semitic legislation in Germany, his destruction of the German labour movement and Mosley's own move to anti-Semitism... [Then there is a discussion on Anti-Semitism, Olympia and the Battle of Cable Street.]

If the use of political anti-Semitism can be seen as a crucial stage in the decline of the BUF from a national movement to a localised racial populist organisation, then its attempt to resurrect its political pretensions in the Peace campaign of 1938–40 merely hastened its inevitable total destruction. The campaign was at best only partially successful in recovering the fortunes of the BUF in 1938–9. As with earlier national campaigns against unemployment and the League of Nations policy of sanctions against Fascist Italy, the role of the BUF in the political history of the decision-making process was non-existent.

4 –   Tom Buchanan, *The Spanish Civil War and the British Labour Movement* (Cambridge, Cambridge University Press, 1991), pp 3, 36, 170

[Attacking the traditional view that the Labour movement was unified in its support for the Spanish Republican Government, Buchanan suggests that] Spain was not an opportunity but a problem. Within the trade-union movement] the catholic minority acted as a storm-centre for opposition to the Spanish Republic...

When British Labour leaders gathered in the summer of 1936 to discuss the military rebellion in Spain it is clear that, beyond issuing general statements of support for Spanish democracy, the issues were far from clear cut. What they knew of Spain and of Spanish labour they did not much like. However, the fact that Spain was so little known gave them considerable latitude in creating a structure for their solidarity... On the other hand, Britain's

Catholic workers were shocked by the outrage against the Spanish church and their numerous voices in opposition to the Republic could not be totally ignored. However, all these problems were overshadowed by the British government's adoption of a policy of Non-Intervention in the Civil War which changed the nature of the problem from a question of internationalism into one of diplomacy, with the threat of war the price of failure. If the debates over Non-Intervention were to provide British Labour with months of acrimonious division, it also saved it for over a year from exposure of the movement's fundamental weakness in its duty of delivering international solidarity...

Bob Walsh, editor of the monthly *Catholic Worker* [stated that] 'The Spanish Civil War, I think, was one of the most heart-rending things that the Catholic workers ever experienced, because of the number of priests and nuns who were killed, and the number churches which were burnt down... religion was attacked and it tended to make quite strongly motivated workers, who normally never sided with anything that might be called fascism, pro-Franco!' [There follows a discussion on the way in which the Catholics both criticized the Labour and trade-union leaders for doing too much for Spain whilst rank and file trade unionists complained of them doing too little. Ernest Bevin and the Transport and General Workers' Union, who provided about £1000 of relief to the Republican side for 'medical and humanitarian requirements', was vehemently attacked by both sides for doing too much or too little. In the end, Labour leaders, except for Clement Attlee, were afraid of Spain and its implications for their organisations. They therefore attempted to remain as neutral as possible.]

5 – R.A.C. Parker, *Chamberlain and Appeasement: British Policy and the Coming of the Second World War* (London, Macmillan, 1993), pp 1–2, 23, 347

The memory of Neville Chamberlain and the idea of 'appeasement' go together. Yet he invented neither the policy nor the word. When Hitler came to power and during the early years of the Third Reich, even while Nazi Germany grew more and more threatening, almost everyone favoured the policy of 'appeasement', the search for peace and the redress of German grievances. Later, however, in 1938 and 1939, it became the personal policy of the Prime Minister. Mr Chamberlain applied it longer than most of his Cabinet colleagues and most of the British people would have done. After February 1938, he personally took the lead in the House of Commons in defending appeasement while the Foreign Secretary spoke only in the less contentious atmosphere of the Lords. Above all, in September 1938, his three visits to Hitler, without any other British minister, applied an adventurous and dramatic style in international affairs and brought him individual fame as the great appeaser. In that month he staked his reputation on success in pacifying the Third Reich. He did so willingly because he believed he could do it. The Munich agreement, he thought, justified his faith.

The policies that led him to Munich had rational grounds to support them; what distinguished Chamberlain was his confidence that these policies had succeeded. Thereafter he became the representative of a dwindling minority who believes that Munich meant peace rather than another in a series of even more threatening crises. His hopes deceived him. His policy failed when war came in September 1939: 'Everything that I have worked for, everything that I have hoped for, everything I have believed in during my public life, has crashed into ruins'. In consequence writers and speakers have misunderstood and under-rated him. He was neither a coward nor a fool; he was neither ignorant nor idle. He was a cultivated, highly intelligent, hard-working statesman, yet he was been written off as a petty, narrow-minded, boring provincial...

To the British 'European appeasement' meant limits on the strength of the German air force and navy. The rest of British policy in Europe was made up of inducements to other countries to join in working for limits on German armed strength. Only in March 1939 did Chamberlain hesitantly turn to attempts to threaten Germany into arms limitation. The United Kingdom favoured the status quo, keeping things as they were...

[From p 307 onwards he discusses the alternatives of using the League of Nations and other means to block Hitler's expansionism, isolationism, a treaty with the Soviet Union, and the idea of giving Hitler a free hand in the East but not the West.]

This book argues that Chamberlain and his colleagues made choices among alternative policies. Those historians who have revised the earlier interpretation of Chamberlain, in which he was written off as an ignorant coward, imply that his foreign policy was dictated by realistic assessment of economic and military weakness and by British opinion. This book suggests that Chamberlain led the government in 1938 and 1939, particularly in the months after Munich, into rejecting the option of a close Franco-British alliance, which might have dealt firmly with Mussolini's pretensions, and might have acted as a nucleus round which those states with reason to fear the Third Reich could assemble to resist it. We still do not know whether or not it was possible to induce the Soviet Union to hinder rather than help Hitler's attempt in 1939 and 1940 to forcibly prevent the Western powers from interfering in eastern Europe. Chamberlain refused to try; he thought collaboration with the Soviet Union undesirable and unnecessary. Yet Chamberlain had no intention of agreeing to a free hand for Germany in eastern Europe. This book suggests that he could have tried to build a barrier to Hitler's expansion. After March 1939 British attempts to do so were either half-hearted or too late. Academically, therefore, this study proposes that the balance of evidence points to counter-revisionist interpretations. Led by Chamberlain, the government rejected effective deterrence. Chamberlain's powerful, obstinate personality and his skill in debate probably stifled serious chances of preventing the Second World War.

6 – Richard Cockett, *Twilight of Truth: Chamberlain, Appeasement and the Manipulation of the Press* (London, Weidenfeld and Nicolson, 1989), pp 186, 188

There is no doubt that the Chamberlain government did consciously set out to control and manipulate the press during those years – it was, after all, an apparent prerequisite of a settlement with Hitler. Furthermore, whilst constantly trying to curb the freedom of the press, the government consistently denied that any attempts were being made to do so – thus, for domestic consumption, maintaining the fiction of liberal democracy with a 'free and independent press'...

What were the consequences of Chamberlain's tight control of the press during the late 1930s? The most obvious consequence was that no alternative policy to appeasement as pursued could ever be consistently articulated in the British press, nor were the facts and figures that might have supported such an alternative policy ever put in front of the majority of the British public. It is a striking fact that only those papers which had absolutely no contact with the government, such as the *Daily Mirror*, were able to oppose appeasement...

The second important consequence of Chamberlain's handling of the press was that he thus managed artfully and successfully to obscure the divisions over his policy that existed not only in Whitehall and Westminster but throughout the country. As this book has shown, editors and proprietors quite consciously suppressed and censored any news or reports that might show such signs of divisions; even 'editorial' writers like Garvin were quite aware of the fact that they were consciously holding back comments and facts for the greater good of pursuing the appeasement of Germany...

Although public opinion polls were in their infancy in the late 1930s... even a most cursory glance of the polls that were taken show that the press, in its support for Chamberlain and appeasement, was dangerously out of step with public opinion. In February 1938, the British Institute of Public Opinion asked the question, 'Do you favour Mr Chamberlain's foreign policy?' This solicited the following answers:

Yes	26%
No	58%
No opinion	16%

7 – Ian Colvin, *The Chamberlain Cabinet* (London, Gollancz, 1971), p 263

It is in some respects not agreeable but necessary to exhume the character of a dominating personality in a recent historical period. As I have said, Chamberlain was rising seventy when these strains came upon him. He was known to all his colleagues as a reserved man and silence may increase prestige, but when his reserve was discarded we discover a certain simplicity of thinking, naive at times as if he had discovered a remedy for international difficulties in a personal diplomacy of his own, difficulties he thought of defining in few words. His was very much the English approach to foreign politics, one of sustained astonishment that some formula could not be found to suit all parties, as if some deep-rooted dispute had never existed.

8 – Martin Gilbert, *The Roots of Appeasement* (London, Weidenfeld and Nicolson, 1966), pp 187–8

'Munich' and appeasement have both become words of disapproval and abuse. For nearly thirty years they have been linked together as the twin symbols of British folly. Together they have been defended as if they were inseparable. Yet 'Munich' was a policy, dictated by fear and weakness, which Neville Chamberlain devised as a means, not of postponing war but, as he personally believed, of making Anglo-American war unnecessary in the future. Appeasement was quite different; it was a policy of constant concession based upon common sense and strength. Whereas the debate over the wisdom of Chamberlain's actions will continue, and the believers in his vision cross words for many years to come with those who consider his actions short-sighted, unrealistic, and dangerous, the debate about appeasement deserves a different fate.

   Although appeasement failed when confronted with the aggressive, irresponsible behaviour of Nazi Germany, it did not, because of this failure, become retrospectively mistaken. It was never a misguided policy, even if it became, by 1938, temporarily an unrealistic one. International affairs do from time to time reach an impasse on account of the total impossibility of agreement between the two conflicting States. But the norm of international affairs remains the assumption that agreement is possible. For as long as this assumption holds good, appeasement is the necessary policy, combining expediency with morality. Just as it was the policy which Britain pursued in Europe after the First World War, so it was with only one exception, Suez, the policy pursued by Britain throughout the world after the Second World War. Only when all the evidence shows, as by 1938 the evidence seemed to show, that the nature of one's protagonist makes appeasement impracticable, should it be abandoned. Nor do those statesmen who abandon before all its avenues have been explored, all its opportunities tried, and all their energy expended, earn anything but the mistrust of their contemporaries and the censure of history.

9 – David Dilks (ed.), *Retreat from Power: Studies in Britain's Foreign Policy of the Twentieth Century, Volume I: 1906–1939* (London, Macmillan, 1981), p 18

After the Rhineland crisis of 1936 came the staff conversations with France, of modest scope but with large symbolic significance because of the conversations which were held to have committed Britain in 1914; after the Anschluss, an acceleration of rearmament... on 27 September 1938, just before the Munich conference, an outright statement that if France fought Britain would join her in the succeeding winter, at last, the decision to build up a continental army after the German seizure of the rump of Czechoslovakia, the guarantee to Poland.

Neville Chamberlain was right to describe this as a 'tremendous departure' in British foreign policy. No administration had previously given a comparable guarantee in central or eastern Europe, to frontiers which Chamberlain's brother once said no British government would ever risk the bones of a British Grenadier... By 1939 the British government was spending unprecedented sums upon arms. There was little choice, in a strategic situation worse than that of 1914. The Cabinet had excellent reasons for averting the contest if they could and for postponing it if not; because foreign policy and defence policy had fallen out of line and the ground was not easily made up.

PRIMARY EVIDENCE AND INFORMATION

10 – 1918 Mosley's Election Manifesto, in numerous sources on the BUF and Mosley

Industry: High wages must be maintained. This can only be achieved by high production based on increased efficiency and organisation. A high standard of life must be ensured by a minimum wage and reduced hours, which are proved to increase rather than curtail production.

Transport: Transportation and electrical resources to be controlled and developed by the State.

Land: The State must acquire land where necessary at a fair price (for soldier's smallholdings).

Housing: In many cases the State must carry out the work (of slum clearance) itself to ensure speed.

Education: Numerous scholarships for higher and university education must be supplied by the State.

Fiscal Policy: Preference on duties already existing and hereafter to be imposed must be granted as a long-solicited act of justice for our colonies. Industries essential to the national well-being must be shielded: unfair competition to British industry... in the form of dumping must be stopped...

Aliens: Immediate legislation is necessary to prevent undesirable aliens from landing; and for the repatriation of those who are now residents in this country.

Empire: Complete unity must be promoted by every means to enable the British Empire to play a leading part in the future League of Nations.

11 – Extract from John Strachey, *Revolution by Reason* (London, 1925), p 12

[This incorporates the ideas presented by him and Mosley to the ILP Summer School in 1925]

We propose first to expand credit in order to create demand. That new and greater demand must, of course, be met by a new and greater supply of goods, or all the evils of inflation and price rise will result. Here our Socialist planning must enter in. We must see that more goods are forthcoming to meet our new demand... The first essential of any successful socialist planning is to see that the new money goes into the right hands...

12 – Mosley Manifesto, issued 13 December 1930, quoted in the *Daily Telegraph*, 14 December 1930

It is impossible to meet the economic crisis with a nineteenth-century parliamentary machine. While the power to maintain or change the government must, of course, be retained by parliament, wide powers to deal with the present economic crisis must be tested in the government of the day for a stated period, subject only to the general control of parliament. The whole organisation of the executive machine, Cabinet, and department structure must be adapted to the present situation. An emergency Cabinet of not more than five Ministers, without portfolio, should be invested with power to carry through an emergency policy...

[The Manifesto then returns to the finance and credit proposals presented in *Revolution by Reason*, and short-term policies such as the removal of 700,000 to 800,000 from the unemployed lists by an early retirement scheme

(280,000), the raising of the school-leaving age (150,000), and by public works schemes (300,000). On long-term policies the following was added that there would be:] a policy of insulating Britain from the rest of the world by imposing import controls and by pumping investments into British and Empire industry... I want now to suggest that the policy of controlled imports can and should be extended to other trades, for this reason: that if we are to build up a home market it must be agreed that this nation must to some extent be insulated from the electric shocks of present world conditions.

13 – Sir Oswald Mosley, *My Life* (London, Thomas Nelson, 1968), pp 287, 321, 336

Fascism was in essence a national creed and therefore by definition took an entirely different form in different countries. In origin, it was an explosion against intolerable conditions, against remediable wrongs which the old world had failed to remedy. It was a movement to secure national renaissance by people who felt themselves threatened with decline into decadence and death and were determined to live, and live greatly. Without these three basic facts it is possible to abuse fascism, but not to make a serious reply to its case and to its spirit...

Fascism does not exist at present, not because it has been answered, but because it belongs to an epoch before the Second World War...

We demand from all our people an over-riding conception of public service. In his public life, a man must behave himself as a fit member of the State, in his every action he must conform to the welfare of the nation. On the other hand, he receives from the State in return, a complete liberty to live and develop as an individual. And in our morality – and I think possibly I can claim that it is only the public morality in which private practice altogether coincides with public protestation... the one single test of any moral question is whether it impedes or destroys in any way the power of the individual to serve the State. He must answer the questions: 'Does this action injure the nation? Does it injure other members of the nation? Does it injure my own ability to serve the nation?' And if the answer is clear on all those questions, the individual has absolute liberty to do as he will...

The fascist principle is private freedom and public service. That imposes upon us, in our public life, and in our attitude towards other men, a certain discipline and a certain restraint; but in our public life alone; and I should argue very strongly indeed that the only way to have private freedom was by a public organisation which brought some order out of the economic chaos which exists in the world today, and that such public organisation can only be secured by the methods of authority and of discipline which are inherent in fascism...

Anti-Semitism was not our policy, for I never attacked the Jews as a people. I never attacked any man on account of race and religion, and I never shall.

14 – Speech by Mosley to 32 attendees of the first meeting of the British Union of Fascists, formed 1 October 1932, in several sources, including Colin Cross, *The Fascists in Britain* (London, 1961), p 67, from which R. Skidelsky quoted it in *Oswald Mosley* (London, Macmillan, 1975), p 293

We ask those who join us to march with us in a great and hazardous adventure. We ask them to be prepared to sacrifice all, but to do so for no small and unworthy ends. We ask them to dedicate their lives to building in this country a movement of the modern age… Those who march with us will certainly face abuse, misunderstandings, bitter animosity and possible ferocity of struggle and danger. In return we can only offer them the deep belief that they are fighting that a great land may live…

15 – Mosley's *Tomorrow We Live* and the fascist response to the decline of Britain, quoted from Sir Oswald Mosley, *My Life* (London, Thomas Nelson, 1968), p 327

British Union emerges from the welter of parties and the chaos of the system to meet an emergency no less menacing than 1914, because it is not so sudden or so universally apparent. British Union summons our people to no less an effort in no less a spirit… A brotherhood of the British was born that in the strength of union was invincible and irresistible. Today the nation faces a foe more dangerous because he swells within… We have been divided, and we have been conquered. Class against class, faction against faction, party against party, interest against interest… Can we recapture the union of 1914 and that rapturous dedication of the individual to a cause that transcends self and faction, or are we doomed to go down with the Empire of history in the chaos of usury and sectional greed?

16 – Mosley's Anti-Semitic Speech at the Albert Hall, 22 March 1936, quoted in *Action*, 26 March 1936

Up to three years ago anti-Semitism was unknown as a strong force in Great Britain. To-day, in any audience in Britain, the strongest passion that can be aroused is the passion against the corruption of Jewish power… the Jew himself has created anti-Semitism – created it as he has always done, by letting people see him and his methods. Even Hitler was not anti-Semitic before he saw a Jew.

17 – Special Branch Report, 7 June 1934 (PRO MEPOL, 2/4319)

The communists and sympathisers who have obtained tickets for the meeting will sit in groups in different parts of the hall. They will act in an orderly way during the opening of the meeting… but after Sir Oswald Mosley has commenced his speech slogans will be shouted by each group in turn, according to a pre-arranged plan. A few men have been told to locate the main lighting switch, with a view, if possible to cutting off the light at a favourable moment.

18 – E.G. ('Mick') Clarke on the prospect of a Fascist march, as reported in PRO: MEPOL 2/3034 and reporting on a speech made in Bethnal Green on 23 June 1937, and taken to the magistrates court

One of them thought that on July 4th we intended to have an unofficial pogrom in East London and persecute the undesirables from our midst and drive them down the docks. Just fancy, a few British people, born in the East End of London, wanting to have a little walk round; and then they want to wind up in Trafalgar Square and hear the voice of a white man… to hear a white man speak and put forward a policy for the British people.

I read that the Jews were going to demonstrate to the Commissioner and the Home Secretary with a view of getting the march banned and apparently they succeeded very well…

In the meantime, boys, I have been trying to ascertain what part of London of ours belongs to Englishmen. What part of England is Jew-land?

19 – The Labour Party Circular on Fascism, 1934, Special cases for attention

LP/FAS/34/ 2-26, LP/FAS/34/20.1, City of Leeds Labour Party (replies to sections of the circular)

Yes, about a month ago, Mosley addressed a packed meeting in the Town hall. Approx. 1500. A good number of these were from outside Leeds. There were about 400 Blackshirts present, most of whom came to Leeds by bus.

Branch of fascist Movement in the City
Estimated 100–200 members.
No regular outdoor meetings.
Hold regular meetings in their own rooms.

No local literature but Fascist Weekly is sold in the streets every week-end.
No excessive press reporting of Fascist activities.

Fascists using corr. columns of local paper with reference to the Olympia affair.

We have taken part in the press controversy.

The Conservative leader has intervened. His attitude is anti-fascist and anti-communist. He said that to an extent the fascist ill-treatment of the Communists was justified because of the Communist attempt to break up meetings.

There is no separate Fascist groups for women but there are a number of women blackshirts.

There is no separate Youth Section but most blackshirts are young people.
No attempt to influence trade union branches.

Very little [support in local politics] amongst politicians. It is said that one or two young Tory Councillors are sympathetic but I have no evidence that this is true.

Several prominent business men are associated and it is sad that undue influence is being used to compel their employees to join.

The Fascists have very large premises at Devonshire Hall. I am informed by one of our Councillors that they are surrounded with Barbed wire. He also says that about 50 or 60 fascists are drilling there regularly.

Another point of interest in Leeds is that the Fascists are threatening to oppose Vyvyan Adams, the Tory MP for West Leeds, who has been so active in the House of Commons in asking questions regarding the Fascists.

LP/FAS/34/235(i/ii) Huddersfield Divisional Labour Party

A Public Demonstration was held in the Temperance Hall, Huddersfield, on Friday, June 15. Speaker J. Beckett. Attendance 300. Our L(eague) of Y(outh)) distributed enclosed leaflet [at end of document].

No indoor/ outdoor meetings.

Youth Movement
Youths are being stopped in the main street of the town and invited to join the fascists, also an office has been opened in town and many youths can be seen going in and out.

LA/ FAS/34/236, The True Meaning of Fascism (Pamphlet)

> Blackshirt, Blackshirt, have you a plan?
> Yes sir, yes sir, we've got two,
> One's for the Master - the other's
> For the Man.

Fascism Exposed
Mosley and Beckett [attack on Mosley] of the other speaker you have heard to-night, John Beckett, we have little to say. This renegade from the ILP, traitor to all the ideals he represented only a very short time ago – whose exhibitionist complex led him to start waving the mace in the House of Commons, has now embraced fascism, the absolute negation of all the ILP'er ever stood for. But enough of Beckett, let us leave him to his conscience.

Programme?
What do the fascists stand for? This is a very difficult question to answer. A lot moan about the need for a strong man at the helm to whit Sir Oswald, and following upon a strong man a rational renaissance coupled with the same renaissance is a lot of vaguely revolutionary talk about the Corporate States, in which both capitalists and workers will subordinate to the State. Thus by stressing the subordination of either capitalists or workers in their talks, according to the audience, fascism can be made palatable to either class.

Facts
[Pamphlet refers to salaries and wages being 35 to 50 percent lower than in 1921.]

The Brutality of the Fascists
Last week there was a meeting of the fascists at Olympia, London. The vicious brutality shown then by the hired strong men of Mosley's private army, has made the name of fascism stink in the nostrils of all decent English people. This sort of thing will not be tolerated here.

Fascist Development
This is nothing more or less than an attempt, by force, to keep things as they are, to prevent any changes in the industrial system of the country that are going to hurt the pockets of our big industrialists and capitalists. Where do you think all the money is coming from to keep Mosley's circus going? Not all of it from Mosley, no he is being subsidised by the capitalist class even as Mussolini, Hitler and Dollfuss were. And subsidised for one end, to prevent the mass of people from having their fair share in the wealth which they create. That is fascism. Nothing more or less. It cannot solve any of our problems – unemployment, poverty, and all the accompanying miseries – all it can do is to drive underground the opposition to these things, and to stifle the demands of the people for that fuller and finer life which they feel is their rightful due.
[There follows a discussion of socialism as the only hope.]
MOSLEY'S MOVEMENT MEANS MENACE and MISERY to the MASSES.

20 – *Bradford Trades and Labour Council Year Book 1937* (Bradford, Bradford Trades Council, 1937), p 3, 11

Having in mind the proposals of the Government for a very considerable increase in the armaments of the country, and also the piling up of armaments in other European countries with a consequent danger of war, the Council in March [1936] passed a resolution calling upon the TUC to discuss measures which might be taken to oppose such an armament programme and to prepare plans for action to prevent the outbreak of war...

We have witnessed a further attempt on the part of the fascist element in Spain to supersede the democratically elected Government of the People of Spain by force of arms. The magnificent fight which the Spanish workers have waged against the Fascists... have been the wonder of the world... the Council organised a Mass Meeting in Bradford to place the true facts before the public, and also opened a Spanish Workers' Relief Fund in conjunction with the TUC Solidarity Fund...

We wholeheartedly condemn the Government's policy of Non-Intervention which has permitted the Fascist countries of Italy and Germany to pour into Spain vast amounts of arms, ammunition, men, whilst it has denied the Spanish Democratic Government the legal right to purchase necessary supplies to defend the State. By its attitudes the 'National Government' has done much to advance the cause of Fascism...

Notes on Chapter 6

1   Communist Party of Great Britain (CPGB), Central Committee (CC), Minutes, 9 March 1933.
2   *Observer*, 7 December 1980, obituary on Mosley entitled 'Britain's Failed Dictator'.
3   R.A.C. Parker, *Chamberlain and Appeasement: British Policy and the Coming of the Second World War* (London, Macmillan, 1993).
4   In the House of Commons, 7 March 1938.
5   M. Gilbert and R. Gott, *The Appeasers* (London, 1963).
6   Martin Gilbert, *The Roots of Appeasement* (London, Weidenfeld and Nicolson, 1966).
7   D. Dilks, '"We must hope for the best and prepare for the worst." The Prime Minister, the Cabinet and Hitler's Germany 1937–9', *Proceedings of the British Academy* (1987) offers one of the best examples of this genre.

Chapter 7

The Second World War: Politics and Social Change 1939–45

Introduction

In May 1940 the Labour Party joined Winston Churchill's Wartime Coalition Government, following the departure from office of Neville Chamberlain. What this ensured is that a wartime political truce would be observed by the major political parties, departing political representatives being replaced, unchallenged, by members of their own party. Only the Communist Party of Great Britain (CPGB), briefly, the Independent Labour Party (ILP) failed to observe this arrangement and forced contests. Other organisations, such as the Common Wealth Party, which included Richard Acland and Tom Driberg, were also active in politics. Nevertheless, politically there was little occurring until the eve of the 1945 general election when the Labour Party, which preserved its organisation, defeated the Conservatives, whose organisation had become moribund in some areas. Yet this situation did not mean that political decisions were not being made. In fact the Second World War is dominated by the issues of consensus and social unity, with historians asking a variety of related questions. Did the war create a new sense of social unity? Did wartime unity provide the blueprint for Labour's post-war welfare state? Did war bring about fundamental social change? On these questions, most of the early accounts of events suggested that there was more social unity than before 1939, that war did provide the catalyst for change, and that it shaped the evolution of the modern welfare state. More recently, however, there has been a tendency to questions such notions, to suggests that there was more continuity with the past, and that the Second World War, by and large, brought about temporary, rather than permanent, change in most areas of social and political life. On balance, this new evidence has stripped away the thin veneer of social unity that was once supposed to have been generated by the war.

In the 1950s, Richard Titmuss argued that social unity and consensus were central features of the Second World War in *Problems of Social Policy*,[1] although he was subsequently at pains to stress that this was only one part of the evolution of social policy within the community (Document 1). He maintained that there was a new mood in the nation which favoured unity and social change, arising out of Dunkirk and the Blitz. The Second World War thus became a 'people's war'. Such views were supported by a variety of writers, including Gordon Wright and Arthur Marwick[2] (Document 4). They, like Titmuss, placed great emphasis upon the fact that more women were employed during the war than before 1939, that there was social levelling as wage differentials narrowed and that the Beveridge Report (Document 7) anticipated the introduction of a social security system that was universal and would ensure that there was a minimum living standard in Britain. Indeed, Marwick stressed that the war caused disruption and destruction, tested the institutions of the community and left the nation in an emotional atmosphere ripe for change (Document 4).

Such views were common currency until the late 1960s, since when detailed research has done much to challenge its various assumptions and arguments. The first major challenge came from Angus Calder's *The People's War* (1969), in which it was argued that whilst there was some evidence of change during wartime it could not be denied that many of the changes were in fact simply the extension of pre-war practices (Document 2). Calder noted that many women had worked before 1939, and that more would have done so, following the established trend, even had there been no war.[3] He further stressed that the Beveridge Report (Document 7), with its commitment to the universal application of the contributory national insurance principle to deal with the exigencies of life, was simply an extension of the practice of the inter-war years, and that there was little that was revolutionary about it. Even Labour's political success of 1945 could be seen in the gradual strengthening of the Labour Party's political position after 1941 and its rising political success in the Gallup polls from the early war years. Effectively, then, the nation was travelling along existing grooves in its social and political development. This lack of unity is a topic he later returned to in *The Myth of the Blitz* (London, Jonathan Cape, 1991), in which he suggested that the mythology of the Blitz became an integral part of the development of a national ideology but bore little relation to reality.

Since Calder wrote *The People's War* almost 30 years ago, the vast majority of relevant material in this prolific area of research – with the notable exception of that written by Arthur Marwick, who has stressed the disruptive nature of war and how it puts institutions to the test (Document 4) – has endorsed the Calder line. Henry Pelling supported Calder's argument in *Britain and the Second World War* (Document 3), suggesting that the war did not raise the level of government expenditure permanently, and that the Keynesian approach to unemployment may not have been responsible for low post-war unemployment levels. Paul Addison, in *The Road to 1945* (London, Pimlico, revised edn, 1994) was also ambivalent towards Titmuss's consensual argument. Whilst he acknowledged that 'The home front organisation for war was becoming a model, and an inspiration for the reorganisation of peace', he doubted whether the atmosphere of optimistic solidarity was as universal as Titmuss suggested.[4] Others have developed this scepticism further, and on specific aspects of the debate. Stephen Brooke, for instance, has doubted the validity of the suggestion that wartime political consensus led to Labour's 1945 victory, in *Labour's War: The Labour Party and the Second World War* (Oxford, Oxford University Press, 1992) and Richard Cockett has examined the anti-collectivist sentiment of the *Conservative Party in Thinking the Unthinkable: Think Tanks and the Counter-Revolution 1931-1983* (London, 1994) There are, indeed, hundreds of publications which now support this alternative, less consensual, view of the Second World War.

In recent years the articles, and edited collections, of Harold L. Smith have been at the cutting edge of this anti-consensual approach. His recent document book, *Britain and the Second World War: A Social History* (Manchester, Manchester University Press, 1996) provides numerous examples, drawn from primary sources, of the way in which health differences, class differences, the discriminatory treatment of women and other aspects of British social life, remained – based upon deep class, ethnic and gender divisions (Documents 9 and 10). Smith's edited collection of essays, *War and Social Change: British Society in the Second World War* (Manchester, Manchester University Press, 1986), also offers a convincing challenge to practically everything that Titmuss and Marwick have suggested. In it, John Macnicol has revealed how the evacuation of school children at the beginning of the war does not seem to have brought about that social unity which Titmuss suggested, that it did little to change the views of Whitehall, and that it probably reinforced the existing social attitudes towards the working class and poverty (Document 5). Others make similar points. John Stevenson suggests that the Beveridge Scheme was hardly revolutionary, a point stressed by some socialists at the time, through *Tribune* and other socialist publications which stressed that it was simply an extension of the insurance principle which had been put forward by the 1911 National Insurance Act (Document 8). Henry Pelling indicates that Labour's victory was not a political revolution; Penny Summerfield suggests that there is a lack of data and a lack of permanence about many of the so-called instances of social levelling that occurred on wartime (Document 6); and H.L. Smith suggests that women's involvement in work was far from being revolutionised by the Second World War, and was far from being made more permanent.[5]

Clearly the extent of social unity and consensus generated by the Second World War has produced a deep and on-going debate. Although no absolute truth has been arrived at, it is clear that certain points have emerged. It is, for instance, clear that the Titmuss view on the consensus produced by the war can no longer be sustained. There is too much evidence to suggest that social levelling was not occurring, that social attitudes remained suspended for the duration in a temporary limbo, and returned to something approaching the pre-war position after 1945, and that social discrimination remained a major part of life in Britain. It also seems that the link between the Beveridge Report and Labour's post-war welfare state is still rather tenuous. Although this topic will be examined in the next chapter, it is clear that the final mix of social reforms which Labour offered drew from its pre-war planning discussions, partly from the inventive mind of Nye Bevan, and also partly from the Beveridge insurance schemes. The Beveridge Report was thus only one contributory factor in Britain's post-war social blueprint. Equally, we should not be surprised at the size of Labour's 1945 victory, for even without the Second World War Labour would probably have strengthened its position, and Labour's victory was still only achieved with a minority vote of 47.8 percent. Thus, if this debate has done anything, it has undermined the notion that one can make sweeping claims for the impact of the Second World War upon British social life. Evidence of social unity and consensus in one direction is often offset by evidence that it did not occur in other directions. Indeed, new research on culture and the media in the war suggests that there was often a marked disparity between the official line and the grass-roots responses.[6]

Documents
SECONDARY SOURCES AND INTERPRETATIONS

1 – R.M. Titmuss, 'War and Social Policy', lecture at London University,, 1955, Chapter 4 in R.M. Titmuss, *Essays on the Welfare State* (London, Unwin University Books, 2nd edition, 3rd imprint, 1960), pp 86–7

The aims and content of social policy, both in peace and in war are thus determined – at least to a substantial extent – by how far the co-operation of the masses is essential to the successful prosecution of the war. If this co-operation is thought to be essential, then inequalities must be reduced and the pyramid of social stratification must be flattened. This is, in part, the thesis advanced by Andrzejewski in a sweeping, untidy but brilliant study recently published under the title *Military Organisation and Society*. In analysing the character of war and its conduct from pastoral and pre-literate societies down to the advent of atomic war, he argued that what he calls the military participation ratio determines the social stratification of society. Mass war, involving a high proportion of the total population, tends to a levelling in social class differences. On the other hand, professional wars, conducted by military leaders recruited from a social élite and depending on support from only a small proportion of the population, tends to heighten existing social inequalities. This study, in my view, effectively answers Herbert Spencer's theory that war conduced to greater social inequalities. It may have been true of some wars in some periods and cultures but not of all wars. However, we must fairly admit that Spencer was writing before the advent of the mass wars of the twentieth century.

The work of these sociologists does, in general, support the arguments that I have advanced: that modern war has had – at least in Britain – a profound influence on social policy and that, reciprocally, the direction of social policy has influenced the way in which war is prosecuted. But this, I am confident – more perhaps by faith than by reason - is not the whole of the story in the evolution of social policy. Man does not live by war alone. To explain the social life of a community in terms of aggression and struggle is to explain only part of 'this sorry scheme of things entire'.

2 – Angus Calder, *The People's War: Britain 1939–45* (London, Jonathan Cape, 1969), pp 17–18, 331, 525–6, 583–5

'This is a war of the unknown warriors' [said Churchill in the summer of 1940]. Subsequently, he contrasted this Second World war with the First, 'The whole of the warring nations are engaged, not only soldiers, but the entire population', men, women and children. The fronts are everywhere. The trenches are dug in towns and streets. Every village is fortified. Every road is barred. The front lines run through the factories. The workmen are soldiers with different weapons but the same courage.' In 1940 and the years which followed, the people in Britain were protagonists in their own history in a fashion never known before; hence the title of this book, *The People's War*.

Those who made the 'People's War' a slogan argued that the war could promote a revolution in British society. After 1945, it was for a long time fashionable to talk as if something like a revolution had in fact occurred. But at this distance, we see clearly enough that the effect of the war was not to sweep society into a new course, but to hasten its progress along the old grooves.

In the shocked Britain which faced defeat between 1940 and 1942 there were very obviously the seeds of a new democracy. Between them, the threat of invasion and the actuality of aerial bombardment had exaggerated a tendency already noted in the previous world war. In a conflict on such a scale, as 1914–18 had shown, the nation's rulers, whether they liked it or not, depended on the willing co-operation of the ruled, including even scorned and underprivileged sections of society, manual workers and women. This co-operation must be paid for by concessions in the direction of a higher standard of living for the poor, greater social equality and improved welfare services. For the conscripts in the armed forces were dangerous enemies to the old social order; jolted out of their acceptance of it by communal travel, hardship and danger. The rifle aimed at the enemy might be turned on the ruling classes, as it was in Russia.

In 1939–45 the people of Britain were called into a participation which was wider, deeper and longer… As for the armed forces themselves, the new techniques of warfare centring on the tank and the aeroplane ensured that the best educated and most socially conscious generation of young men in Britain's history was increasingly courted as well as bullied by the military hierarchies, cajoled into a more skilled and more conscious role that their fathers had played in the First World War. [Yet they took over much of the role themselves, and demanded a fairer system of food rationing and involvement in the decisions of war production.]

So the people surged forward to fight their own war, forcing their masters into retreat, rejecting their nominal leaders and representatives and paying homage to leaders almost of their own imagination – to Churchill, to Cripps, to Beveridge, to Archbishop Temple and to Uncle Joe Stalin. The war was fought with the willing being and hearts of the most vigorous elements in the community, the educated, the skilled, the bold, the active, the young, who worked more and more consciously towards a transformed post-war world…

In conscripting women, Britain went further than any other nation – further than Stalin's Russia and far further than Hitler's Germany…

Yet, as so often with features of wartime life which evoked cries of horror and admiration from contemporaries, what had happened, above all, was the exaggeration of peacetime trends. Certain of the lighter industries – the northern textile mills were the best known example – had long relied on women for half or more of their labour force. Nearly five and a half million women had been in employment before the First World War, which had raised the figure to seven and a half million. Afterwards, a great proportion had left the factories as swiftly as they had invaded them, but a slow rate had been resumed in the 'twenties and 'thirties.

In mid-1943, the proportion of the nation's women between fifteen and sixty who were in the forces, munitions work and essential industries was about double that in 1918, at the corresponding stage in the previous war. Nearly three million married woman and widows were employed, as compared with a million and a quarter before the war. It was calculated that, among those between eighteen and forty, nine single women out of ten and eight married women out of ten were in the forces or in industry. Those women left over were mostly looking after the nation's young children, but hundreds of thousands of women were in part-time employment, many of them in improvised offices and workshops in village halls, and even in drawing-rooms, which took the work of those who could not leave their own home for long.

It was estimated, however, that if peacetime trends had continued without any assistance from Hitler, about six and three-quarters million women would have had jobs outside the home in 1943. Since the official estimate of those employed stood at around seven and a half millions, the number of extra women who were working was no more than about three-quarters of a million – a considerable, but hardly an overwhelming figure. Nor does it follow that those who now worked and who could not have done so without the war necessarily accepted this in the spirit of grim dutifulness...

The first impetus for the Beveridge report had come from the TUC which in February 1941 had sent a deputation to lobby the Minister of Health on the inadequacy of the existing provision for health. Since health insurance could not be treated in isolation, the committee appointed by Arthur Greenwood on June 10th, 1941, with Beveridge as its chairman and eleven civil servants representing the Government departments concerned, had been entrusted with a comprehensive survey of all existing social insurance schemes.

The need for such a survey was obvious. In 1938–39 nearly twenty-one million people had been covered by the state's old age pensions scheme; fifteen and a half million workers by unemployment insurance; and twenty million people – but no more than half the population – by National Health Insurance. The benefit given under the different schemes were theoretically meeting the same need but in fact greatly needed. [This is followed by an outline of the main points of the Beveridge Scheme, with its commitment to universal provision based upon a contributory system of insurance.]

Yet the scheme was nothing like so revolutionary as Beveridge, and some of his admirers, liked to pretend. In the first place, in A.J.P. Taylor's words, he 'finally rejected the socialist doctrine of a social security provided by society'. His scheme was contributory of course, and the contributions involved were to be paid on a flat rate, applying to all income levels, which was essentially a retrogressive arrangement. The scheme provided a minimum level of security for those who could afford no better; but the well-to-do could still buy better provision if they wished. Secondly, it was abundantly clear by 1942 that the existing social insurance schemes must somehow be rationalised and co-ordinated, and there was a wide measure of agreement on the left and centre of British politics that the elimination of poverty must be an aim. Beveridge's scheme expressed this consensus. The civil service experts who advised him generally sympathised with his ideas. From January to October 1942, the committee took evidence from no less than a hundred and twenty-seven individuals and organisations, and Beveridge himself emphasised that witnesses as far apart in their interests as the TUC, the employers in the Shipping Federation, and the social scientists of PEP, made proposals of their own agreeing on 'practically all' the main principles of the report...

The vagaries of the electoral system had exaggerated Labour's advantage into a landslide. For the party's supporters, this was a moment of joyful tears. 'POWER!' exclaimed a columnist in Manchester's *Labour* journal. 'The revolution without a single cracked skull. The pioneers' dream realised at long last. Nothing to stand in the way of laying the socialist foundation of the new social order.'

The Gallup Poll now asked the public whether it thought that the results meant that the British people wanted Labour to govern 'along existing lines only more efficiently, or to introduce changes such as nationalisation?' Fifty-six per cent made the second assumption, as compared with only thirty per cent favouring the first.

But revolution was not on Attlee's agenda. For six years, Attlee would remain Prime Minister, presiding over a valiant economic recovery, Productivity would soar, exports would exceed the dreams of the wartime planners. 'Full employment' would be maintained... The transition from war to peace would be made, in the short run, with conspicuous success.

Labour would fulfil its programme of nationalisation; but the only major item which would prove sufficiently controversial to provoke the Conservatives into repealing it would be the takeover of steel. The coal mines and railways, physically weakened by the war, were not worth saving by private enterprise...

There was, of course, the welfare state, which would have its symbolic birthday on July 5th, 1948, when the new National Insurance scheme and the National Health Service would come into operation simultaneously. It would seem, for ten years or more, that the war on Beveridge's Five Giants had been completed. Disease, certainly, would lose much of its vitality. Ignorance, for all the limitations of the 1944 Education Act, would continue its steady retreat. But Want, Squalor and Idleness would covertly maintain a grim empire in the midst of increasing affluence. In the 1960s, seven or eight million people, representing one Briton in seven, would be living below the standard of living on which national Assistance was based, and the numbers would not be dwindling, but growing...

Indeed, those to have the best service from the welfare state would be the well-to-do. Under R.A. Butler's ingenious dispensation, one child in seven from the middle classes would proceed to university in the 1950s, as compared to one in sixteen before the war; the proportion of students from the lower-paid sections of the working class would remain the same. Free hospital treatment would be a boon for the middle-class budget, but after promotion, there would still be expensive hospitals providing more exclusive standards.

3 – Henry Pelling, *Britain and the Second World War* (London, Fontana, 1970, 1976), Chapter 12

The impact of the war on British domestic history – on the nation's economy, its politics, its social conditions and its cultural life – is extraordinarily difficult to determine, for any attempt to draw up an assessment involves us at once in problems of hypothesis. If the war had not occurred, what would have happened in the six years, 1939 to 1945?... Too frequently it was assumed, at the end of the war or shortly afterwards, that changes which had occurred since 1939 were the direct outcome of the war. As time goes by, however, we are able to get a clearer picture of the long term trends, and in many cases we then discover that what people have ascribed to the impact of war really has more deep-seated causes...

The first question to which we may address ourselves is whether the very great increase in public expenditure, which was such a feature of the war, had a permanent effect in the post-war years. The ordinary taxpayer might think so, as the standard rate of income tax, which had not been above 5s 6d in the pound in the period 1923–1939, was never thereafter below 7s 9d. Looking at the matter from the other side, we find that government expenditure in the inter-war period, before the beginning of re-armament, rarely amounted to more than 25 per cent of the gross national product, whereas since the war it has never fallen below 36.5 per cent. [He discusses the displacement effect of war.] A sociologist, Professor S. Andreski, has put the matter in a slightly different way: in his view, modern wars have called for an increasingly large participation by the people as a whole, and as a price for their support the people in one way or another secure compensation in the form of increased social welfare...

The main problem with such views is that there is no reason to suppose that, in the absence of total war, government expenditure would have remained constant as a proportion of the gross national product. In Britain there was a rapid increase in expenditure in the years 1900 to 1914, and there has been a considerable increase again in the years since 1955. Unfortunately for the supporters of the theory of the military participation ratio, in neither of these two periods was it assumed by the government that war, if it came, would require the active participation of the bulk of the population. If, instead of looking at all government expenditure, we examine separately the expansion of the social services, we find that the growth of expenditure per head of population has been remarkably uniform since the beginning of the century. This is partly because commitments assumed by legislation tend to build up gradually as time goes on...

It is generally maintained that the most important single change in the economy effected by the war is the existence of full employment – a condition introduced in Britain (though not in Northern Ireland) by the demands of total war, and then maintained in peacetime, so it has been argued, by Keynesian policies of stimulating demand, to which all the British political parties became committed when they accepted the Full Employment White Paper in 1944. There is no doubt about the fact of full employment: between the wars the proportion of the unemployed to the total labour force was rarely less than 10 per cent, whereas since 1945 it has rarely been as high as 2.5 per cent. This has had a dramatic effect upon strengthening the trade unions, providing far greater opportunities for women's work, and leading to a constant inflation of about 4 or 5 per cent per annum, with an annual 'wage round' as one of its more prominent features. But whether full employment has been entirely, or even largely, the result of the application of Keynesian ideas may be doubted, as the government has been constantly under the necessity of taking demand out of the economy, and has never been able to do any 'pump priming' of the kind that Keynes advocated...

In the hectic days of 1940, it was quite common for people to suppose that the war was affecting a social revolution in Britain. Many of the wealthy thought so... By 1941 Harold Nicolson was shocked to think that he would 'have to walk and live a Woolworth life hereafter'. This was an absurd exaggeration, but undoubtedly he had to live a somewhat reduced existence. By contrast, the wages of nearly all manual workers rose faster than the cost of living, and with the advantages of overtime opportunities for work by married women, and general full employment their families were usually better off than before the war. Left-wing publicists like J.B. Priestley and Sir Richard Acland were glad to believe that social distinctions were being eroded, and argued that the process should be deliberately encouraged in order to 'release fresh stores of energy and enthusiasm' for the war. But to Conservatives this argument seemed to be a case of the wish being father to the thought; and the government was mindful of the fact that Parliament still had a Conservative majority...

Undoubtedly the war brought into existence for a time a stronger sense of community throughout the country than normally existed in peacetime. Dunkirk, the Battle of Britain and the blitz produced a 'back-to-the-wall' solidarity that transcended class barriers and brought together all sorts of people in the Home Guard, Civil Defence and air-raid shelters, even to some extent the factories.

But it would be a mistake to make too much of all this. Some of the interest in serious culture was quite fortuitous: that is to say, it arose out of the temporary absence of some of the lighter forms of entertainment. The BBC did not find, from its audience samples, that the market for serious music was expanding rapidly, but rather it was growing slowly as it had done before the war...

The explanation of all this may lie in the fact that, in spite of the shocks of 1940, the Second World War made much less impact on the British mind than the First World War had done. In 1914 the country was not prepared mentally for the trials that it had to undergo – the appalling suffering of the trenches and a rate of casualties never previously experienced. But in 1939 most people feared a repetition of the First World War, and so there was psychological trauma resulting from the sacrifices that it eventually involved. The average Britain might be impressed... by what he took to be the exceptional military prowess of the Soviet Union, and wonder what the reason for it was; but the war did not really weaken his adherence to his own distinctive national institutions and customs. Parliament, the political parties, the Civil Service local government, the press, the law, the trade unions – all emerged from the war with slightly different surface features, but basically unaltered.

4 – A. Marwick, 'My Views on the Consequences of the War for Britain', in *World War II* (Milton Keynes, Open University, 1973), p 56, 57, 58, 59–60, 61–2

The two most recent comprehensive studies of Britain during the Second World War have both taken a rather negative view of the consequences of the war for British society. Dr Pelling condemns those who have attributed social change to the war as having 'failed the commonest of historical pitfalls, the fallacy of post hoc, ergo propter hoc'. Dr Calder has maintained 'that the effect of the war was not to sweep society on to a new course, but to hasten its progress along old grooves'. The debate is not between those who argue that the war brought 'good' consequences, and those who argue that the war brought 'bad' consequences, but it is between those who argue that the war was a positive agent for social change, and those who do not see the war as having had any significant influence, as compared with long-term trends. [He then suggests that whilst bombing may not have created the social mixing sometimes suggested, its consequences in terms of evacuation revealed to the middle and upper classes the social deprivation that existed.]

By late 1941 a preoccupation with the problems of social reform was apparent at all levels of society. In that year were founded both the Conservative 'Post-War Problems Committee' and the '1941 Committee' of upper class liberals and socialist intellectuals; in 1943 the Common Wealth party was founded, and, standing on a platform for radical social reform, proceeded to win a number of by-elections from Conservative supporters of the Coalition Government. The Federation of British Industries declared in May 1942 that 'we are on the threshold of a new world, and the theories and practice of the past cannot be taken for granted in the future'. Most significant, perhaps, was the role of the Army Bureau of Current Affairs which distributed a fortnightly journal *Current Affairs* as a basis for discussion among British troops; from September 1942 *Current Affairs* show a growing concern with the problems of reconstruction and social reform. In May 1941 in response to Trade Union pressure, the government appointed a specialist committee to study 'existing national schemes of social insurance and allied services'. Hoping to silence for the time being a tiresome and opinionated administrator, Sir William Beveridge, the government put him in charge of the survey. But Beveridge was able to appeal to gathering public sentiment and his Beveridge Report not only recommended a comprehensive social insurance system for the entire nation, but also postulated a National Health Service, avoidance of mass unemployment, child allowances, and enlightened national policies for housing and education. Beveridge's blueprint for a 'universalist' welfare state (one in which social services would be available to all, rich as well as poor) became, despite Churchill's hostility, a matter of public debate and widespread enthusiasm...

[Turning to women and the war he points out that, unlike the First World War, they were now conscripted, and that the civilian employment of women expanded greatly. By the end of the war there is evidence that employers were more favourable to the employment of married women. As a result, there has been a debate about the extent to which the war transformed the position of women.]

And this debate over the question of the effects of the war on women really brings one to the heart of the whole question of whether war brought about significant social and economic changes. In my view the manner in which society reacts to war to bring about just such changes can be summarised in the form of a four-tier model. First, the war produced disruption and destruction, creating new patterns of behaviour, and calling forth a need for reconstruction. Second, the war provided a direct test of existing institutions, provoking where they proved inadequate to the needs of war their destruction, or their transformation. Thirdly, the war required the participation of underprivileged classes in the community, who correspondingly benefitted from the new needs the community had for their services, both in the form of guided change (direct rewards from the government), and unguided change, resulting from their stronger market position, and from the new sense of status that they acquired irrespective of guided government action. Finally, the war aroused a powerful psychological and emotional responses favourable to change.

Bombing and all its implications forms the most obvious example of the disruption and destructive effect. Another example is the billeting throughout most of the war of almost half a million foreign troops on British soil rising to one and a half million at the time of the Normandy landings...

The test effect of war is well exemplified by the case of the hospital system, which before the war was rent by the petty rivalries between the 'voluntary' hospitals and the local-authority hospitals. To deal with the student influx of air-raid casualties, the government had to create a unified Emergency Hospital Service, providing free treatment. Gradually the scope of the service has extended, so that by the end of the war it provided a solid basis upon which the future National Health Service could be built...

The underprivileged groups in the community who benefitted from being drawn into participation in the war effort were exactly the same groups as underwent a similar history in the First World War: the working classes, women and children, and young people. The working classes benefited because of their strong market position when labour power was an essential ingredient to success in the war; they benefited because the government knew it was vital to secure their full support and co-operation...

In blunt terms the consequences for British society of the Second World War were rather similar to those of the First World War for France. Technically, there was victory; and without doubt there were positive social changes. But there were heavy physical losses which made more difficult the realisation of the social aspirations aroused by the war. Above all there was the basic problem of 'we won didn't we', a reluctance to face the fact that the institutions which survived the battering of war were not necessarily, thereby, perfect institutions with which to meet the post-war world. Those who judged everything by the highest standards of human brotherhood and efficiency will continue to feel that there was little 'real change' in Britain. Those who accept the imperfections of human systems, and who recognise that change is not necessarily always in the one direction, will perhaps recognise that, even without the drama and tragedy of an occupation and resistance, the Second World War nonetheless did have a considerable impact upon the British people.

5 – John Macnicol, 'The Effect of the Evacuation of Schoolchildren on
Official Attitudes to State Intervention' in Harold L. Smith (ed.), *War
and Social Change: British Society in the Second World War* (Manchester,
Manchester University Press, 1986), pp 27–8

This chapter has tried to show – in the space available – how complex was the
evacuation experience. It was an episode that affected the children in many
different ways. But running through the diversity of experience was the trauma
of family separation and the culture shock of coping with a new environment.
These difficulties were greatly exacerbated by poor civil defence planning. A
minority of children – the exact proportion cannot be established – displayed
symptoms of the poverty and deprivation that had been quite commonplace
in the 1930s, and significantly under-recorded by government reports; these
medical and social symptoms horrified many hosts in the reception areas precisely because they seemed to epitomise wider urban-rural cultural differences. In a sense evacuation did provide a shock to public consciousness and a
'throwing together of social classes' (though it must be remembered that most
hosts, like most evacuees, were working class). However, it is difficult to find
evidence that this brought about fundamental ideological shifts on the part
of different groups – notably, with Whitehall. Evacuation required the help
of a large number of middle-class voluntary workers in the rural areas who,
perhaps more than any other section of the population, had very fixed ideas on
social propriety; it was this lobby that propagated the wildly exaggerated and
inaccurate stories of the evacuees' condition. In short, the social debate on evacuation probably served to reinforce existing analyses of working-class poverty
rather than to change them; for conservative social observers it confirmed
their view that the bulk of the problems were caused by an incorrigible under-
class of personally inadequate 'cultural orphans' for whom a Welfare State
could do little. Evacuation shows us that the ideological consensus of wartime, so stressed by Titmuss and some historians, was something of a myth.

6 – Penny Summerfield, 'The Levelling of Class', in Harold L. Smith
(ed.), *War and Social Change: British Society in the Second World War*
(Manchester, Manchester University Press, 1986), pp 201–2

What can we conclude from this review of surveys and accounts pertinent to
this issue of the 'levelling of class'? I should like to end by drawing together
three main points.

Firstly, permanent 'levelling up' of the working class, as depicted by both
defenders of middle-class status and advocates of a 'classless' society in the
1940s and '50s, is thrown into doubt by the absence of any guarantee of the

permanence of relatively enlarged working-class incomes and by the beginning of the late 1940s of the reversal of fiscal policies which had favoured the working class during the war.

Secondly, on the other hand, there were certainly some wartime changes in social stratification and there is no doubt that some groups of manual workers improved their pay position markedly, relative both to other groups of manual workers and to some groups of salaried workers. In addition, it seems that working-class women undertook paid work to a greater extent... All the same there were wider variations in the income levels of different working-class groups – for example, aircraft workers and servicemen's wives – and little sign of any 'levelling' within the working-class household. Likewise, some middle-class groups, such as 'managers and administrators' fared better than others, such as 'professionals'.

Thirdly, evidence of differences in saving patterns within and between the classes suggests that when class is seen in relation to property, rather than income, the war gave rise to very little movement out of the working class via accumulation, and it may even have encouraged the widening of property differentials, both within the middle class and between it and the working class.

PRIMARY EVIDENCE AND INFORMATION

7 – Beveridge Report (Report on Social Insurance and Allied Services, 20 November 1942, CD 6404)

9. The third principle is that social security must be achieved by co-operation between the State and the individual. The State should offer security for service and contribution. The State in organising security should not stifle incentive, opportunity, responsibility: in establishing a national minimum for himself and his family...

17. A scheme of social insurance against interruption and destruction of earning power and for special expenditure arising at birth, marriage or death. The scheme embodies six fundamental principles: flat rate of subsistence benefit; flat rate of contribution; unification of administrative responsibility; adequacy of benefit; comprehensives and classification... Based on them, and in combination with national assistance and voluntary insurance as subsidiary methods, the aim of the Plan for Social Security is to make want under any circumstances unnecessary...

22. The second view is that whatever money is required for provision of insurance benefits... should come from a Fund to which the recipients have contributed and to which they may be required to make larger contributions, if the Fund proves inadequate...

8 – Extract from *Tribune*, 4 December 1942

Sir William Beveridge is a social evangelist of the old Liberal school. He is an honoured member of the Reform Club, and the horizon of his political aspirations is, therefore, not boundless. He specifically disavows many of the tenets of revolutionary Socialism. But he has a good heart and a clear, well-stocked head, and he has discharged his task with Liberal fervour and even a trace of Liberal innocence.

What kind of world would the honest Liberal like to establish? He would like to make a truce between private enterprise and State ownership. He would like the two to work in harness together, but above all, he would like, by resolute action, to appease the most obvious pains and succour the most grievous casualties which capitalism produced. From this dangerous angle Sir William has approached his task. He would like to establish a tolerable minimum standard of security for every citizen, for the injured worker, for the widow, for the aged, for the unemployed, for the sick and for the growing child.

This is a commendable ambition, and the desire to achieve it is certainly not confined to those who have dabbled or delved into Socialism. But the merit and novelty of Sir William is that he has set down with the authority of a statistician and on Government note paper the conditions which must be satisfied if this modest ambitions is to be achieved. Here it is in black and white – a plain description of men's necessities, how much (or how little) he must have in his pocket if fear and want and hunger are to be lifted from his car. In short, Sir William has described the conditions in which the tears might be taken out of capitalism.

9 – Joint Committee of the Royal College of Obstetricians and Gynaecologists and the Population Investigation Committee, Maternity in Great Britain (Oxford, Oxford University Press, 1948)

In all aspects of maternity care well-to-do mothers get better attention than those who are poor. They come under the antenatal supervision earlier, can afford a nursing home bed if no hospital one is available, and are more often given analgesia. While the well-to-do owe their privileges largely to being able to afford private care, they are also more aware of the need for medical supervision during and after pregnancy, and are seldom prevented by household ties from making the maximum use of the services available. They have, on the average, fewer children than poor mothers, are more able to obtain domestic help during pregnancy and the lying-in period and retain it for a longer time. There is, however, in all classes room for improvement in the standard of maternity care and domestic help.

10 – Mass Observation, *People in Production* (London, John Murray, 1942), p 15

The most striking feature of the industrial situation here is the survival of strictly peacetime procedure in the conflict between the employers and men, which is still today the predominant conflict here. One looked and listened in vain for any sign of unity binding all parties in the fight against Germany. From the men, one got the fight against the management. From the management, one experienced hours of vituperation against the men. Both sides claim to be concerned only with improving the situation to increase the strength of the struggle against Fascism, but, nevertheless, the real war which is being fought here today is still pre-war, private and economic.

Notes on Chapter 7

1   Richard Titmuss, *Problems of Social Policy* (London, HMSO, 1950).
2   Gordon Wright, *The Ordeal of Total War 1939–1945* (London, 1968); A. Marwick, *Britain in a Century of Total War* (London, Bodley Head, 1965).
3   Angus Calder, *The People's War: Britain 1939–45* (London, Jonathan Cape, 1969).
4   Paul Addison, *The Road to 1945: British Politics and the Second World War* (London, Jonathan Cape, 1975), p 15.
5   John Macnicol, 'The Effect of the Evacuation of Schoolchildren on Official Attitudes to State Intervention', John Stevenson, 'Planners' Moon? The Second World War and the Planning Movement', Henry Pelling, 'The Impact of War on the Labour Party', Penny Summerfield, 'The "Levelling of Class"' and Harold L. Smith, 'The Effect of War upon the Status of Women' in Harold L. Smith (ed.), *War and Social Change: British Society in the Second World War* (Manchester, Manchester University Press, 1986), pp 3–31, 58–77, 129–48, 179–207, 208–29.
6   Nick Hayes and Jeff Hill (eds), *Millions Like Us* (Liverpool, Liverpool University Press, 1999/2000).
7   This is out of copyright and may be freely reproduced, but I would like to thank the Controller of Her Majesty's Stationary Office for help in reproducing this extract.

Chapter 8

'Never Again': Attlee, the Post-war Labour Governments 1945–51 and the Politics of Consensus 1951–79

Introduction

The years between 1945 and 1979 saw important political changes in British politics and society. The Attlee Labour Governments presided over the creation of the modern welfare state, both the Conservative Party and the Labour Party ran the country for about seventeen years each on very similar policies, promoting the idea that there was political consensus; and the small Liberal and nationalist parties remained on the margins of power, even though their vote in general elections began to increase. The only major threat of change came when Margaret Thatcher became Prime Minister in May 1979, committing herself to breaking the existing political consensus and challenging the trade unions and the welfare state, as noted in Chapter 9. Up to 1979, however, the lasting experience of the post-war years was the sense of agreement about the direction, if not the fine detail, of British politics.

Although there are many debates, and sub-debates, revolving around the politics of these years, there are four which are broad-ranging. The first concerns the contributions made by the Attlee Governments between 1945 and 1951. Should one see the Attlee years as the apogee of the Labour Party's history or the nadir of socialism? Was Labour ahead of the electorate, behind it, or in tune with its hopes and ambitions? The second concerns the decline of the Labour Party since 1951. This was a topic for writers in the late 1950s and early 1960s, and once again in the 1980s, but has dipped as an interest since Tony Blair's Labour Government came to power in 1997. The third debate relates to the view that there was political consensus between the Conservative and Labour Parties on most policy issues – such as defence and welfare – with only minor political eddies to diminish it. Was this the case? Most writers would say yes. However, the consensus was thrown into sharp context by Margaret Thatcher's declared aim, in 1979, to challenge many of the institutions upon which such equanimity had been founded, in order to reverse Britain's relative economic decline. The fourth, rather less debated, issue concerns the role of small political parties in British politics. Given that about 97.1 percent of the voters voted for the two major parties in 1951, and that this had fallen to 76.6 percent in 1974, 82.1 percent in 1979 and 71.8 percent in 1983. Did the smaller political parties in Britain have a rising political role to play between 1945 and 1979?

Debates

The Attlee Governments have been the real locus of debate for Labour historians in recent years. In 1979 Phillip Williams wrote a book on Hugh Gaitskell, and in 1982 Kenneth Harris produced a monumental work on Attlee (Document 2),which explains how Attlee rose, almost accidentally, to become Labour leader and Prime Minister. Since then, various writers have produced books on Attlee, John Campbell has written a critical one on Nye Bevan, and yet others have written on the history of the period. Most notably, Peter Hennessy's book *Never Again* recaptured the mood of the age, using the title of Labour's attack on the Conservatives in the 1945 general election.[1] The list of articles and books connected with this period would fill most of this chapter.[2] Many of these writers have tended to treat the Attlee years with respect, viewing them variously as evidence of planned socialism, of the shift to the left, of the working out of liberal policies forged in the 1930s and the Second World War, or even as a period of Conservative social reform – 'Butskellism'. Yet if the Attlee years have been the apotheosis of Labour's planned socialist economy for many politicians, this is not a view held by many historians. They have been less sympathetic, willing to challenge the mythology which has been built around the events of 1945–51.

Recent interpretations have raised two major questions about Attlee's Labour Government, the first major area of debate. First, to what extent was the early legislation a product of a social blueprint laid down by the Second Word War? Secondly, and more vitally, were the Labour leaders committed to introducing socialism and taking Britain into new directions?

Paul Addison, Ralph Miliband (Document 3) and other historians have implied that Labour's socialist programme owed much to wartime radicalism and planning, and relatively little to genuine demands from Labour political pressure to introduce socialism.[3] The Labour leaders were seen to be Addison's 'social patriots' carrying out the wartime measures demanded by a radicalised electorate or, in Miliband's less generous estimation, mere managers of the demand for the state capitalism which had emanated from the Second World War. These are views which Kenneth Morgan and Henry Pelling dispute, feeling that Labour offered more than wartime radicalism required.[4] These issues, dealt with in the previous chapter, have been re-examined in a recent book by Steven Fielding, Peter Thompson and Nick Tiratsoo[5] (Document 1). This notes that Labour politicians asked what went wrong, following the Labour Party defeat in the 1951 general election, and what has gone wrong since. It suggests, from the evidence provided by various mass observation surveys and other cultural evidence, that in 1945 Labour was ahead of the electorate, not behind it. Indeed, it appears that the social unity and radicalisation of the Second World War period has been greatly exaggerated. Labour won in 1945 because of other factors, such as the poor organisation of the Conservative Party, rather than because it was offering socialism. What went wrong between 1945 and 1951 had much to do with Labour's flawed perception that the electorate supported socialism when in fact it simply wanted the pre-war conditions without high unemployment. Once this was realised, Labour leaders were reluctant to go further in offering socialist measure.

In this, and other works, the same authors have also questioned the ability of the Labour leadership to deliver their social promises because they did not understand how to manage the economy. This seems unfair to governments which did so much to recapture the lost trade and output of the pre-war years in extremely difficult circumstances. However, this is supported by Jim Fyrth's edited collection of essays entitled *Labour's High Noon*.[6] In this, authors such as John Saville and Michael Cunningham suggest that Labour did not know how to operate the economy, and that Labour's economic planning was a failure.[7] John Foster suggests that the Keynesian economic management that Labour adopted 'demanded the practical demobilisation of working-class organisation at its basic level: on wages and conditions' if it was to work.[8] Thus it was perhaps just as well that the Labour Governments did not press too far with socialist reforms, given that they were incapable of delivering the necessary economic growth to sustain them.

There is, inevitably, a deep difference between the Morgan line and the Fielding, Thompson and Tiratsoo one, for while the former maintains that Labour achieved much, the latter sees Labour as going further than the electorate wanted, being unable to afford further socialist policies, and having therefore to modify its position. To Morgan, then, the Attlee Labour Governments were, not surprisingly, the most effective since the passage of the Great Reform Act of 1832.[9]

Seen in these terms, the difference of opinion between Labour and Marxist historians seems irrelevant. Marxists might deny Labour's efforts and the Labour Party supporters admire them but, given that the electorate may have felt that Labour's socialist measures were too advanced, it is not surprising that Labour had to trim its sails to the political wind. The economic crises of 1947 and 1949 also helped Labour leaders to consolidate their existing reforms, rather than to introduce new ones, after July 1948 when both the National Health Service (NHS) and the national insurance scheme came into force.

There is no doubt that the Beveridge Report (1942) provided the blueprint for the introduction of the contributory insurance principle, although there is equally no doubt that Attlee's Labour Governments went further than Beveridge and wartime radicalism demanded in the socialist measures they offered. Indeed, both points can be seen with regard to the formation of the NHS. The Beveridge Report deliberated upon the need for a comprehensive health and rehabilitation service, and emphasised the need for a universal contributory scheme of health provision which would make medical and dental treatment immediately available whether in private or public health hospitals. There was an acceptance, however, that contemporary provision of private and public health systems might be better organised.[10] The Labour Party's *A National Service for Health* (1943) accepted these ideas, although it anticipated 'a national full-time salaried and public service' for general practitioners.[11] Henry Willink, Churchill's Minister of Health, offered a scheme which contemplated some state control over doctors. But none of these reports or scheme ever envisaged the nationalisation of the hospitals which Bevan's National Health Service Bill intended, nor the extent to which GPs would be drawn into the NHS on a quasi-salaried basis. These proposals put Nye Bevan into conflict with Herbert Morrison, Lord President of the Council, in building up a scheme to nationalise hospitals and the medical services, and in maintaining the NHS without charges. Bevan was also involved in a famous battle with the doctors to get them to join the NHS. In the end his non-contributory NHS scheme was implemented, replacing the previous fear implicit in his book *In Place of Fear* (Document 9).

On the basis of the NHS, then, Labour's social measures were more than simply a response to the blueprint suggested by Beveridge for it is clear that this socialist commitment went well beyond the contributory and limited public control scheme that he and others envisaged (see Chapter 1). The Attlee Governments ought to be seen as successful administrations that went well beyond the limits of wartime radicalism, as suggested by Keith Laybourn (Document 4). This view accords with those of Fielding, Thompson and Tiratsoo, although the emphasis is different.

The second debate concerns Labour's apparent political decline after 1951. Looking back from around the turn of the century, it is clear that the

Labour Party has not collapsed and that it is still electable. Nevertheless, this
was not apparent throughout the 13 years of continuous Conservative rule
between 1951 and 1964, and again in the 18 years of Conservative rule
between 1979 and 1997. Indeed, in 1960 Mark Abrams and Richard Rose
asked the question *Must Labour Lose?*[12] This followed Labour's third successive general election defeat in 1959. In the eight years leading to that defeat,
Labour had been divided in opposition. A group of 50 or so 'Bevanites'
demanded more immediate left-wing responses to the issues of the day, and
in 1955 Bevan was almost expelled from the Labour Party. Thereafter there
was greater unity which saw Hugh Gaitskell, who replaced Attlee as leader
in 1955, finally join up with Bevan, who became Labour's deputy leader. Yet
even this did not resolve the problems of the Labour Party. Indeed, Gaitskell
had been convinced that Tony Crosland's *Future of Socialism* (1955) was the
correct analysis of the future. It argued that the application of new technology
had solved the problem of production, and that public ownership was now
less relevant than before. What was required, it was suggested, was that
socialism should emphasise equality, a classless society, and the development
of welfare provision (Document 5). Any doubts about this were dispelled
with Labour's general election defeat in 1959, which led Gaitskell to attempt
to remove Clause Four (on public ownership) from the Labour Party
Constitution at the 1959 Labour Party Conference. The attempt was unsuccessful, although he subsequently battled, successfully, to get the Labour
Party to reinstate its commitment to multilateral, rather than unilateral,
nuclear disarmament.

Despite Gaitskell's failure to get the Labour Party to remove Clause Four,
Morgan Phillips, the General Secretary, did decide to review Labour's policies
(Document 10) *en route* to producing *Signpost for the Sixties* (Document 11).
Unfortunately, Gaitskell was not to see the results of these changes. He died
in 1963, and was replaced as Labour leader by Harold Wilson, who led
Labour to victory in the 1964 General Election with his demand to trans-
form the economy with 'white-heat' technology[13] (see the end of Document
11). Labour's wilderness years were over and, though replaced in office by the
Conservatives between 1970 and 1974, the feeling that Labour would never win
again did not reappear until after Thatcher's general election victory of 1983.

The years of the Wilson and Callaghan (Callaghan was elected as Labour
Leader in 1976 after the retirement of Wilson as both Prime Minister and
Labour Leader) leaderships between 1963 and 1979 initially promised a great
deal for Labour, but were constricted by one economic crisis after another.
Whilst Wilson had come to power in 1964 committed to oversee the
expansion of science and technological innovation within a modern and
dynamic economy, it is clear that his Government faced serious economic
problems which led it to adopt a siege mentality. In 1967, following upon

wage controls and the devaluation of the pound, trust was destroyed between the Labour Government and the trade unions. This led to trade-union opposition to Barbara Castle's proposals to curtail strike action and the withdrawal of her White Paper *In Place of Strife* (see Chapter 9). In the 1970s, the attempt to form a voluntary system of controlling wage demands through the Social Contract failed when the Wilson and Callaghan Governments failed to deliver the increased social spending that was promised as a means of narrowing income differentials. Indeed, the severe economic crisis and the run on the pound forced Denis Healey, the Chancellor of the Exchequer, to seek financial help from the International Monetary Fund, which insisted upon substantial spending cuts in 1976. At this point, the Labour Government effectively abandoned its commitment to spending large sums of money to guarantee full employment.

Faced with an increasing trade union rebellion, and having to be propped up by Liberal support from 1977, the Callaghan Government was eventually defeated at the general election of May 1979 following the industrial unrest now known as the 'winter of discontent' of 1978–9. Labour's political decline then continued throughout the 1980s and 1990s.

Despite the fluctuating fortunes of Labour, and indeed the Conservative Party, there seemed to be remarkably little differences in their general approach to the welfare state, domestic issues and foreign policy. Many historians and writers have referred to the period 1951–79 as one of political consensus, when all political parties accepted the capitalist-based welfare state of Britain. Dennis Kavanagh has particularly stressed this point in contrast to the politics adopted by Margaret Thatcher in the 1980s (Document 6). However, not all would agree that such consensus existed, and this is the basis of the third debate referred to here. Even those who accept consensus as the defining basis of British politics define it with qualifications. Historians and political writer such as Dennis Kavanagh, P. Morris,[14] Ralph Miliband, Tony Benn and David Marquand have accepted that there was some type of consensus in British politics after the Second World War, although they often differ over whether or not it was a pre-war feature of British politics or a post-war development. Ranged against them, however, are Ben Pimlott and Michael Fraser,[15] both of whom reject the idea that consensus could mean anything in a society in which politicians were so fundamentally divided on policies. Thatcher, to them, merely sharpened the divides that already existed. Kavanagh, on the other hand, would simply argue that Thatcher's commitment to principle in politics sought to negate most of what had happened before.

Reflecting on the pre-war situation, it is wise to remember that in most issues of policy there was agreement between the two political parties on broad principles, if not necessarily in the fine detail. This was true of the mixed economy, for Labour pushed no further with nationalisation, and the Conservatives removed only the steel industry from public ownership. Both parties continued to retreat from empire, supported NATO, wished to work with the trade unions and approved of a minimalist welfare state based upon social security. While the fine detail of policies might differ, the broad principles of policy remained the same. It was thus a shock when Thatcher challenged the welfare state and the trade unions, and further pushed forward the demand for freedom in the face of socialism.

The Conservatives had shared parliamentary power almost equally with the Labour Party between 1945 and 1979, although they were subsequently to remain in office for a continuous period of 18 years. Although not a central debate – indeed rather a sub-debate – the question has been asked why the Conservatives were so successful. A variety of historians, including Brendan Evans and Andrew Taylor, suggest that it is because the party has remained politically flexible and pragmatic, not hooked upon principles, although identified with traditions.[16] John Ramsden, whilst accepting this point, has also suggested that it was the result of good party organisation, and that the party has done well out of economic expansion in the southern part of England (Document 7).

There may have been several factors responsible for the fact that there were Conservative Governments between 1951 and 1964 and from 1970 to 1974, but what is clear is that these had relatively little to do with the success of the Conservative Party in government. Under Churchill, Eden, Alec Douglas-Home and Edward Heath, the Conservatives formed governments which faced serious difficulties. Most obviously, they presided over Britain's decline as a world power, a fact most marked in the Suez Crisis in 1956 when, having invaded Egypt with the French to protect British interests in the Suez Canal – still the routeway to the Far East – the Anglo-French forces were forced to withdraw as a result of American pressure. This was partly responsible for the resignation of Sir Anthony Eden and his replacement by Harold Macmillan, whose own retirement in 1963 was prompted by the fact that he faced both cancer of the prostrate and the Profumo crisis, a sexual scandal with security implications. When Edward Heath became Prime Minister in June 1970, he was immediately faced with industrial unrest and economic problems. The introduction of the Industrial Relations Act of 1971 did not help matters, and the miners' strikes of 1972 and 1974 eventually helped to bring about the defeat of the Conservative Party. Thus, although the Conservatives won the approval of the electorate, it faced many of the same types of problem in office that the Labour Governments endured.

Indeed, both Labour and Conservative Governments were faced with the serious problem of Britain's relative industrial decline (see Chapter 9) and falling international status. Even Macmillan's (Supermac's) suggestion that 'most of our people had never had it so good' rang hollow when Britain faced rising inflation and living standards that were declining in relation to her major industrial competitors. Nonetheless, the electorate fluctuated between the Conservative Party and the Labour Party in its desire to improve Britain's financial and political position.

The success of the Labour and Conservative Parties raises the issue of the other political parties, the fourth debate indicated in the introduction. Apart from winning some political kudos at parliamentary by-elections, and through an alliance in 1977 with James Callaghan's Labour Government, the Liberal Party had a very limited presence in the House of Commons. Nevertheless, in line with some other small political parties, there was a general trend towards an increasing non-Labour/Conservative vote, although this was not reflected in the House of Commons as a result of Britain's 'first-past-the-post electoral system. In 1979, however, there was a setback for that trend, although minority political parties have done well since (Document 8). In the years 1945–79, though, the minority political parties carried very little meaningful influence in British politics.

Conclusion

Politics changed considerably in the years 1945–79. The Attlee Labour Governments created the welfare state, which owed as much to their own ideology as it did to the Beveridge blueprint. Nevertheless, it created a mixed economy, and it may well have been that the Attlee Governments limited the advance of the socialist state because of the hesitancy of the electorate, although financial difficulties and the need to implement the new schemes must have been considerations. Defeated in 1951, the Labour Party began to doubt whether it would ever be elected again, a doubt which resurfaced after 1979. For this reason, its leader attempted, in 1959, to abandon Clause Four of the Labour Party Constitution, advocating public ownership. Even though this was not actually abandoned until Tony Blair pressed the party to do so in the mid-1990s, it is clear that the Labour Governments of Harold Wilson and James Callaghan were not prepared to venture further. Indeed, with both the Labour and the Conservative Parties steering a middle course it is hardly surprising that the years between 1951 and 1979 saw something of a political consensus, subsequently rudely disturbed by Margaret Thatcher's commitment to the principle of an anti-socialist and anti-state policy. In the meantime, the smaller political parties played an almost infinitesimal part in British politics, even though their electoral support was expanding rapidly. Until 1979, then, politics generally shifted to the left, with more state involvement than previously suggested before the Second World War. This contrasts with the years since 1979, which have seen a shift to the right under the Conservative administrations of Thatcher and Major and the Labour administration of Blair. The abandonment of Clause Four and the promotion of Blair's 'third way' policies since the 1990s, perhaps indicates that the policies of Gaitskell and Crosland have won over the Labour Party, and that there is now a new consensus which is far to the right of that which operated until 1979. Nevertheless, one must acknowledge that the views of Crosland/ Gaitskell and Blair are different. Whilst Crosland advocated the end of Clause Four, he did not believe in the need for social welfare and redistribution of wealth through state action. Blair's 'third way' has abandoned the idea of redistribution and Keynesian interventionism as a way to ensure full employment.

Documents
SECONDARY SOURCES AND INTERPRETATIONS

1 – Steven Fielding, Peter Thompson and Nick Tiratsoo, *'England Arise!' The Labour Party and Popular Politics in 1940s Britain* (Manchester, Manchester University Press, 1995), pp 210–14, 217–18

By the beginning of the 1960s memories of 1945 had been clouded by the internal struggle over nationalisation and Labour's repeated electoral failures. Writing at the time, the journalist Anthony Howard reflected the Party attitudes to the Attlee Government:

Occasionally late at night at a Labour Party conference – or in the small hours of the morning at the most strenuous gathering of the TUC – the cry can still be heard. 'Where,' a plaintive, maudlin voice will ask, 'did it go wrong?'

Most historians of the 1945–51 Labour Governments have tried to answer this question. In so doing, they have often assumed one or other of the embattled positions adopted within the Party during the 1950s. Consequently, many accounts of the Attlee years suggest that if only ministers had acted in a different manner – a bit more or less nationalisation here, or a more rigorous or flexible set of controls there – then electoral success would have been guaranteed. Thus, failure can be reduced to an examination of the Labour leadership and Cabinet decision-making. One important corollary of this approach has been the widespread, but barely substantiated belief amongst historians that wartime public sentiment was conducive to the implementation of radical policies. There is, in fact, little difference in the way defenders and critics of the Labour Party have interpreted popular politics during this period. Whereas the former have considered that Labour reflected the people's mood, the latter have stated that the Party was much more the conservative force. That the people's politics may have inhibited Labour's attempt to build socialism has never been seriously countenanced.

It should be clear by now that this study is critical of accounts which view Labour's time in office exclusively through Cabinet minutes, Commons debates and Trade Union Congress reports. Any complete history of the period has to take account of such matters. However, to exclude other subjects from view seriously distorts our understanding of politics in the 1940s. Evidence derived from a range of sources, in particular Mass Observation, opinion polls and social surveys also needs to be given adequate weight. These take us beyond the charmed circle of enlightened civil servants and the politically engaged and allow some assessment to be made of the actions and opinions of the vast majority of the British people...

In order to emphasise the case made in this work it is now appropriate to recapitulate its argument. The war's impact was widely misconstrued both by many influential contemporaries and later historians. Whilst the conflict promoted the desire for social harmony and a new political settlement in the minds of the minority, in others this was clearly not the case. First, though the evacuation of working-class children may have temporarily bridged social differences in some households, in others, it actually reinforced pre-existing class antagonisms. Similarly, German bombing of Britain's urban centres often failed to bridge status distinctions within the working class, let alone overcome those more profound differences which divided classes. Second, the political radicalisation, much commented upon at the time and subsequently, has been greatly exaggerated... As some pessimists noted at the time, the experience of the Second World War – whether it was spent in the factory or at the Front – did not imbue people with a new conception of public affairs.

Analysis of Labour's 1945 victory, still in terms of constituencies won the Party's greatest triumph, confirms this conclusion. Invariably interpreted as evidence of the public's radicalisation, Labour's achievement in fact relied upon a number of other, more mundane, factors. The Party clearly won the positive support of a large number of voters who wished to see the implementation of substantial reforms. Labour exploited this advantage to the full because, as Conservatives alleged, Transport House's organisation was, perhaps uniquely better than their own. The party also was, perhaps, uniquely, better than their own. The party also benefited from the support of those more disenchanted with the Conservatives than enthused by Labour's promise of socialism. As a consequence, Attlee's Commons majority gave the impression of a landslide which, on the basis of the popular vote, was not merited.

Many of those who considered that Dunkirk and the Blitz had fundamentally changed social and political attitudes were Labour-inclined writers who viewed war in the light of their own hopes for the future. This version of events was also embraced, a few doubters apart, by the majority of Labour leaders and members. To interpret the war as an ethical breakthrough suited their conception of socialism. Thus, the Second World War was seen as supplying the missing sense of purpose that had barred Labour's route to power before 1939. The social solidarity and political engagement believed to define the wartime mood were thought to be the means by which socialism would emerge after the war. Labour's 1945 victory was presented as proof of this view. Once installed in office, it was Labour's peacetime task to promote the consummation of wartime developments...

Labour's inability to make socialists on the scale anticipated in 1945 demonstrated the extent to which the effect of the Second World War had been misinterpreted. Whilst Labour's promise of full employment and social security encouraged voters to support the Party in unprecedented numbers few would be willing to embrace its ethical vision...

Pressing electoral considerations forced the Labour leadership to come to terms with this popular indifference...

This study argues, therefore, that something did go 'wrong' during 1945–51. The basic problem, however, was not Party policy. Instead, the answer to the question 'what went wrong?' lies in the more fundamental issue of Labour's flawed perception of the electorate. Due to the effects of the Second World War, many Labour leaders and activists believed that the British people had become uniquely responsive to ethical socialism. Yet, in 1945 most voters simply wanted to return to pre-war conditions, albeit without the insecurity induced by high unemployment and inadequate public welfare. Consequently, they approved of the practical reforms outlined in *Let Us Face the Future*. However, whilst Labour members saw this programme as merely the first step towards the responsible society, even a majority of Labour supporters had no wish to embrace ethical change. The electorate's fundamental indifference to Labour's wider vision was only recognised by a few in the Party. Inheritors of a nineteenth century political tradition predicated on a forward march to an ineluctable end, Labour activists in particular refused to accept the legitimacy of popular feeling. After the crisis of 1947 the leadership responded to Labour's electoral unpopularity by proposing to temporarily 'consolidate' the Government's achievements. This was opposed by those in the Party who remained confident that voters would eventually be forthcoming. They wanted to advance further down the road to socialism without regard to public opinion. If Labour was losing support, they argued, this was because too little, not too much, socialist legislation had been passed... [They then go on to argue that traditional working-class culture was not homogeneous, and was far from reaching some type of pinnacle in 1945.]

A sceptical reader might consider that the preceding chapters have been unduly negative. It has been argued that the war did not transform social and political attitudes to the extent once thought; that Labour members failed to accurately interpret the moment; that the Party was unable to fully connect with popular concerns. This would not be an entirely accurate impression. The Labour Government, after all, implemented a reform programme without precedent in spite of this... Yet, Labour's hopes for a socialist transformation were never fulfilled. Overlooking the Party's appeal for new morality, voters were, instead, attracted by the prospect of a welfare state and full employment. This was only half of what was on offer in 1945.

2 – Kenneth Harris, *Attlee* (London, Weidenfeld and Nicolson, 1982), pp 565, 566, 567–8

Attlee believed in Clause IV to the end of his days. He hoped that society would become less the product of profit motive and more the projection 'of the zeal to work for the good of the community'. But he was not in a hurry to see it happen, or ever certain that it would. 'My own view is that where the leadership is good, whether in the private or public sector, the response is satisfactory'...

One of Attlee's greatest strengths as leader was that he did not represent any of the contending groups in Labour's perennial struggle for dominance. His membership of a trade union was a formality, and his connection with the ILP did not survive that body's decision to leave the Labour party in 1931. He was not associated closely with the Socialist League, nor with the enduring Fabian tradition of the party. His rise to leadership demonstrated that the lack of a power base in some sections of the party may not be a handicap to an aspiring Labour leader, though a safe seat is an inestimable advantage. He became deputy leader only because nearly all his seniors were defeated in the 1931 election. Only through the inability of rival camps to agree did he become leader in 1935, and the same rivalries sustained his leadership at the next test in 1945. He was thus an 'accidental' prime minister, as his denigrators have been ready to point out...

Bevan, Bevin, Morrison, Cripps, Dalton as leaders would have caused conflict...

He was laconic and lacked charisma... He was not 'a great man'; he was not exactly 'the common man'; he was, in fact an ordinary middle-class figure, and yet he was leader of the country. If it could happen to him, it could happen to anybody...

As a statesman, Attlee's record is very good, registering one complete failure, some weaknesses, some successes and one epoch-making achievement.

3 – Ralph Miliband, *Parliamentary Socialism* (London, Merlin Press, second edition 1972, first edition Allen and Unwin 1961), p 288

In regard to nationalisation, there was no ambiguity at all. From the beginning, the nationalisation proposals of the Government were designed to achieve the sole purpose of improving the efficiency of a capitalist economy, not as marking the beginning of a wholesale transformation, and this was an aim to which many Tories, whatever they might say in the House of Commons, were easily reconciled, and which some even approved – with the exception of iron and steel.

4 – Keith Laybourn, *The Rise of Labour: The British Labour Party 1890–1979* (London, Edward Arnold, 1988), pp 136–7

Recent writers have been right to attack the political myths which have surrounded the Attlee governments of 1945 to 1951. In no way can it be correct to see these administrators as calmly, and with deliberate intent, introducing the planned socialist state devised by democratic socialists and agreed to by the nation as a whole, as some contemporary writers and recent politicians would have us believe. There was much less planning than the myths allow for and far too much hesitancy, produced by the acute financial difficulties within which these administrations worked...

Historians have been no less partial than politicians in examining the Attlee years in ways which suit their own political perspectives. Marxists have, on the whole, denigrated the achievements of the Labour government due to the fact that their ideology rejects the view that democratic parliamentary socialism could ever be other than inefficient and prone to compromise... Those who are more right-wing are inclined to accept that the Attlee governments had their faults but did achieve a significant shift in the attitude and role of government in society. Morgan, very much in the moderate Labour mould, acknowledges the great achievements of the Attlee years...

[There follows a discussion of Bevan's distinctive contribution to the NHS.] Equally, there is no doubt that Attlee and his colleagues did envisage the creation of a socialist state. But as democratic socialists they did not seek to transform the nation overnight... And it is widely agreed that the Labour programme of 1945 to 1947 was one of the most ambitious and successful to be introduced by any post-war administration...

Indeed, the successes of the Labour governments should not be overlooked. They offered the most effective evidence of what could be achieved by a democratic socialist administration. They brought about a change in the direction for the British nation, and moved government towards a more humanitarian concern for its people, committing it to the maintenance of full employment – a strong contrast to the events that followed the First World War. These achievements were considerable and formed the basis of the policies of successive governments, at least until 1979.

5 – Brian Brivati, *Hugh Gaitskell* (London, Richard Cohen Books, 1996), p 287–8, 293, 295–6, 339–40, 444–5

… the very success of the Attlee governments gave rise to many problems, the most compelling of which was how the Labour Party was to move on. There were different kinds of responses. For some the Attlee governments represented a beach-head in the invasion of capitalism: the task was to break out of the beach-head and gain control over the remains of the private sector. For others, the achievements of the Attlee governments had settled the domestic balance of the economy, the mixed economy was the new reality and the challenge was the effective management of the mixed economy to promote greater equality – an objective which might or might not be achieved by gaining greater control in the form of nationalisation.

This second school came to be known as the 'revisionists', after Eduard Bernstein's classic text *Revising Marxism*. The irony was not lost on Tony Crosland, one of the key players amongst the revisionists. Some years later when helping to organise the Gaitskellite Campaign for Democratic Socialism, Crosland used to add Bernstein's name to lists of possible supporters. Revisionism was a mixture of economics, political philosophy, practical proposals and party propaganda. Gaitskell embraced it, helped to shape it and championed it practically; his theoretical contribution was, however, rather more limited.

Gaitskell always began his analysis of British socialism by considering its roots. Thus, in a *Political Quarterly* piece published in 1956, on the 'Economic Aims of the Labour Party', he opens by reminding his readers that 'Labour 'has never been encumbered by a precise and rigid collection of dogmas set out in the works of the socialist fathers'… [Brivati then examines the views of Gaitskell which distance the Labour Party from Marx, emphasises the links with the trade unions and suggests that its inspiration came from the Fabians and the Independent Labour Party.]

What is striking when reading Crosland and Gaitskell's work… is the confidence they expressed that the economic problem of wealth creation had been solved. This optimism is matched by an astonishing faith in the power of indicative planning and demand management. But Crosland also believed that it was the affluence of the new society which had contributed to the defeat of the backward-looking Labour Party and that if the party were to win it had to stress modern visions of socialism, like social welfare, and had not to harp on about 'nationalising the commanding heights of the economy'.

The new society, brought about by the development of world markets in the twentieth century and by the Second World War, had produced a new economic organisation. Crosland called this the 'mixed economy', to imply a mixture of state and private ownership, and he was adamant that the Labour Party must adapt its vision of socialism to this new situation if it was ever to win power...

For both the working-class and middle-class activists the success of the Attlee governments in fulfilling many of the demands of the 1930s created a psychological barrier against accepting the need to change socialism. The experience of government, the very creation of a partially socialist state, meant that many of the old dreams were dead. [There was thus confusion about party objectives in the future.] Crosland saw the way out of the confusion and the first step in re-establishing the agenda of socialism as the production of a modernised definition of socialism. Gaitskell was to latch on to this later when he asked for a revision of the Labour Party's basic aims. Crosland believed that the only constant element, 'common to all the bewildering variety of different doctrines which had been known as socialism', consisted of certain 'moral values and aspirations'; and people had called themselves socialists because they shared these aspirations. Therefore a belief in the 'possible future that designates socialism' rather than an attachment to a particular set of means was what was important.

The values that Crosland identified were as follows: a protest against the material poverty and physical squalor which capitalism produced; a wider concern for social welfare for the interests of those in need or oppressed or unfortunate for whatever cause; a belief in equality and the classless society and especially the desire to give the worker his or her just rights and a responsible status at work, rejection of competitive antagonism, an ideal of fraternity and co-operation and a protest against the inefficiencies of capitalism as an economic system. Gaitskell echoes many of these concerns directly in his 'Amplification of Aims' and in his speech at the post-mortem Conference after the 1959 general election.

The most obvious omission from this list of socialist values was the question of the 'ownership of the means of production, distribution and exchange'. As socialism was not defined in Marxist terms of ownership, adherence to nationalisation was not a key criterion for socialism. Moreover, simply as a means to an end – the end not specified – nationalisation could, Gaitskell and Crosland argued, be used to justify types of society which had little to do with socialism. Ownership was not central to socialism; but social welfare aspirations and equality were...

[After Labour's defeat in the 1959 General Election it was argued by some that nationalisation, which was unpopular, was one of the major reasons for Labour's defeat. This was an argument which Gaitskell accepted, in line with his revisionist views. As a result he spoke, unsuccessfully, against Clause Four, the public ownership section of the Labour Party's constitution.]

On Saturday 28 November 1959 Gaitskell delivered the speech to the Party Conference in Blackpool. The circumstances were unfavourable. There was no platform position; Gaitskell spoke for himself alone. Even his initial procedural decision to push the reforms through Conference were probably mistaken…

Gaitskell spoke later on the first day. The key section of his speech argued that Clause 4 in its current form was inadequate and 'lays us open to continued misrepresentation… It implies that we propose to nationalise everything, but do we? Every little pub and garage? Of course not. We have long come to accept a mixed economy… the view… of 90 per cent of the Labour Party. Had we better say so instead of going out of our way to court misrepresentation?…'

The touchstone for Gaitskell was rationalism. He believed in equality because it made sense and because he was confident that he had the macroeconomic ideas that could make a more equal society a reality…

As the history of the Labour Party has unfolded since January 1963 so there have been a number of manifestations of Hugh Gaitskell to add to the views of him abroad in his lifetime. The first picture to come into focus was the Mr Butskell caricature of the 1950s – which took more concrete form in the 'desiccated calculating machine' image of the anti-unilateralist. At the very end of his life and in his death, the man came through the image as both a hero and a lost leader for a generation of radically minded people. The hero was given his monument in Philip William's official life, finally published in 1979. After this, with the Labour Party dividing and the SDP quietly claiming his mantle, he descended into political obscurity. As collectivism ended and the Labour Party switched from the intellectual powerhouse of post-war contemporary history to the intellectual hoarder of other people's ideas, so Hugh Gaitskell slipped from political actor and influence into history: the kinder, gentler, more tolerant and more egalitarian world he tried to make, and then was robbed of the opportunity of making, slipped with him.

6 – Dennis Kavanagh, *Thatcherism and British Politics: The End of Consensus* (Oxford, Oxford University Press, 1987), pp 5, 6, 7, 9, 34, 308–9

In coming to power in 1979, Mrs Thatcher made no secret of her determination to break with what *The Times* called the clubbable consensus. Mrs Thatcher herself was the product of a change in British politics and, in turn, she gave voice and direction to the new policies. One always has to take care in analysing the rhetoric of politicians… A reader of Mrs Thatcher's speeches, however, does not need to be so careful. She is what she says she is. A content analysis of her speeches in the 1979 general election campaign reveals an emphasis upon two themes. The negative one is 'socialism' and the positive one is 'freedom', or a 'free society' or 'freedom under the law'. In her rhetoric she scorns consensus politics and proclaims her determination to scrap many aspects of it…

Consensus is not an ideal term because it can be used in so many different ways. My main interest is to identify a set of politics and values which, to a large extent, were shared by all post-war governments until 1979. Trevor Smith [*Politics of Corporate Economic* (Oxford, Martin Robertson, 1979)] has fairly objected to the use of the term consensus which he associated with agreement by deliberation or conscious bipartisanship. He thinks a more accurate term in this context is policy coincidence…

Mrs Thatcher has clearly wanted to break with many old policies. In a prepared speech in the 1979 general election she compared herself to the Old Testament Prophets, who did not say 'Brothers I want a consensus', and she proclaimed the importance of conviction and principles in politics – as if these were incompatible with consensus. In 1981 in Australia, she replied to criticisms from Mr Heath that she was abandoning consensus politics. 'For me, consensus seems to me the process of abandoning all beliefs, values and policies'…

[Suggesting that Thatcherism tends to mean anti-consensus, strong government which resists pressure groups, and opposition to high inflation and trade-union militancy, Kavanagh suggests the following.]

The term Thatcherism has three different contexts. The first refers to Mrs Thatcher's no-nonsense style of leadership and hostility to the premium placed on gaining agreement by consensus. As a leader she is remarkable for regarding politics as a suitable arena for the expression of personal beliefs. In contrast to Harold Macmillan, who thought that people should turn to bishops for moral leadership, Mrs Thatcher sees the expression of fundamental beliefs as part of the leader's task…

By the early 1950s it was already possible to refer to a post-war consensus about many, though not all policies. In foreign affairs there developed a general agreement about such issues as Britain's role as a nuclear power, membership of NATO and decolonisation… Until 1961 there was front-bench agreement that Britain should stand aside from the European Community…

The package of policies on the domestic front is familiar: full employment budgets, the greater acceptance – even conciliation – of the trade unions, whose bargaining position was strengthened by increased membership and full employment…

The old consensus had its admirers among various lobbies, senior civil servants, front benchers, and opinion formers. It would be quite wrong to assume that leaders lacked conviction or belief in the policies they pursued... However, the post-war consensus had its critics too, particularly among Labour's left and the free market wing of the Conservative party. The political agenda is always in a state of transition and like a paradigm, the old Butskellite, Social Democratic, Keynesian models have gradually been abandoned as more and more anomalies have crept in. In recent years the political party, economic interests and groups most closely associated with the collective consensus have all declined. And, of course, the country's economic failures have all gnawed at the foundations of the old consensus. An increase in political polarisation and adversarial politics between the parties has probably been an inevitable reaction of the new situation.

This writer's expectation is that there will be a new 'consensus' on social and economic policy, though it may be more difficult to obtain... and that the new policy will include most of the social and welfare elements of the old one and some of the economic thinking of Thatcherism.

7 – John Ramsden, 'The Conservative Party Since 1945' in Anthony Seldon (ed.), *UK Political Parties Since 1945* (London, Philip Allan, 1990), pp 21–2, 32

The most obvious and important continuity is the fact that the Conservatives have remained a generally successful party. By the end of the 1987 Parliament, the Conservatives will have governed for about 29 out of 46 years since the war, all the time in a single party government and with an effective working majority. This is in itself not new: in the century since the 1886 Irish crisis effectively re-balanced British politics, the party has also governed for about two-thirds of the time. The near despair of 1945 and acute party crises of 1965 and 1975 must both be set against this record of success – and the expectation of success.

The Conservatives have always enjoyed an organisational lead over other parties, not apparent in 1945 but certainly re-established by 1950 and ever-present since. By any measurement, such as the number of members and activists, the number of party employees, the amount of money available for electioneering, that lead has been continuous. Much of the advantage doubtless accrued to the party simply as the best defender of industry and property, but much too owed to a readiness to innovate. In this field the Conservatives have been the least conservative of all the British parties: the poster campaigns run by Colman, Prentis and Varley in 1958–9, use of opinion polls and panel surveys in the sixties and co-ordinated down-market campaigning through Saatchi and Saatchi in 1978–9 are all examples of Conservative experiments that other parties had to follow...

It was in the perpetuation of the loyalties and instincts of unionism that Conservatives remained strong in such places as Liverpool and Glasgow, and it is no accident that no alternative basis for Conservative strength was found when religion and nationality ceased to be dominant issues in such places in the sixties.

With these exceptions, the regional basis of the strength has remained remarkably constant. Conservatives have consistently done better in the southeastern half of England, suburban constituencies and rural areas, than in Wales and Scotland, northern England or the inner cities. The distribution of the seats in 1983 roughly matched that of 1935, when the Conservatives and Labour won a similar share of the seats. What did change though was the number of seats in the party's southeastern stronghold region, as economic development tilted the balance of population. Now that half the population of Britain live to the south of Birmingham, it is a greater political benefit to have strong roots there. The southeastern counties and London suburbs, always the best Conservative areas since the days of Peel and Disraeli, had 165 MPs in 1935 but 235 MPs by 1983 – an increase of over 40 percent. It is no wonder that the party of 'Selsdon man' – and indeed of 'Finchley woman' – has prospered...

[Much of the rest of the essay deals, briefly, with the recovery of Conservative confidence between 1945 and 1957, the administrations of Sir Anthony Eden, Harold Macmillan and Alec Douglas Home, and the Heath experiment of 1965–75. This is followed by a brief analysis of Margaret Thatcher and Sir Keith Joseph – her mentor, whose speeches of 1974–5 were issued as *Reversing the Trend* – who rejected the policies which postwar governments had pursued. The Centre for Policy Studies which he formed with Thatcher in 1974 provided the pressure group for free market ideas.]

Much of the character of the Conservative Party at any time is derived from its leader, who sets the tone and much of the acceptable agenda. Nobody would now underestimate that fact in Margaret Thatcher's case. It is though still easy to underestimate how far she is a product of the party's shift of direction as well as the fuel in the machine. After 1974 it was clearly what the party desperately wanted.

8 – John Stevenson, 'The Liberal Party Since 1945' in Anthony Seldon (ed.), *UK Political Parties Since 1945* (London, Philip Allan, 1990), pp 40–41, 43

The Torrington by-election [of 1958, in which Mark Bonham-Carter won the seat from the Tories] marks the beginning of the second phase of Liberal politics since the Second World War. Where the years between 1945 and 1958 seemed to continue the process of decline evident between the wars, after 1958 the party began a revival marked by a series of spectacular by-election results and a gradual increase in its share of the vote. Between 1929 and 1958 the party did not win a single by-election. After 1958 the party was to receive needed publicity and welcome boosts to its confidence through its ability to overcome large majorities at by-elections. The party was entering a period when it could act as a vehicle for anti-government protest. But there was a more substantial basis to the Liberal revival shown in an increased share of the vote in the 1959 general election to 6 per cent and the doubling of its voting strength. In 1962 the party achieved another spectacular by-election success when Eric Lubbock won Orpington - the first Liberal breakthrough in the Conservative suburbs and a source of considerable optimism.

The history of the party in the 1960s was one of continued by-election successes... and a slow, painful increase in its share of the vote at general elections and in the number of MPs elected: nine MPs in 1963, rising to 12 in 1966. However, the decade ended with a setback when in 1970 the party was reduced to only six seats and its vote fell, demonstrating the fragility of the Liberals as a parliamentary force...

In 1977 he [David Steel] was given a chance when the ailing administration of James Callaghan sought a pact with the Liberals. The Lib-Lab pact gave the Liberals a consultative role in government but no seats in Cabinet nor any formal promise of proportional representation...

When the Labour government fell in 1979 following the Winter of Discontent the Liberals found themselves smeared by their association with the Labour Party. The party only returned eleven MPs and its vote fell by two millions to 14 per cent of votes cast. The revival seemed stalled.

PRIMARY EVIDENCE AND INFORMATION

9 – Aneurin Bevan, *In Place of Fear* (London, Heinemann, 1952),[17] pp 75–6

When I was engaged in formulating the main principles of the British Health Service, I had to give careful study to various proposals for financing it, and as this aspect of the scheme is a matter of anxious discussion in many parts of the world, it may be useful if I set down the main considerations that guided my choice. In the first place, what was to be its financial relationship with National Insurance; should the Health Service be on an insurance basis? I decided against this. It had always seemed to me that a personal contributory basis was peculiarly inappropriate to a National Health Service. There is, for example, the question of the qualifying period. That is to say, so many contributions for this benefit, and so many more for additional benefits, until enough contributions are eventually paid to qualify the contributor for the full range of benefits.

In the case of health treatment this would give rise to endless anomalies, quite apart from the administrative jungle which would be created. This is already the case in countries where people insure privately for operations as distinct from hospital or vice versa. Whatever may be said for it in private insurance, it would be out of place in a national scheme. Imagine a patient lying in hospital after an operation and ruefully reflecting that if the operation had been delayed another month he would have qualified for the operation benefit. Limited benefits for limited contributions ignore the overriding consideration that the full range of health machinery must be there in any case, independent of the patient's right of access to it...

10 – Morgan Phillips, *Labour in the Sixties* (London, Labour Party, 1960), p 3, 24

Since last October the Labour Party has been immersed in an internal controversy about the causes of its defeat, which has sapped its energies and damaged its morale. It is essential that we should end this sterile inquest...

It has been said that the Labour party is faced with an intolerable dilemma – either to sacrifice its principles in order to win power or to retain its principles and find itself forever in the wilderness. The NEC rejects this dismal view. It believes in a Socialist victory...

Summary of Action Points
1. The National Executive Committee will, during the next two years, survey the major foreign and domestic problems now facing the British people. These will be the subject of reports at Annual Conference.
2. A major drive will be launched in January 1961. The aim will be both to strengthen the Party membership in those areas and groups traditionally loyal to Labour and to extend Party membership into industries and groups where our hold is weak.
3. The National Executive Committee will consult with affiliated Unions on:

(a) measures to broaden the social and occupational base of the Movement and to counteract contracting out;

(b) effective means of getting the ideals, policies and activities of the Labour Movement over to the public;

(c) the development of new machinery for regular consultation between the Party and the Unions;

(d) measures to increase the Party's income.

4. Constituency Parties will be asked, in addition to the recruiting drive, to concentrate upon these tasks:

(a) political training and discussion;

(b) increasing the membership and participation of women;

(c) further expansion of Young Socialist Groups;

(d) improvement of Party premises;

(e) increasing of Party's income.

5. Labour Groups will be asked:

(a) to undertake a review of local government activities with the purpose of:

(i)   humanising local government administration;

(ii) developing services to meet new and emerging needs.

(b) to review their Standing Orders.

(c) to improve their public relations activities

The task will be the subject of more detailed guidance from the National Executive Committee during the course of this year.

11 – Labour Party, *Signpost for the Sixties* (London, Labour Party, 1961), pp 5, 7

At Scarborough last year the Annual Conference received with enthusiasm the pamphlet *Labour in the Sixties* which had been prepared by Mr Morgan Phillips; and accepted unanimously the action points with which it concluded. The first of these runs as follows: 'The National Executive Committee will, during the next two year, survey the major foreign and domestic problems now facing the British people. These will be the subjects of reports to Annual Conference.'

In fulfilment of this pledge to 'report on the major domestic problem now facing the British people,' the National Executive has prepared *Signposts for the Sixties* and will seek approval for it at this year's Conference. In recommending it to the Party, we would emphasise that we have not tried to draw up a comprehensive programme...

Our single aim has been to make good an important deficiency in the formulation of Socialist policy, to which *Labour in the Sixties* pointed. 'What the Party need today,' Mr Phillips wrote, 'is not another batch of policy documents or detailed blueprints but a clear statement both of our distinctive attitude to postwar capitalism and of the new direction we would give to the nation's affairs'. We concur; and that is why so many important topics have to be excluded from this document. Instead of covering all the ground, we prefer to highlight five main themes – planning and economic expansion, the use of our land, a new approach to social security, equality of educational opportunity and fair taxation. These issues, we believe, are becoming increasingly significant and they illustrate both our critique of the Tory Affluent Society and the Socialist remedies we recommend.

We live in a scientific revolution. In the sixteen years since the war ended, man's knowledge and his power over nature – to create or destroy – have grown more than in the previous century. In such an epoch of revolutionary change, those who identify laissez-faire with liberty are enemies, however unwitting, of democracy. The enlargement of freedom which we all desire cannot be achieved by opposing State intervention but only by assuring that the national resources are wisely allocated and community services humanely planned. Indeed, the three main ways of achieving this must be: first, to harness the forces released by science in the service of the community; secondly, to plan and supervise the balanced growth of the economy; and, thirdly, to ensure that the ever-increasing wealth created by modern techniques of production is fairly shared.

Notes on Chapter 8

1   Peter Hennessy, *Never Again, Britain 1949–1951* (London, Jontahan Cape, 1992).
2   See Bibliography.
3   Paul Addison, *The Road to 1945: British Politics and the Second World War* (London, Jonathan Cape, 1975); Ralph Miliband, *Parliamentary Socialism* (London, Merlin. 1972 edition)
4   Kenneth O. Morgan, *Labour in Power: 1945–1951* (Oxford, Clarendon Press, 1984); Henry Pelling, *The Labour Government 1945–51* (London, Macmillan, 1984).
5   Steven Fielding, Peter Thompson and Nick Tiratsoo, *'England Arise!' The Labour Party and Popular Politics in 1940s Britain* (Manchester, Manchester University Press, 1995).
6   Jim Fyrth (ed.), *Labour's High Noon: The Government and the Economy 1945–51* (London. Lawrence & Wishart, 1993).
7   Michael Cunningham, '"From the Ground Up"? The Labour Government and Economic Planning' in Fyrth (ed.), *Labour's High Noon*, pp 3–19.
8   John Foster, 'Labour, Keynesianism and the Welfare State' in Fyrth (ed.), *Labour's High Noon*, p 34.

9   Morgan, *Labour in Power*, p 503.
10 Social and Allied Services, *Report by William Beveridge* (London, HMSO, 1942), pp 158–60.
11 Pelling, *Labour Government*, p 103.
12 Mark Abrams, 'Why Labour has lost the Election' in *Socialist Commentary*, May 1960, June 1960, July 1960, August 1960; later published as Mark Abrams and Richard Rose, *Must Labour Lose?* (London, Penguin, 1960).
13 S. Fielding, '"White Heat" and White Collar: the Evolution of "Wilsonism"' in R. Coopey, Steve Fielding and Nick Tiratsoo (eds), *The Wilson Government 1964–1970* (London, Pinter Publishers, 1993), pp 29–47.
14 D. Kavanagh and P. Morris, *Consensus Politics from Attlee to Thatcher* (1989).
15 M. Fraser article in P. Hennesey and A. Seldon (eds), *Ruling Performance, British Governments from Attlee to Thatcher* (1989).
16 Andrew Taylor and Brendan Evans, *From Salisbury to Major: Continuity and Change in Conservative Politics* (Manchester, Manchester University Press, 1996).
17 Heinemann Educational Publishers, a division of Reed International and Professional Publishers Ltd have no objection to the use of this material, although no copyright holder could be found.

Chapter 9

Britain's Industrial Decline, the Welfare State and Social Problems 1945–79

Writers have, for many years, examined Britain's relative industrial decline, often describing it as the 'British disease', an epithet used to emphasise the uniquely British nature of the problem. The nature and cause of this decline, particularly in manufacturing, has, of course, been subject to intense debate. Foreign competition, the loss of empire, limited technological innovation, strikes and trade unionism, the burden of the welfare state, British cultural attitudes, and even the fall in profitability (Document 1), have been offered in explanation. Solutions have also emerged in abundance as economists and politicians have attempted to address the problem. These range from the removal of the 'nanny' welfare state, on the assumption that the decline has become marked since 1945, to the development of ever-wider world-wide trading regions (Document 3).

In the meantime, while more permanent solutions are being sought, the social consequences of decline are obvious for Britain. The lower rate of economic growth that Britain has often faced has meant that wage levels and standards of living have been falling relative to those of other industrial nations. The assumptions – made by Tony Crosland, Hugh Gaitskell and Harold Wilson in the 1950s and 1960s – that poverty could be defeated by the application of new technology and that living standards would grow constantly have been undermined. In other words, Britain's industrial decline can be seen in the continuation of poverty, and in what seems at present to be the widening of the gulf between the 'rich' and the 'poor'. Britain's industrial decline and its social consequences are thus issues of vital importance to the country, although perhaps more so since the mid- and late 1960s than before, since these factors call into question the viability and continuing existence of the British welfare state. Is the welfare state a burden that Britain cannot afford, or is it an essential part of Britain's economic growth, necessary in order to ensure the proper distribution of wealth throughout society in order to tackle poverty?

The issue of Britain's decline was highlighted by Bryan Gould MP when he addressed a conference at Leeds University in March 1994. He accepted that international trading competition from other rapidly industrialising nations inevitably meant Britain's relative industrial decline, but could not understand why Britain 'should now be doing so much worse than they [other competing industrial nations] are doing'.[1] This is a fair point, since the classic explanations, that international trade competition and the maturing of the economy reduce the rate of growth, should also apply to other maturing nations as well as Britain. The assumption is, therefore, that there is some-thing distinct, if not unique, in Britain's industrial decline.

Nevertheless, the starting point of any explanation of Britain's industrial decline must be seen in terms of her long-term international trading com-petition. Britain was the leading industrial nation at the beginning of the nineteenth century, and inevitably faced the loss of its pre-eminent position as the United States, Germany and other nations industrialised in the mid-dle and later years of that century (Documents 3 and 4). Eric Hobsbawm wrote about this loss at some length in *Industry and Empire* (1968), suggesting that the decline was evident in the late nineteenth century, and that it was at this point that Britain retreated from industry into trade and finance. Nicholas Kaldor, who advised Harold Wilson's Labour Governments of the 1960s, took this further by suggesting that the difference in Britain's perfor-mance was largely to do with the stage which the various industrial economies had reached in their development from immaturity to maturity, but that Britain's industrial future depended largely upon its effective use of 'trained manpower' (Document 4). These ideas on decline have been stressed by other historians who have complained of too little production,[2] or too few producers.[3] Indeed, the interpretations of decline have focused upon the rel-ative contraction of the industrial sector and the move to the service sectors of the economy, a move which, of course, can be interpreted as economic maturing. There is an inevitability about this process, although many writers feel that Britain should be able to retain a higher level of manufacture, out-put and growth than is being achieved.

In recent years, however, there has been an increasing tendency to suggest that there are more specific causes of Britain's decline. Many right-wing historians, such Correlli Barnett, Max Beloff and Lord Robert Blake, have suggested – driven by their ideological opposition to the welfare state – that

Britain's recent industrial decline has been the product of the country's commitment to welfare through Beveridge.[4] 'Blake argues that the vain and egotistical as well as very clever' Beveridge lobbied, with the aid of Keynes in the Treasury, for Britain 'to pursue a course of social reform which she could not afford'.[5] Corelli Barnett, in *Audit of War* and, more recently, *Lost Vision* has endorsed this view. The solution of Britain's problems for these historians is the scaling down of the welfare state, a policy which found favour in the rhetoric, if not the practice, of Mrs Thatcher's administrations in the 1980s.

The origin of these ideas dates back to the end of the Second World War, to the work of Freidrich von Hayek, who felt that liberty and equality were in direct conflict with collective measures. This was developed by politicians such as Enoch Powell and Ian Macleod, to an argument about the economic burden on the welfare state. Powell's views were endorsed by the Institute of Economic Affairs, a right-wing think-tank, which produced a pamphlet entitled 'Towards a Welfare State' (1967), were amplified by Margaret Thatcher at Conservative Party conferences, and amplified in Rhodes Boyson's *Down with the Poor* (1971). Given the economic problems of Labour Governments in the 1970s, it is hardly surprising that James Callaghan also began to question the ability of the nation to support the welfare state at the 1976 Labour Party Conference. Increasingly, then, monetarist ideas began to challenge the twin pillars of welfare politics – the Keynesian ideas of expanding out of slump and the belief that a welfare state was necessary in order to overcome poverty and inequality. By the 1960s, the right were arguing that poverty had ended, despite the contrary views of Peter Townsend, Sir Douglas Black and many other researchers (Documents 8) Above all, however, they argued that the welfare state was not necessary, since it imposed a massive economic burden upon Britain which she could ill afford.

The new right believed that the economic growth of the country was inextricably interlinked with the growth of the welfare state. Economic growth had been held back by the burden of welfare, which had imposed an impossible economic burden. This had to be rolled back. In a version of the classical wage-fund theory, they argued that governments fixed the rate of inflation through the control of the money supply, whilst trade unions fixed the corresponding rate of unemployment through the medium of their wage bargaining. Therefore, if trade-union wage demands were pitched too high, this would result in the loss of their members' jobs. Conversely, the rate of unemployment could be lowered by labour market reforms, that is by pricing oneself back into work. Once government relinquished responsibility for unemployment then the *raison d'être* for budget deficits would disappear and the Public Sector Borrowing Requirement, seen as an important contributory factor to the excessive growth of the money supply, could be cut back. Traditionally, Conservatives have always disliked the public sector, and such cutbacks, it was argued, would not only reduce inflation but also enable direct taxation to be reduced. This in turn would improve the supply side of the economy through improved work incentives and the opportunity for higher personal savings – what Gladstone, in the nineteenth century, saw as allowing money to fructify in the pockets of the people. Finally, and of vital importance, a retreat from the welfare state would remove the threat to liberty which liberal conservatives have always associated with the continuous expansion of the state. Once this 'rolling back of the frontiers of the state' had been accomplished then there would be, it was hoped, a return to the classical political and moral virtues of individual responsibility and prudent housekeeping.

The ideas of the new right are, of course, enveloped within the philosophy of individualism. The welfare state was, and still is, viewed with distrust by it for several reasons. First, the welfare state denies people a choice of service; it exemplifies the coercion inherent in a system that dictates universal ideals of equality, or in other words it sets maximum standards.[6] Indeed, 'The British welfare state has logically and ineluctably become the main instrument for the creation of equality by coercion'.[7] Secondly, it diverts resources away from 'wealth creating' sectors of the economy.[8] Thirdly, it results in high taxation and government borrowing, leading to a spiral of inflation. This is due to peoples' expectations, of their reliance on a 'dependency' culture', and government's unwillingness to put necessary unpopular policies into action. Fourthly, welfare undermines the work ethic and culture: the unemployed have no incentive to work.[9] Fifthly, 'the [national] insurance principle is fraudulent, as a mechanism used to introduce back door socialism... [and] imposing higher taxation... In practice... contributions are a tax on employment'.[10] For these reasons, the new right in general, and Sir Keith Joseph in particular, saw a situation in Britain that was described as 'dysfunctional democracy'. Out of this situation the 'overload thesis' was developed.

This thesis is crucial in understanding the new right perspective on the welfare state in the 1970s. It argues that the post-war boom created consumer confidence and general prosperity. Expectations were high that standards of living would increase, as would social welfare systems and benefits. However, there was a general decline in deference and respect for authority, due in part to new affluence, 'free welfare, health and education'.[11] This in turn weakened individual work and incentives, while aspirations for state egalitarian principles became more pronounced. The plurality of groups in welfare social democracies pressed the government to intervene to protect their interests by offering higher wages, employment security, and contrasting high and low interest rates and prices. To secure power, the political parties promised to fulfil the desires of the competing interest groups. In the 1960s and 1970s, it is argued, the contradictions in policy were all too apparent. To placate the trade unions and to alleviate social disturbances, the governments of the day attempted to juggle with the economy. Price freezes, wage freezes, reflation, deflation and similar actions became the order of the day. In 1968, Wilson's Labour Government attempted to bring in incomes policy legislation, as did the Heath Conservative Government of the early 1970s and the Labour Government of 1974 to 1979. Nonetheless, aspirations continued to rise, and were reinforced by each successive government. 'Appeasement strategies', according to the new right, 'lead to even more state agencies'.[12] These included health and welfare service increases which led to an ever-increasing circle of public spending and spiralling costs. The expansion of the state's welfare mechanism not only destroyed individual motivation, due to the development of dependency and higher taxation, but it also – if Bacon and Eltis are to be believed – left the system with too few producers to pay for the services of the welfare state.[13] Only by rolling back the state's involvement can prosperity be assured.

Such an interpretation has naturally been rejected by socialists. However, one of its main critics is Alan Sked, who suggests that the creation of a welfare state does not necessarily lead to the economic ruin of a country (Document 2). According to Sked, Britain's expenditure on welfare services has been comparable with that of other economies, of which some were expanding. Income tax was also less of a burden than has been described, and tax rates constantly compared favourably with those in Europe. Taxation does not necessarily discourage hard work; rather, according to the OECD, it makes people work harder.[14] Also, in 1967 a government working-party concluded that 'high taxes do not discourage savings', and this can be seen by increases in domestic savings during a period in the 1970s when taxation actually rose.[15]

New right critics expressed the view that the welfare state leads to an enforced and coercive equality. By this they mean universal equality. Nothing could be further from the truth. Equality – using a socialist framework – means more than universal welfare initiatives. It means a totality of relationships, some economic, some social and some personal. It is essentially about power, not about welfare. The new right have failed to appreciate the very nature of the welfare capitalism they are attacking. The welfare state was introduced to remove the most obvious social disadvantages of capitalism without necessarily changing the relationships that are part and parcel of the construction of capitalism.

Sked (Document 2) writes that welfare benefits are complementary to growth and efficiency. A healthy work-force is a productive one. Welfare social benefits, such as the 'dole' or supplementary benefit do not necessarily create a dependency culture or work-shyness. Sked points to the reviews by the National Assistance Board in 1951, 1956, 1958, 1961 and 1964, and to the reports by the Supplementary Benefits Commission in 1978 to provide evidence for his arguments. Both of these authorities showed clearly that only a small minority of claimants benefited from the welfare system, and of these most were disabled, ill, or unable to work due to personal problems.[16] This being the case, the welfare state has been cleared of some of the charges levelled against it by its new right critics, most obviously that it has produced a breed of 'scroungers' or 'beggars' who take advantage of the system.

The fact is that the new right and the anti-collectivists needed to explain why Britain was no longer a leading industrial nation. The past was seen as the yardstick for the future. What the nation did in the nineteenth century could, for those who believed in the new-right analysis, be reproduced now. The laissez-faire economic approach could be reborn. The implications of this, of course, were that the major social problems had been tackled, that the welfare state could be rolled back, and that the conditions of the early and mid-nineteenth century recreated.

This view, of course, conflicted with the left wing in Britain, which felt that there was more need for welfare provision, and feminists, who believed that the British welfare state was male-oriented, to the disadvantage of women. It also conflicted with the work of those, particularly in the 1970s and early 1980s, who began to reveal that there was still acute and marked poverty in British society. Poverty had not vanished.

Professor Peter Townsend, Sir Douglas Black, Joanna Mack, Stewart Lansley and others have maintained that the welfare state had not eradicated poverty. Townsend's late 1960s survey, which appeared as *Poverty in the United Kingdom*, suggested that Britain still experienced relative poverty of about 25 to 30 percent, based on the fact that this proportion of the population were deprived of the lifestyles enjoyed by the average family (Document 8). His relative poverty was based upon a survey of 2000 families, using 60 items of family life in Britain such as diet, fuel and light, clothing, housing, family support. From this he produced a 'deprivation index' based upon 12 major items. Townsend's findings were supported by the Black Report, researched in 1980. Although strongly criticised at the time for the techniques that it adopted, Sir Douglas Black's enquiry into the health of the nation suggested that at all stages of life those in households where the head was an unskilled manual worker were disadvantaged compared with others. Indeed, men and women in unskilled households had a two-and-a-half times greater chance of dying before reaching retirement age than their professional counterparts. Also, infant mortality rates for those born into unskilled families was over three-and-a-half times professional ones. Being poor in Britain in 1980 was still very much a matter of life and death. In effect, the gap between the death rates of the poor and the rest of the nation had not changed since 1900.

The Government severely restricted the circulation of this embarrassing report, attacked the notion of relative inequality, and suggested that the benefits system ensured that no one lives in poverty in Britain. Yet these criticisms were partly answered by Joanna Mack and Stewart Lansley, whose book, *Poor Britain*, was produced (by George Allen & Unwin in 1985) in conjunction with the London Weekend Television series 'Breadline Britain', which appeared in the summer of 1983. They examined poverty from the point-of-view of the 'general social perception of need'. In other words, they moved to an objective assessment of poverty based upon the subjective view of a cross-section of society. They found that the 'poor today are too poor', that there were about four million adults and two-and-a-half million children living in poverty, and that another four-and-a-half million were living on the margins of poverty. In other words, something between 14 and 22 percent of the nation were living in poverty in Britain during the early 1980s. The implications were clear: welfare capitalism had failed, because it had not solved poverty. This was a far cry from Mrs Thatcher's assumption that there was no poverty in Britain because any absolute poverty was dealt with by the provision of state benefits.

Conservatives, apart from blaming the expense of the welfare state for Britain's economic decline, have also focused upon the destructive strike record of trade unions as a cause of industrial loss and innovative inhibition. Mrs Thatcher came to power in May 1979, following on from the 'winter of discontent' of 1978-9, when there was an outbreak of strike activity, including some well-publicised municipal strikes. Indeed, in response to the view that trade unions were a major factor in causing the 'British disease', their strike activity restricting the free development of laissez faire, the Conservatives introduced legislation to control trade-union activities. Between 1979 and 1990, the Conservative Governments introduced eight acts – including the Wages Act and the Public Order Act, both in 1986 – which have brought about a radical change to the employment laws of Britain and thrown trade unions onto the defensive. The introduction of new legislation designed to make trade unions more accountable was central to the new government's economic philosophy, which aimed to deregulate and 'free' the economy from constraints in order to achieve the economic renaissance of Britain. In other words, the attack upon trade-union power was part of the process of rolling back the modern welfare state and state control which was perceived to be the cause of Britain's post-war economic decline. The Labour Party clearly felt some concern about the high strike activity of the late 1960s (Document 11), and in 1969 Barbara Castle introduced the ill-fated White Paper *In Place of Strife* to address the issue by introducing 'effective company or plant agreements' (Document 9). It was rejected by a trade-union movement concerned about restrictions upon its freedom to strike. Yet it was the Conservative Party which was to adopt a more aggressive attitude to trade unions and strike activity under Margarate Thatcher. The Conservative view on strikes was provoked in the mid-1970s by the Bow Group, a small fringe group which saw the need to deal aggressively with trade unionism (Document 10). With the industrial action of the winter of discontent and the arrival of Thatcher as Prime Minister, the views of this fringe group assumed a more central role within Conservative policy in the move to free up the economy and make it more competitive.

The assumption that Britain's high strike levels and trade-union militancy was a major cause of Britain economic decline is not borne out by the evidence. It is often noted that the British work longer hours than their European neighbours, that strikes form only a very small percentage of the working days lost to the nation, and that Britain does not necessarily have the worst per capita strike record of the industrial world. In any case, Peter Nolan, in his survey of recent writings on British trade unions suggest that they have a positive rather than a negative impact on output and efficiency, in that they force management to adopt new techniques (Document 5). In this situation, then, it would appear that other factors, such as the failure of industrial training (Document 6) and the limited and misdirected use of capital might also have had an impact. Indeed, many writers have argued that Britain's relative industrial decline is the responsibility of entrepreneurs and managers who have ignored the need for education and training; it is this neglect that accounts for the British disease. Indeed, there is much to suggest that Britain's educational and cultural attitudes might also have restricted industrial growth (Document 7). Combined with a poor system for the redistribution of wealth, this has meant that poverty has risen, most markedly since the 1960s, and that Britain has not addressed the problem of industrial decline.

There is still no clear and unchallenged explanation of Britain's economic decline, particularly for the period since the Second World War. Nevertheless, pointers are emerging, as well as suggestions that can be dismissed. The most obvious factor is that Britain's relative economic decline has been continuing for more than a century, as other nations have industrialised. That decline was inevitable. But it begs the question why Britain, having scaled down to a new level, proved unable to sustain even that in comparison with other industrial nations. What is clear is that it has very little to do with the laziness of the workforce, the burden of the welfare state or the impact of strikes and trade-union activities. Even in a period of weakened trade unionism the problem of economic decline still persists. Therefore, it is clearly other factors, perhaps in combination, that are to blame. The lack of social investment by government, the failure of training, and the failure to identify and invest readily in new and expanding industrial sectors is problematic. Above all, however, it must be recognised that Britain's balance of economic activity is changing, particularly from the manufacturing to the service sector, and that the maturation of a small industrial nation like Britain has something to do with it. Belonging to a wider trading region may, as Andrew Gamble suggests, be the only way to maintain a position or reverse the process of decline (Document 3).

Documents
SECONDARY SOURCES AND INTERPRETATIONS

1 – Andrew Glyn and John Harrison, *The British Economic Disaster* (London, Pluto Press, 1980), pp 1–2

At the end of the sixties, the Labour party seemed to many to be formally established as a respectable party of government, likely in coming years to alternate with the Tories in a Tweedledum and Tweedledee act in which one performer could barely be distinguished from the other. Yet by the end of the seventies the party, as represented by annual conferences, was committed towards a thoroughgoing process of internal democratisation and a radical left-wing programme. It was at war with its parliamentary leadership.

Underlying all this was a sharp deterioration in British capital's performance. The best single indicator of the intensifying... difficulties is the collapse in the rate of profit, which fell to about 12 per cent in the early sixties and to some 4 per cent in the late seventies. If the pundits are right it will be down to 2 per cent in 1980.

So it is hardly surprising that employment in the manufacturing backbone of the economy fell throughout the decade, that around one in two people is now out of work and production is falling. Nor should it come as a great surprise that the traditional workers' party, whose rationale during the fifties and the sixties was the ability to offer reforms to workers without endangering the fabric of capitalism, has been catapulted into a state of crisis.

2 – Alan Sked, *Britain's Decline: Problems and Perspectives* (Oxford, Basil Blackwell, 1987), p 72, 77, 81–2

By the 1960s progress, especially economic progress, was no longer taken for granted in Britain. The balance of payments crisis of 1964 – leading to devaluation in 1967 – together with the debate over entry into the Common Market, brought home to the British that however well they had been doing, others had been doing better. Thus, even if the economy since 1945 had grown faster than ever before, it was performing less well than that of Britain's main economic competitors. The result was a feeling of profound concern and an acceptance of relative decline, which was taking place on a massive scale. By 1980 Britain had been progressively overtaken in terms of gross national product (GNP) per head of population by Norway, Iceland, Finland and Denmark... In 1985 she was overtaken by Italy. Her present situation, as summed up by one of the leading economic historians, is as follows: 'Britain is no longer counted amongst the economically advanced nations of the world. A wide gap separates her from the rest of the industrialised Europe. The difference as measured in national product per head between Britain, and say, Germany, is now as wide as the differences between Britain and the continent of Africa'...

Before the 1960s British self-confidence had been boosted by victory in two world wars, the successful transformation of Empire into Commonwealth, a world role in international affairs, and a consciousness of parliamentary government and the rule of law going back over centuries... Since the 1960s, however, most British political institutions... have experienced public criticism. The result is that the 'Westminster model' is no longer displayed to all and sundry as an object of automatic emulation and has itself been modified. Indeed, the range of modification has been considerable: the introduction of the referendum on major matters of debate (continuing membership of the Common Market, the retention of Ulster within the United Kingdom, proposed devolution for Scotland and Wales)...

All this is significant because it surely proved that the 'British disease', whatever else it may be, is not one of failure to respond to public pressure for institutional change...

Yet in the organisation of is own welfare services, [Britain] is said to be facing a 'crisis of legitimacy' which has apparently been brought about by a backlash against a welfare system responsible, so it is said, for Britain's economic decline both by burdening the economy and by creating social attitudes which undermine enterprise. It has also been claimed, however, that the real crisis in welfare arises simply as a result of the cuts imposed by the recent lack of economic growth, and that the decline of the welfare state is part of the decline of Britain. Let us therefore examine these issues. Has the welfare state undermined Britain's economy? Is it now in any sense in crisis? How, once again, does Britain compare with other Western societies in this respect?

According to statistics collected by the European Commission in the 1970s, Britain appeared to be faring relatively well in the battle against poverty compared with her continental neighbours... [This is followed by a survey of education and other issues which suggest that the welfare state has improved living standards although not equality. After surveying a number of theories about Government and welfare depriving British industry of profits he argues that this was not the case and seems to accept that the welfare state has been a positive force for growth.]

The first part of the criticism is based on the Bacon-Eltis thesis: the view that production in Britain fell by more than half in 1965–75 compared with the previous decade as a result of a shift in employment from manufacturing towards public services. In short, a declining manufacturing base had to finance a growing service one, in which huge pay rises were conceded to local and central government workers. This led to economic decline: since the trade unions ensured that wages in the private sector also went up and since the extra costs could not be passed on for fear of foreign competition, the end result was decreased profit, reduced investment and less modernisation of industry. The only answer to this was reduced public spending. [There were objections to this: some questioned why British industry's productivity was so low in the first place.] Finally, it has been shown that the decline in the profitability of British industry began in the early and mid-1950s when the public sector was small and that there was no shortage of capital in the 1960s and 1970s. Hence it is difficult to see British industry was being deprived of either labour or capital by government.

3 – Andrew Gamble, *Britain in Decline* (London, Macmillan, 1981, 1985), pp xiv, xv–xvi, 230

Britain has now been in decline for a hundred years. It has become the most observed and analysed decline in modern history, provoking a speculative literature of enormous dimensions. Few explanations have not been proffered, few causes not dissected, few remedies not canvassed at least twice. The decline has been the central fact of British politics for a century, a major preoccupation of its political intellectuals and intermittently, but increasingly, of its political leaders. Two processes stand out – the absolute decline in power and status of the British imperial state, and the relative decline of the British economy with its long-standing failure to match the rates of expansion of its rivals.

The starting point of Britain's decline was the position of unrivalled dominance it had achieved during the nineteenth century. By 1900 Britain controlled over one-fifth of the world's land surface and ruled one-quarter of the world's population...

The slope of Britain's descent has not been uniform. There have been periods of recovery, even of advance and success, but the underlying trend has been inexorable; the problems surrounding Britain's future have accumulated whilst the reserves for meeting challenges of all kinds have dwindled. This is why the decline in world power and the relative decline in economic performance appear inextricably linked. At every crisis of the economy the prospects for lasting recovery have looked bleaker, the strait-jacket of decline tighter. Speculation burst out afresh at such times about the 'British disease', an incurable malady that lies so deep in British psychology and British culture and has taken hold of the body politics that no cure may be possible.

The most common diagnosis of this 'disease' in the 1960s and 1970s was that the country was living beyond its means. The British consumed too much and worked too little. Britain was portrayed as the New Rome, over-burdened by taxation, bureaucracy, and excessive public and private consumption, and suffering rampant inflation and paralysing internal struggle over the distribution of wealth and income. Sometimes these writers differ as to the identity of the barbarians at the gates; many believed they were already within the city; but all agreed that the British had become morally dissolute. Notions that the British are lazy and refuse to work harder, whilst demanding ever greater quantities of things to consume, were commonplace. As one Labour minister put it: 'For generations this country has not earned an honest living'... [Gamble then argues that alarmist judgements like this have rested upon the balance of payments, public spending and pay. These have produced crisis after crisis, although the real problem has been why British capital has been so weak in the twentieth century despite all efforts to overcome the problem. The general argument is that Britain chose the path of international trade in the nineteenth century and has not adjusted to the loss of empire and competition which has undermined her old hegemony. In this respect, none of the major political parties have adapted Britain to the needs of a more competitive age.]

Socialists in Britain face a major task in helping to defend those communities and groups of workers threatened by the kind of restructuring which policies inspired by the social market strategy necessarily impose, and at the same time forging a new popular conception of socialism. But if there is to be any alternative at all to the present direction of world affairs, they must also find ways of building new political and economic links between all those communities, regions... throughout the world system which have an interest in creating a new global economic and political order. British problems are not national problems and will not be solved in a national context. The perils facing all countries are more grave and more evident than at any previous time. Only a political transformation of the present institutions and structures of the world system can lift their shadows.

4 – Nicholas Kaldor, *Causes of the Slow Rate of Economic Growth of the United Kingdom* (Cambridge, Cambridge University Press, 1966), republished in David Coates and John Hillard, *UK Economic Decline* (London, Prentice Hall, Harvester Wheatsheaf, 1995), pp 50–1

Britain having started the process of industrialisation earlier than any other country has reached 'maturity' much earlier – in the sense that it has attained a distribution of the labour force between the primary, secondary and tertiary sectors at which industry can no longer attract the labour it needs by drawing on the labour reserves of other sectors. There are disadvantages of an early start, as well as advantages – as is shown by the fact that some of the late-comers of industrialisation have attained higher levels of industrial efficiency even before they became fully industrialised.

But once it is recognised that manpower shortage is the main handicap from which we are suffering, and once our thinking becomes adjusted to this, we shall I hope, tend to concentrate our efforts on a more rational use of manpower in all fields.

5 – Peter Nolan, 'Trade unions and productivity' in David Coates and John Hillard, *UK Economic Decline* (London, Prentice Hall, Harvester Wheatsheaf, 1995), pp 130, 136

Have British trade unions impeded cost cutting changes in production, as proponents of orthodox economic analysis claim? Or are they more usefully viewed as a potential force for economic dynamism, among other things by blocking low wage, labour intensive routes to profitability? What does the research evidence reveal?…

Two main conclusions emerge from the above discussion. First, the research on unions and productivity for Britain does not demonstrate a clear, unambiguous negative link. If anything it points in the opposite direction: that is against the commonplace idea that unions lower the level and growth rate of productivity. Yet the available evidence remains too impressionistic, and too limited by a conceptual framework which separates unions from the other dynamic factors which bear on productivity outcomes to be reliable. More conceptual refinement, and more attention to the dynamic effects of institutions, is urgently needed to enhance our understanding of the complex role of unions in contemporary capitalist economies.

Second, it has been argued that a decade or so of hostility towards trade unions has done little to reverse the deep seated weakness of industry in Britain. There has been no sustainable improvement in the productivity, efficiency or competitiveness of Britain's economy, and the industrial structure has continued to develop in a direction which will make it more, not less, difficult to participate in the expanding markets for high research, high technology products. Hence the prospect for industrial renewal in Britain looks remote at present. In the medium term it looks likely that the Government's cheap labour policies will dominate the competitive strategies of firms and industries located in Britain.

6 – David Finegold and David Soskice, 'The Failure of Training in Britain: Analysis and Prescription', *Oxford Review of Economic Policy* 4, 1988, p 21

We will argue that Britain's failure to educate and train its workforce to the same levels as its international competitors has been both a product and a cause of the nation's poor relative economic performance: a product because the ET (education and training) system evolved to meet the needs of the world's first industrialised economy, whose large, mass production manufacturing sector required only a small number of skilled workers and university graduates, and a cause, because the absence of a well-educated and trained workforce has made it difficult for industry to respond to new economic conditions.

The best way to visualise this argument is to see Britain as trapped in a low-skills equilibrium, in which the majority of enterprises staffed by poorly trained managers and workers produce low-quality goods and services. The term 'equilibrium' is used to connote a self-reinforcing network of societal and state institutions which interact to stifle the demand for improvements in skill levels… [The main theme is that the staying-on rate in Britain for those aged between sixteen and nineteen is small compared with most other industrialised nations.]

7 – Margaret Mathieson and Gerald Bernbaum, 'The British Disease: a British Tradition', *British Journal of Educational Studies* 26, 1988, pp 126–7

Central to our argument is that an arts based, Christian notion of gentlemanliness, which excludes, and even opposes science, technology and commerce, dominated high status educational institutions in the nineteenth century. This literary Christian notion both reflected and consolidated the values of Victorian society, which conferred the highest status upon the ownership of land, and the style and manners associated with gentlemanly distance from the daily labours on that land, and from what were regarded as the sordid features of industrialisation and urbanisation. Special emphasis will be placed upon the antipathetic response to science and technology which was, and continued to be, represented in the values embodied both in the arts based curriculum and in the relationship of the education system to other parts of society.

PRIMARY EVIDENCE AND INFORMATION

8 – P. Townsend, *Poverty in the United Kingdom* (Harmondsworth, Penguin, 1979), p 31

Individuals, families and groups in the population can be said to be in poverty when they lack the resources to obtain the type of diet, participate in the activities or have the living standards and amenities which are customary, or at least widely encouraged or approved, in the societies to which they belong. Their resources are so seriously below those commanded by the average individual or family that they are, in effect, excluded from ordinary living, customs and activities.

9 – *In Place of Strife: A Policy for Industrial Relations*, Cmnd 3888, presented to Parliament by Barbara Castle, Secretary of State for Employment and Productivity, January 1969 (London, HMSO, 1969),[17] paras 3, 55, 81

Until action is taken to remedy these defects [in industrial relations] conflict in British industry will often be damaging and anti-social. The Government places the following proposals before Parliament and the nation convinced that they are justified on two main grounds. First, they will help to contain the destructive expression of industrial conflict and to encourage a more equitable, ordered and efficient system, which will benefit both those involved and the community at large. Second, they are based on the belief that the efforts of employers, unions and employees to reform collective bargaining need the active support and intervention of Government...

The Industrial Relations Bill will lay down the principle that no employer has the right to prevent or obstruct an employer from belonging to a trade union. This principle will become part of the contract of employment...

The fundamental solution [to strikes] lies in the re-structuring of our present system of collective bargaining when it is disordered and defective. Many strikes would not take place if there were quick and effective methods of resolving the matter in dispute...

Reform of collective bargaining will remove many of the causes of strikes. Comprehensive and effective company or plant agreements will solve many existing difficulties. Better procedure will resolve disputes before the impatience of those concerned leads to a strike.

10 – Richard Barber, *The Trade Unions and the Tories* (London, Bow Group, 1976),[18] pp 1, 12

The biggest single obstacle to the return of a Conservative Government is the... widespread belief that through inability to work with the Trade Unions it would be unable to govern. Not surprisingly, the present Labour Government and Trade Union leadership have skilfully sought to perpetuate this belief and they have been assisted by the regular failure of the Conservative Party to formulate a strategy to defend it.

The threat the Trade Unions pose to the Conservative Party has two distinct strands. First there is the threat that a Conservative Government could not pursue a successful economic policy because of the inability to control wage demands. The problem can almost certainly be overcome. Secondly, there is the threat that unless a Conservative Government pursues democratic policies approved by the Trade Unions the latter will begin a fresh round of strikes and industrial unrest of a kind which succeeded in destroying the last Heath administration...

The current Conservative policy towards Trade Unions appears to consist of persuading their leadership that they have nothing to fear from a Conservative Government and that their legislative privilege will remain intact... The weakness of this policy is more likely to persuade voters that there is little to be gained by a change of Government and that they might just as well support the Party which is unequivocally subservient to Trade Union interests...

Conclusion
The electoral problem which the Conservative Party faced in relation to Trade Union power is not insoluble. However, the present low-key approach is misconceived for it serves to perpetuate the damaging impression that the power of Trade Unions is such that only a Government subservient to their wishes can hope to rule.

Main Points
(1) Force trade unions to face the economic consequences of their action.
(2) New Industrial Relations Act needed.
(3) Closed Shop should be outlawed...

(4) Postal ballots should be mandatory for all Trade Unions elections of Officers above a certain level...

11 – Strike Statistics 1965–1980, drawn from a variety of sources, including Keith Laybourn, *A History of British Trade Unionism 1770–1990* (Stroud, Sutton, 1992), pp 169, 201

Year	Number of Strikes	Number of Workers involved (000s)	Number of days lost lost (000s)
1965	2354	876.4	2925
1966	1937	543.9	2398
1967	2116	733.7	2787
1968	2378	2258	4690
1969	3116	1665	6846
1970	3906	1801	10,980
1971	2228	1178	13,551
1972	2497	1734	23909
1973	2873	1528	7197
1974	2922	1161	14,750
1975	2282	570	6012
1976	2016	444	3284
1977	2703	785	10,142
1978	2471	725	9405
1979	2080	4121	29,474
1980	1338	1326	4266

Notes on Chapter 9

1   David Coates and John Hillard (eds), *UK Economic Decline: Key Texts* (London and New York, Prentice Hall and Harvester Wheatsheaf, 1995), p 3.
2   Andrew Shonfield, *British Economic Performance Since the War* (London, Penguin, 1958).
3   Walter Eltis, 'How Public Sector Growth Can Undermine the Growth of the National Product' in W. Beckerman (ed.), *Slow Growth in Britain* (Oxford, Oxford University Press, 1979).
4   Correlli Barnett, *The Audit of War: The Illusion and Reality of Britain as a Great Nation* (London, Macmillan, 1986); M. Beloff, *Wars and Welfare* (London, Edward Arnold, 1984); Robert Blake, *The Decline of Power 1915–1964* (London, Granada, 1985).
5   Blake, *The Decline of Power 1915–1964*, p 284.
6   V. George and P. Wilding, *Ideology and Social Welfare* (London, Routledge, Kegan Paul, 1985), p 37.

7   *Ibid.*, pp 37–8.
8   A. Sked, *Britain's Decline: Problems and Perspectives* (Oxford, Blackwell, 1988), p 77.
9   *Ibid.*, p 77.
10 George and Wilding, *Ideology and Social Welfare*, p 41.
11 *Ibid.*, p 232.
12 *Ibid.*, p 232.
13 R. Bacon and W. Eltis, *Britain's Economic Problem: Too Few Producers* (1978).
14 Sked, *Britain's Decline*, p 77.
15 *Ibid.*, p 78.
16 *Ibid.*, pp 76–80.
17 Crown copyright is reproduced with the permission of the Controller of Her Majesty's Stationary Office.
18 Also quoted in Keith Laybourn (ed.), *British Trade Unionism c. 1770–1990: A Reader in History* (Stroud, Sutton, 1991), pp 196–7.

Bibliography

This section lists a few of the many books and articles relevant to each chapter. Some extracts from these articles and books are included in this volume.

The Liberal Reforms 1905-14: Voluntary Help and the State

Derek Fraser, *The Evolution of the British Welfare State* (London, Macmillan, 1984).

J.R. Hay, *The Origins of the Liberal Welfare Reforms 1906–1914* (London, Macmillan, 1978).

David Howell, *British Workers and the Independent Labour Party 1888–1906* (Manchester, Manchester University Press, 1983).

Keith Laybourn, *The Evolution of British Social Policy and the Welfare State* (Halifax, Ryburn, then Keele UP, now Edinburgh UP, 1995).

Keith Laybourn, *The Guild of Help and the Changing Face of Edwardian Philanthropy: The Guild of Help, Voluntary Work and the State* (Lampeter, Edwin Mellen, 1994).

Pat Thane, *The Foundations of the Welfare State* (London, Longman, 1982).

Class Politics or Accident of War? Liberalism and the Rise of Labour 1916–18

Michael Bentley, *The Climax of Liberal Politics: British Liberalism in Theory and Practice 1868–1918* (London, Edward Arnold, 1987).

P.F. Clarke, *Lancashire and the New Liberalism* (Cambridge, Cambridge University Press, 1971, republished 1996).

Keith Laybourn, *The Rise of Labour* (London, Edward Arnold, 1988).

R. McKibbin, *The Evolution of the Labour Party 1910–1924* (Oxford, Oxford University Press, 1974).

Henry Pelling, *The Origins of the Labour Party* (London, Macmillan, 1954).

Duncan Tanner, *Political Change and the Labour Party 1900–1918* (Cambridge, Cambridge University Press, 1990).

Trevor R. Wilson, *The Downfall of the Liberal Party, 1914–1935* (London, Colleens, 1966).

The First World War: the Impact of War Upon British Politics and Life 1914–18

J.M. Bourne, *Britain and the Great War 1914–1918* (London, Edward Arnold, 1989).

Keith Dockray and Keith Laybourn (eds), *Representation and Reality of War, The British Experience: Essays in Honour of David Gordon Wright* (Stroud, Sutton, 1999).

Bernard Waites, *A Class Society at War: England 1914–18* (Leamington Spa, 1987).

Trevor Wilson, *The Myriad Faces of War* (Cambridge, Polity Press, 1986).

J. M. Winter, *Socialism and the Challenge of War* (London, Routledge and Kegan Paul, 1974).

J.M. Winter, *The Great War and the British and the British People* (London, Macmillan, 1986, reprinted 1987).

Britain on the Breadline: Slump, Poverty and the Politics of Realignment During the Inter-war Years 1918–39

D.H. Aldcroft, *The Interwar Economy: Britain 1919–1939* (London, B.T. Batsford, 1970).

Stuart Ball, *Baldwin and the Conservative Party: the Crisis of 1929–1931* (London, Yale University Press, 1988).

Stuart Ball, *The Conservative Party and British Politics 1902–1951* (London, Longman, 1995).

Robert Blake, *The Conservative Party* (London, Eyre & Spottiswoode, 1970).

Bentley B. Gilbert, *British Social Policy 1914–1939* (London, B.T. Batsford, 1970).

Chris Cook, *The Age of Alignment: Electoral Politics in Britain 1922–1929* (London, Macmillan, 1975).

Keith Laybourn, *Britain on the Breadline: A Social and Political History of Britain 1918–1939* (Stroud, Sutton, 1998).

David Marquand, *Ramsay MacDonald* (London, Jonathan Cape, 1977).

Margaret Mitchell, 'The Effects of Unemployment on the Social Conditions of Women and Children in the 1930s', *History Workshop*, 1985.

John Stevenson and Chris Cook, *The Slump: Society and Politics During the Depression* (London, Jonathan Cape, 1977).

Richard Thurlow, *Fascism in Britain: A History 1918–1985* (Oxford, Basil Blackwell, 1987; London, I.B. Tauris, 1998).

Charles Webster, 'Healthy and Hungry Thirties', *History Workshop*, 1982.

L. MacNeill Weir, *The Tragedy of Ramsay MacDonald* (London, Secker & Warburg, 1938).

Industrial Relations and the General Strike 1919–39

Keith Laybourn, *The General Strike of 1926* (Manchester, Manchester University Press, 1993).

Keith Laybourn, *The General Strike: Day by Day* (Stroud, Sutton, 1996).

Margaret Morris, *The General Strike* (London, Penguin, 1976).

Gordon Phillips, *The General Strike* (London, Weidenfeld and Nicolson, 1976).

Patrick Renshaw, *The General Strike* (London, Eyre Methuen, 1975).

C.J. Wrigley (ed.), *A History of British Industrial Relations, Vol. II 1914–1939* (Brighton, Harvester, 1987).

The Reaction to Fascism at Home and Abroad in the 1930s and the Politics of Appeasement 1938–9

Tom Buchanan, *The Spanish Civil War and the British Labour Movement* (Cambridge, Cambridge University Press, 1991).

David Dilks (ed.), *Retreat from Power: Studies in Britain's Foreign Policy of the Twentieth Century: Volume One 1906–1939* (London, Macmillan, 1981).

Martin Gilbert, *The Roots of Appeasement* (Weidenfeld and Nicolson, 1966).

Sir Oswald Mosley, *My Life* (London, Thomas Nelson, 1968).

R.A.C. Parker, *Chamberlain and Appeasement: British Policy and the Coming of the Second World War* (London, Macmillan, 1993).

Robert Skidelsky, *Oswald Mosley* (London, Macmillan, 1975, 1980, 1990 editions).

The Second World War: Politics and Social Change 1939–45

Angus Calder, *The People's War: Britain 1939–45* (London, Jonathan Cape, 1969).

Henry Pelling, *Britain and the Second World War* (London, Fontana, 1970, 1976).

Harold L. Smith (ed.), *War and Social Change: British Society in the Second World War* (Manchester, Manchester University Press, 1986).

R.M. Titmuss, *Essays on the Welfare State* (London, Unwin University Books, 2nd edition, 3rd imprint, 1960).

'Never Again': Attlee, the Post-war Labour Governments 1945–51 and the Politics of Consensus 1951–79

Aneurin Bevan, *In Place of Fear* (London, Heinemann, 1952).

R. Blake and W.R. Louie (eds), *Churchill* (Oxford, Oxford University Press, 1996).

Brian Brivati, *Hugh Gaitskell* (London, Richard Cohen Books, 1996).

B. Evans and A. Taylor, *From Salisbury to Major: Continuity and Change in Conservative Politics* (Manchester, Manchester University Press, 1996).

Steven Fielding, Peter Thompson and Nick Tiratsoo, *'England Arise': The Labour Party and Popular Politics in 1940s Britain* (Manchester, Manchester University Press, 1995

Keith Harris, *Attlee* (London, Weidenfeld and Nicolson, 1982).

Dennis Kavanagh, *Thatcherism and British Politics: the End of Consensus* (Oxford, Oxford University Press, 1987).

A. Lawrence and P. Dodd, *Anthony Eden 1897–1977* (Greenwood, 1995).

Kenneth O. Morgan, *Callaghan: A Life* (Oxford, Oxford University Press, 1997).

Ben Pimlott, *Harold Wilson* (London, HarperCollins, 1992).

Britain's Industrial Decline, the Welfare State and Social Problems 1945–79

Andrew Gamble, *Britain in Decline* (London, Macmillan, 1981, 1985).

Andrew Glyn and John Harrison, *The British Economic Disaster* (London, Pluto Press, 1980).

Keith Laybourn, *A History of British Trade Unionism 1770–1990* (Stroud, Sutton, 1992.

Alan O'Day and Terry Gourvich (eds), *Britain Since 1945* (Macmillan, 1991).

J. Ramsden, *The Winds of Change, Macmillan to Heath: The Conservative Party 1957–1975* (London, Longman, 1996).

Alan Sked, *Britain's Decline: Problems and Perspectives* (Oxford, Basil Blackwell, 1987).

Index